With *Wings*, There Are No Barriers

With *Wings,* There Are No Barriers

A Woman's Guide to a Life of Magnificent Possibilities

Sue Augustine

PELICAN PUBLISHING COMPANY

Gretna 1997

*The word "Pelican" and the depiction of a pelican are trademarks
of Pelican Publishing Company, Inc., and are registered
in the U.S. Patent and Trademark Office.*

Library of Congress Cataloging-in-Publication Data

Augustine, Sue.
    With wings, there are no barriers : a woman's guide to a life
of magnificent possibilities / Sue Augustine.
      p.   cm.
    ISBN 1-56554-195-2 (alk. paper)
    1. Women—Life skills guides. 2. Women—Psychology. 3.
Success.   I. Title.
HQ1221.A86 1996
646.7'0082—dc20
                                        96-30364
                                            CIP

Unless otherwise indicated, all Scripture quotations are taken from
the *King James Version* of the Bible.

Scripture quotations marked TLB are taken from *The Living Bible*
©1971 by Tyndale House Publishers, Inc. All rights reserved.

Manufactured in the United States of America
Published by Pelican Publishing Company, Inc.
1101 Monroe Street, Gretna, Louisiana 70053

*This book is dedicated with gratitude to my husband, Cliff Zaturski,
and my daughters, Sheila Fulton and Lori Page,
who have strengthened my wings with their encouragement,
patience, and love,*

*and to my three precious grandchildren,
Kurtis, Aaron, and Alexandra, who,
with their unconditional love and adventurous spirits,
are teaching me to fly higher into a world of fun,
playfulness, and total abandonment.*

Contents

Acknowledgments 9
Letter to My Readers 11
Introducing a Life of
Magnificent Possibilities 13

Chapter 1 The End 25
Chapter 2 Worth 63
Chapter 3 Insight..............................107
Chapter 4 Nurturing 133
Chapter 5 Goals 191
Chapter 6 Strategies.........................227
Chapter 7 The Beginning 257

A Personal Word 275
Summary...277
About the Author.............................279

Acknowledgments

I would like to thank all those who helped make this book possible by supporting me in spreading my wings and enabling me to fly to new heights.

In particular, I thank the great people at Pelican Publishing Company for trusting in my work and believing in my message. I am grateful for the opportunity they have given me to touch hearts and encourage thousands of others to spread their wings through my writing.

I owe a special thanks to all those who played a role in getting me started in my speaking and writing career by believing in me and being inspiring examples themselves of flying up and over the barriers—Joanne Wallace, Clinton Howard, David Beck, Perry and Angela Catena, Bob Proctor, Mark Victor Hansen, Jack Canfield, and the late Rev. Jack Counsell.

I would also like to give credit to the many great trainers, speakers, and authors who have made a contribution to this book through either a seminar, an article, a sermon, a speech, or a conference. I have had the privilege of sitting in the audience and learning from, as well as sharing the platform with, some of the best of our time. I have taken an abundance of notes and collected articles through the years, which sometimes makes it difficult to give credit to the exact source of my information and inspiration.

I want to express my appreciation to my husband, Cliff Zaturski, and my daughters, Lori Page and Sheila Fulton, for their role and assistance in the operation of my business and also for their constant encouragement and outstanding dedication to spreading this message of hope, transformation, and renewal.

I feel a deep sense of gratitude to my mother, who pushed me to strive for excellence and continues to encourage me so I can reach new heights, and to my late, warm, caring father. I would also like to acknowledge my sisters, Lois Galloway, Carol Tuttas, Ticha Augustine, and Ruth DeBruyn, for being living expressions of what it means to go soaring into a life of magnificent possibilities.

A special thank you goes to my close friends for their positive reinforcement and for standing behind my vision, especially: Liz Purser, for lovingly nurturing this book from conception to completion; Norma Theissen, for consistently expressing her belief in me and the message I want to share; Diane King, for her infectious enthusiasm; Molly Harding, for her generous assistance in editing; Eva McCarney, for her thoughtful suggestions; Barbara Pohorly, for reminding me to nurture myself; and so many others, too numerous to mention, for their faith in this work.

Most of all, I thank the women who so openly shared their ideas and deepest thoughts with me to be included in this book in the hopes that they would inspire you to soar to new heights, too.

Finally, I thank my many corporate clients and audience participants for their trust in my material and for expressing to me the tremendous need for this book.

Letter to My Readers

During my travels as a speaker, I began telling audiences I was writing a book for women on the topics of building self-confidence, conquering inner turmoil, and surmounting life's barriers. Many women responded by saying, "If there's a need for an entire book about this, then apparently I'm not alone . . . and somehow that's comforting to know." Their sentiments reminded me of the words to a song written by Barry Manilow called "All the Time," where he wishes that someone would have promised him he wasn't alone.

In a very special way, it's reassuring to realize that, directly or indirectly, we are connected because all of our lives have been touched by insecurities and doubts, by grief and sadness, by anxiety and fear. In one way or another, we've all had to deal with the inner barriers of loneliness or embarrassment. Some of us have had to face the external ones of an unfair boss, the death of a loved one, family breakdowns, or some form of abuse. Whether our personal challenges come from the heartache of a failed relationship, a wayward teenager, a family suicide or illness, or whether they result in divorce, abortion, or substance abuse, we've all shed private tears. We've all released our pain with sighs of despair. Yet there truly is some solace to be found in knowing we are not alone; that someone, somewhere, has shared our hurt and desperation. Like a soothing balm or a healing ointment, it helps to ease the pain and make it bearable.

Even so, this book was not written with the masses in mind. It was written just for you. If you were the only one in the world to read it, it was worth the effort, the long hours of research and study, the many interviews, and the intense moments of personal reflection. Of the thousands of books published each year that you could be holding in your hand right now, you are reading this one. I am convinced that there are no coincidences. I believe that you are here not by chance, but because God is about to unfold a wonderful plan for your life. And I am glad to be part of your journey. I appreciate these words by Emily Dickinson: "If I can stop one heart from breaking, I shall not live in vain."

Thank you for the opportunity to share my thoughts, ideas, and impressions this way in the hopes that your heart is that one.

Introducing a Life of Magnificent Possibilities

Even as a child I dreamed of being able to fly! Every chance I got, I would lie on the cool grass in summertime, staring up into the treetops, studying the birds and the butterflies. I was fascinated as they moved effortlessly through the air with wings gently moving, flitting from treetop to treetop, or flower to flower. I knew in my heart that someday, somehow, I too would spread my wings and fly. I never considered the possibility that perhaps it was only a dream. I didn't "wish" that I could fly. I didn't "hope" to fly. I just knew I would.

And so it is with all our dreams. With our steadfast belief that what we want to happen is really possible, dreams can come true. I was sharing this with my daughters not long ago, and they pointed out that, in fact, my dream had become a reality since I now *fly* internationally as a conference speaker and workshop leader. I regularly fly back and forth across continents. I have to use an airplane to do it, of course, but I really am flying.

My particular dream became a reality in an even deeper sense, though. You see, it takes wings to coast above life's barriers. It takes wings to rise up and over daily obstacles or roadblocks and to view seemingly impossible hurdles as golden opportunities. It takes wings to abandon old beliefs and self-limiting behaviors and to go soaring high into a life of magnificent possibilities. In an amazing way, I've grown my wings and you can, too.

Perhaps you have a childhood dream. Maybe there's something you've been longing to do, something that makes your heart do giant flip-flops every time you think about it. You have the opportunity to see that dream come true.

Not that there won't be barriers. Some of the barriers in my life took the form of situations that appeared nearly impossible. There didn't seem to be any solution to the obstacles I faced in my former marriage. There didn't appear to be an answer to my financial dilemma or my ill health or the constant feelings of listlessness I experienced.

Without the tools, techniques, and knowledge of the principles

I'm going to share with you, those situations might have indeed *been* impossible. They might have stayed that way and held me back from achieving my ideal life. When we have our wings, we can advance boldly and with confidence to meet our dreams. With wings, we can make a difference in our homes and families. With wings, we can go out and contribute more to our community and to world goals of peace and prosperity.

The purpose of this book is to encourage women everywhere to learn and grow from the experiences life offers them. We don't necessarily learn from others' experiences, although it's possible, but we almost always learn from our own. For most of us, this takes a special type of courage and self-motivation, since life's lessons often come disguised as insurmountable barriers.

> Resiliency is an important factor in living. The winds of life may bend us, but if we have resilience of spirit, they cannot break us. To courageously straighten again after our heads have been bowed by defeat, disappointment and suffering is the supreme test of character. (Anonymous)

In these pages, you will discover the principles to create a full, rich life and the inner strength and faith to conquer the barriers along the way. Although many of the techniques are not new, and some have been practiced for centuries, I have attempted to present them with a fresh perspective, in such a way that you will be encouraged to embrace them and act on them.

When you do, they will enable you to move to a new plateau of inspiration and achievement. To inspire means literally to enliven the spirit, to stimulate creativity and arouse one to greater productivity. To *be* inspired means to take action with a renewed sense of energy, purpose, and enthusiasm. The word "enthusiasm" is derived from the Greek *en theos,* meaning the spirit of God within you. Inspired women come to life with passion when they are propelled by this spirit. My greatest desire is to encourage you, inspire you, and bring you new hope through a heightened awareness of your own amazing potential.

WINGS—AN OVERVIEW

In the 1970s, while I was attending a seminar much like the programs I now present, a simple phrase came to my mind: "With wings, there are no barriers." I jotted it down quickly, because, although I had no idea then that it would someday be the title for a book, I had learned that new thoughts and creative ideas often come like the butterfly. They alight but for a moment, and then just as quickly fly away. If we don't capture them instantly, they disappear, and may never come again.

Even though I thought I might give the idea to someone who could use it in a poem or a song, year after year I transcribed those words in my new journals and never did give them away. Their impact became more and more meaningful. Wings seemed to me to represent freedom. I imagined a butterfly approaching a garden wall, and simply flying up and over! Nothing could keep her from going where she wanted to go, or prevent her from fulfilling her purpose in life.

That type of freedom is something many women tell me they are truly searching for. It's almost always the answer women give when I ask for their definition of success—freedom from such pressures as self-doubt, guilt, anxiety, fear, time restraints, relationship problems, boredom, and exhaustion; freedom to enjoy life to the fullest. How liberating it would be to live with complete abandon, every day a new adventure. Women, today more than ever, have a deep craving for the inner harmony that this type of liberty would bring.

Since the mid-1980s, I have conducted numerous seminars and workshops on attaining personal and professional excellence. When asked to prepare a program for women focusing on the areas of self-image and positive risk taking, I was delighted to have the opportunity to offer some of the special tools I have discovered that we, as women, need if we are to achieve the peaceful life this freedom would provide.

Now, as I speak to women internationally about overcoming the barriers to a liberating and prosperous life, I am increasingly aware that there are certain human qualities that consistently affect our ability to do this.

1. **Worth**—Only with a sense of personal value do we believe that our dreams can become realities.

2. **Insight**—By learning to trust our inner wisdom, our spiritual connection to God, we can formulate insightful ways to conquer the challenges life puts in our pathways.

3. Nurturing—When we cherish and nurture ourselves, then we will have the energy to tap our insights and the willingness to continue giving to those we love and care about.

4. Goals—A true sense of purpose along with specific targets and objectives strengthen us to make the exciting choices that will transform our lives.

5. Strategies—Life-patterning systems, or action plans, will set those goals in motion.

Not long after I began presenting this program internationally I realized, to my delight, that these five success keys to overcoming barriers formed the acrostic "wings":

Worth
Insight
Nurturings
Goals
Strategies

Soon I noticed that women everywhere were "getting their wings" and reporting astounding results in their lives. Some of their stories I will share with you on these pages. Although they involve real individuals, I have changed names and other particulars to protect their privacy.

Many forward-thinking corporations and organizations now invite me to present the principles to their employees, both men and women, realizing the importance of addressing personal issues as well as professional ones. Corporations everywhere are beginning to recognize that attaining balance—mentally, physically, and emotionally—is crucial to all of us to give peak performance on the job.

Now, I am delighted to be able to offer this information when audiences ask for it in book form. For those who cannot attend my programs, this book can be your seminar. For those who have attended, this will be a great refresher, or perhaps a gift of new life for the mothers, sisters, and friends you love and care about. The principles presented here literally have the power to transform your life, as they have mine and thousands of other women like me. The results you experience as you follow this flight path will be astounding.

My goal is to introduce to you key ideas, concepts, and principles that will enable you to create the life that, until now, you've only dreamed about. By applying the five simple steps to get your "wings," you can achieve a life filled with excitement, energy, contentment, and inner peace—no matter how grand or humble your personal goals.

IN PRAISE OF WOMEN

Some may ask why, in this era, there is still such a need for a success book specifically for women. In spite of the great strides toward equality and the emphasis on the status of women, I believe there are a number of valid reasons.

Over the years, historic gender roles in society have dictated how women should behave. In stories, women were portrayed as either sugary and syrupy or the *wicked witch*. We often saw women waiting to be rescued while the men did the rescuing. Even our parents and teachers expected boys to be independent, hardworking, and responsible while girls were encouraged to be sheltered and taken care of. Until now, success books and manuals have been geared almost exclusively toward male business executives. In the past, books specifically for women often referred mainly to their roles as homemakers, wives, and mothers. *These roles are essential and will always be valid choices for women.* But the omission of any reference to a female role in industry or professions is an indication that women have been classified as passive followers or spectators, cheering men from the sidelines, rather than as team members involved in a joint effort.

It is also a sign of the difference in the times—then and now. More women today are attempting to balance two lives at once. Striving for excellence in our careers and homes can put almost unbearable pressure on even the most confident, organized, and efficient woman. Along with balancing home and work, strained family and personal relationships, demanding bosses, poor diet, lack of exercise, health matters, and money concerns are leaving us exhausted. We feel stretched too thin. Finding time alone is almost impossible, resulting in stress that weighs us down or wears us out. These struggles deserve some attention. It's time to recognize and learn from the endeavors of enterprising women who are becoming good at survival, and to discover the secrets they use to cope successfully with chaos.

During the course of my research, I found that some women see change and challenges as wonderful opportunities and believe that this is a fabulous era in which to be alive. Others, though, view change as a threat. They feel trapped and helpless, and see no other choices for themselves. They struggle through life with negative attitudes and depression, wondering why it's all happening to them.

While some women have determined to take charge of their lives and create their own happy, prosperous futures, many others feel dissatisfied and see themselves as *forever victims* of their circumstances. What is it that makes the difference?

The most common reason is that, sadly, few women truly realize what extraordinary human beings they are. They don't see themselves as brimming with possibilities. There are incredibly talented women everywhere who simply need to burst through their cocoons and discover their wings in order to experience the confidence that will help them use their natural abilities.

Because of traditional stereotypes and assumed gender roles, women, and men as well for that matter, have been inhibited in dreaming of a life beyond the norm. We have not been motivated to recognize our many possibilities, options, and alternatives. Often, the gender roles assigned to us have become our reality, not so much because we are incapable of doing more, but because we have accepted and believe in them.

The good news is that the efforts of many concerned people, both men and women, are gradually changing our perceptions of these roles and helping us to upset the status quo.

I see a wave of change coming in this era. Instead of trying to be more like men, or being threatened by men, women are beginning to appreciate their unique feminine qualities—attributes that are not only valuable, but vital in our homes, the workplace, and society. We're realizing that it's time to go beyond fighting for women's rights or blaming men for our lack of success and happiness, and take a more active stand in asserting the value of feminine traits.

In many cases, men's traits, such as aggressiveness and competitiveness, are more accepted and appreciated in society and, for this reason, command better pay and more prestige. The characteristics women are often criticized for—being strong-minded, persistent, firm, and definite in making tough decisions—would be praised in a man.

Other feminine traits such as tolerance, sensitivity, empathy, emotional openness, and being "others oriented" are also valuable and contribute a great deal to our world every day, whether in the workplace, community, or home. Unfortunately, however, they are not always acknowledged.

It is time to recognize and enjoy the benefits of being a woman. Let's not overlook the many advantages we have. Men often assess their own worth in terms of their positions, income, and other external rewards. Women are less likely to shape their identities by their job titles. Because of their multiple roles, women have more opportunities for personal gratification. For example, we often enjoy deeper personal relationships and have more interests that are not job related. Both of these can provide a refreshing solace and personal support system when challenges arise, as they do in everyone's life.

Aside from the personal benefits, women have an opportunity to contribute to the community and the world by helping to improve conditions for women *and* men in society in general. Because of traditional sex roles, equality is not a problem only for women. Both sides have been restricted and each can benefit by learning from the other.

What a tremendous freedom we will finally experience when we can recognize, encourage, and enrich the special gifts of each gender, rather than being intimidated, hindered, or threatened by them. When we overcome these barriers, we'll find that we can build a better world, with men and women learning from each other.

External barriers are not the only ones to overcome. With wings, you will soon be able to overcome the internal ones of

self-doubt, self-consciousness, and inhibitions

anxiety, irrational fear, and excessive worry

emotional pain and injury from your past

personality conflicts

lethargy, exhaustion, and burnout

procrastination, self-sabotage, and resistance to change

Most of all, with wings, you'll be able to experience total freedom, and truly enjoy being you!

HOW TO READ THIS BOOK FOR MAXIMUM RESULTS

As you read each chapter, think of your current situations, challenges, and interests, whether at home or at work, and relate the information to your life. Ask yourself, "How can I use these concepts to overcome the obstacles I face? How can they directly improve the quality of my life?"

Use your imagination and actually see yourself applying the new techniques and strategies. As you go through the book, continually adapt the procedures and ideas to your own style and life situation.

Years ago, someone suggested I do these two things when reading. They have greatly enhanced the value of every book I've read since and I'm sure they'll do the same for you.

1. Use a special marker to highlight key ideas that stand out and are especially meaningful. That way, when you go back later to review, you can spot those concepts right away.

2. Keep a pen and spiral-bound note pad handy. Put the title of the book on the front cover, and as you read each chapter, make summary notes of those points that are particularly pertinent to your life. By doing this, what you'll end up with is a shorter version of the book with only those ideas that you plan to adapt to your life situation. It will be easy to review and you will have it available any time you need a "quick refresher."

FLYING IN TWENTY-ONE DAYS

Another idea for getting the most out of every book is to read with a sense of purpose. It seems that we read best when we read with some personal goal in mind. Be clear on what you intend to do differently as a result of reading this book. Complete the exercises as they are presented and use the information as a personal goal planner.

Most important of all, put new strategies and techniques into practice regularly and as soon as you can. The quicker you implement a new idea, the sooner it will become a habit. Don't allow yourself to become overwhelmed. It's natural to feel uncomfortable when attempting anything new or different, so don't be discouraged. It generally takes approximately three weeks to develop a new habit—not a long time when you consider how long you've been waiting for your wings! You should begin to fly in twenty-one days.

Growing your wings fully could happen quickly; however, taking flight doesn't always occur in an instant. Seeing my dream come true took decades. Your dream may also span many years. And, like me, once you take flight you may even break a wing or two during the process. But every worthwhile dream is worth the effort, the pain, the heartache of setbacks and failures, and the time invested. I urge you to believe that you can fly. You will begin to experience the ecstasy of being free, totally free, to soar to new heights!

It is my privilege to share these thoughts and ideas with you. I believe they have the power to refresh your heart, renew your spirit, and kindle a sense of passion in your soul. The rest is up to you. You have the potential to expand your boundaries and see your life transformed into one of peace, joy, and love.

With *Wings*, There Are No Barriers

Be like the bird
That, pausing in her flight
Awhile on boughs too slight,
Feels them give way
Beneath her and yet sings
Knowing that she hath wings.

Victor Hugo

CHAPTER 1

The End

> Old things are passed away; behold, all things are become new.
> (2 Cor. 5:17)

PERHAPS "THE END" WOULD SEEM to you to be a peculiar way to start a book. Yet, I encourage you to be prepared as you read these words, for your life as you know it may be coming to an end. If, until now, your existence has been one of frustrations, self-doubt, disappointments, exhaustion, or heartache, then I believe that you already know intuitively that something has to end. Life can't stay the way it is *and* improve at the same time. If you are truly ready to emerge from your cocoon, spread your wings, and begin soaring into a life of magnificent possibilities, the old life must die. Then, when you become a new creation, you can begin building a fresh life—a victorious one brimming with inner peace, love, abundance, and prosperity.

Every ending brings us naturally into a place of renewal—a time to start over, a chance to begin again. I am convinced that God challenges us with wonderful opportunities that have been brilliantly disguised as impossible situations. My mother used to say that nature had a way of preparing us for new beginnings. There will always be a little discomfort—sometimes a lot of discomfort—when it is time to end some old way or leave some familiar pattern in our lives. And it is this discomfort that encourages us to pursue the new possibilities. It's the annoyances that plague us that actually cause us to long for and look forward to change. Depending on how we act or react, pain and anguish can be gifts that lead us into a better way.

Mom's favorite example, after raising five daughters, was that as each girl entered her teens, the friction would begin. This friction, she believed, helped everyone in the household not only to prepare for the time that the daughter would leave the nest, but actually to look forward to it. And, sure enough, it worked every time. Can you imagine, Mom would ask, what would happen without that friction? Why, these five daughters might still live at home!

ARLENE'S STORY

Not long ago, my friend Arlene moved away to begin a wonderful new career. Until recently, she was immensely fulfilled in her position as a sales manager in a large and progressive organization. It probably never entered her mind to look "up" to new and better possibilities. After all, she had everything a woman could want in a career—all the benefits including a company car and regular holidays, plus prestige and a great salary along with commissions. As a single parent, she earned enough to pay for a lovely home and support two children on her own. They enjoyed a luxurious life-style.

At work, she was pretty much in command of her time, and controlled the types of training programs she wanted to introduce to her sales representatives. Indeed, there were always dreams hovering in the back of her mind, dreams about doing and being more, and the longing to try her wings at something beyond her comfort zone. But she had a good team to work with, people with lots of drive and initiative, and her job to motivate them provided her with just enough of the challenge she needed to create a satisfying career for herself.

Then, management changed. Policies and staff changed. In fact, the whole operation was reorganized. Things became increasingly uncomfortable. Arlene started feeling "stressed" much of the time, something she wasn't used to. Even small predicaments irritated her. Nothing seemed to go as smoothly as it once had.

Arlene suddenly found herself questioning her own abilities. She had a hard time staying positive—something that had never been a problem before—and this concerned her. Her job became one of settling disputes and putting out fires. No matter what approach she tried, things got worse. Although trials were nothing new in Arlene's life, she'd always found creative ways to work things out. This time there didn't seem to be any answer. For the first time in years, she found herself close to tears much of the time. She dreaded going to work most days, and began to wonder what it would be like to work somewhere else.

At about that time, she decided to respond to an ad for a similar position in another city, offering more responsibilities and new challenges. Although it meant a total upheaval for the whole family—selling their home, moving to an unfamiliar area, and basically starting over—the increase in salary and benefits, along with the added responsibilities and exciting opportunities this job offered, made it worth the effort. She applied for the position and, with her background and expertise, was hired almost immediately. Arlene is now settled in her new position and sees it as one of the best things that could have happened. This position has opened up a whole new realm of possibilities for her. But without the necessary tension caused by the changes in her former position, would she have taken the steps to check into this new opportunity? Chances are, the answer is no. So in essence, "The End" signifies new opportunities, new growth, and new beginnings.

Certainly we prefer security over the unknown, but endings must occur in order for improvements to be made. Besides, is there really such a commodity as security?

ON THE WINGS OF CHANGE

To end anything naturally means change. We need to clear out the old to make room for the new. The very law of nature is change and change means growth. Every living thing is in the process of being transformed. We know this and yet in most cases we continue to resist transformation.

Change and growth must become something we love instead of something we merely endure. To stop changing is to stop living. That's when we become stagnant, just like a river or a stream if it were to remain motionless.

Women who adapt easily and quickly to change are enthusiastic and energetic. There's a freshness about them. They even thrive on the challenges that accompany change. Those who resist change often end up leading dull, tedious lives. They stop growing and developing. Some become lethargic and resigned to their lots in life.

Change and growth often come into our lives disguised as impossible hurdles or major tragedies. Yet, progress of any sort usually includes a few stumbling blocks. These hardships often serve to end some period of our life that was waiting to be ended; close some door that was ready to be closed; strengthen us in preparation to turn the page to the next chapter. Every exit is also an entrance to a new place.

These trials often become our guides for later experiences in our lives. Change usually breaks off certain accustomed ways of living and helps us to form new ways that may be necessary for our growth. Change and hardships are pathways, not roadblocks!

When we fall in love with change and the results it can produce in our lives, we actually look for it and move toward it. We are continuously moving in one direction or the other anyway. We never simply coast or stay in one spot. Change is what keeps us moving *forward*. A new beginning has the potential to be richer and more exciting than the past because of the many ways we have grown through our trials and life experiences.

The Three Stages of Change

Change doesn't happen in an instant. It seems there are three particular phases we go through when faced with every ending.

1. In the present stage, old ways are comfortable, familiar, and controllable. They may or may not be doing us the most good but, in any case, they do happen naturally and with ease. Because the present stage doesn't demand a lot of conscious thought or effort, we are tempted to stay there, even in our darkest hour of adversity, even at the cost of moving on to a more rewarding place.

When the butterfly is still at the *larva* stage, it obviously has a more difficult time surmounting obstacles than if it had wings. Perhaps the caterpillar appears to us to be in a comfortable rut, but it eventually senses that the time has come to experience a dramatic transformation. We, too, have a natural, inborn inclination to become all we were created to be, and we can never be satisfied until we do. "One can never consent to creep when one feels an impulse to soar" (Helen Keller).

What will motivate us to move on to that next stage? Often, it's what I will refer to as *best-worst* situations—those times when we say, "This is the worst thing that could happen to me!" Then later, we realize it was all for the best. These seemingly hopeless catastrophes can cause deep suffering. At the time, we just can't see that any good could ever come out of them. It's not until they've passed that it becomes clear it was actually the best thing to happen because it brought about some personal change or new opportunity that might have eluded us otherwise.

Most of us have weathered at least one *best-worst* incident. If you have, you know that even tough times can have positive results. I know I have had my share, and I admit it's difficult to believe that upsetting or challenging circumstances may have come into our lives for our benefit. What usually happens is that the pain we experience causes us to hunger and thirst for a better way. It's when we are weakest that we have the most powerful motivation to learn how to be strong. We might not be thankful at the time, but neither would we be grateful for the pain caused by scalding soup on our tongues! Yet we have to admit that without it we might continue eating and later suffer even more. *Could it be that the very discomfort that has caused you to seek your wings is a gift?*

2. The transition stage is where we begin to think of leaving comfort behind in search of something better. It means getting out of old ruts and taking on a new perspective. It's a time of stretching, developing, and growing. Often this is a painful place. We're moving into unexplored territory, where new ways are unfamiliar and often frightening. What we need is a time apart, a chance to go to a place where we can be sheltered from the storms for awhile, until we are fully transformed, ready to meet the world again.

A *chrysalis* is the case that encloses and shields the caterpillar during its transition. We, too, need a special covering to protect us during this dormant stage preceding transformation. Since the shift for us is predominantly an internal struggle, our chrysalis during this fragile stage might be a fresh, new belief in ourselves, a sense of positive expectancy, our faith in God, or a feeling of hope for a more triumphant future.

During this stage, we could be tempted to turn back to the familiar, where we have been getting "comfortable" results. And yet somehow, like the caterpillar, we know intuitively that if we are ever to take flight and experience spectacular results, we must stay in this new place for a season, in spite of the uncertainty, regardless of our fears.

This stage can seem as though it will last forever. Yet we know that nothing in life is endless. Everything is temporary. Nothing is permanent aside from God and His love.

So, what does it take to push through this stage? You can use this time to grow—emotionally and spiritually. An ancient Bible principle states that you will know the truth and the truth will set you free. The truth is that, above all else, you and I are spiritual beings. Knowing this, we have newfound strength and freedom to rise out of our limiting beliefs and old thinking patterns. Change may seem disruptive, but we can have the assurance that a new way of life is emerging, just as it should.

When I was having some major renovations done to my home, all I saw for quite a long while was what appeared to be nothing more than chaos and confusion. If I hadn't known what was taking place and why, I might have given up hope that there would ever be any semblance of order in our home again. But I realized this apparent lack of order wouldn't last. It was all part of the process and something that had to happen before the new could arise.

Whether it's a lost job, a divorce, the death of a loved one, or even moving away, endings are at the very least disruptive, and at most devastating. Even though our society encourages us to withdraw and mourn for a time, no one really teaches us how to prepare for new beginnings and start over. Staying flexible allows you to look for the lessons to be learned in everything that happens along the way. Ask yourself how your life will be different now or how your situation can help others. What will you be able to contribute to the world as a result of conquering this tough time?

In other words, choose to focus more on the opportunity for personal growth than on what you are leaving behind. It's not always easy but you can take advantage of the situation by exploring the many opportunities that present themselves in every hardship. Believe it or not, they are there in even the most traumatic circumstances. It's natural to mourn your loss and live in the past for awhile, but it's always your choice whether you grow wings from the experience or hold onto the adversity longer than necessary. Are you ready to burst out of that old life and begin anew? At this stage, there is little to lose and much to gain.

3. In the breakthrough stage, after you finally push through, it becomes easier to accept new roles and situations. Risks are still scary but are exhilarating, too. You've shed the layers that are no longer necessary, and you feel recharged. It's in this stage that you are able to willingly open up to new ideas and possibilities. Now that you're transformed, you begin to welcome change and see it as a pathway to a new and brighter future. It's now that you're able to pursue your aspirations and realize your dreams.

In the life of the butterfly, the *imago* is the final and perfect stage after leaving the protection of the cocoon. This represents our own new life. We are no longer limp and helpless, tossed about by every wind. We are exhilarated and intensely eager, yet peaceful and satisfied all at once. We're finally able to fly up and over any barrier.

However, change is sometimes a slow process and requires patience. We can't simply attach wings to a fuzzy caterpillar and expect it to fly. Trying to speed things up in our lives only results in frustration.

Breaking through a cocoon demands stamina and commitment. Yes, it is a struggle, but it's in pushing through the barriers that we strengthen our wings. Imagine for a moment coming upon a butterfly with her wings fully formed, pushing to break open her cocoon. Feeling sorry for her, you might try to make things easier by breaking it open so she won't have to fight anymore. She would emerge easily, it's true, but with wings all shriveled, weak, and drooping. Eventually she would die, for it's in the struggle that her wings are strengthened. It's in the fight for freedom that she becomes beautiful and powerful. This is all part of the transformation process, and yet we wish someone would come along and take away our obstacles. We long for an easier pathway to freedom. We say, "God, I shouldn't have to struggle like this." And God asks, "Why not?"

The word "transformed" comes from the Greek verb *metamorphoun,* "to change, to transfigure, to alter in appearance." Our word *metamorphosis* is derived from this Greek root. One definition of the word metamorphosis is "an abrupt developmental change in the form or structure of a creature, such as a butterfly, occurring subsequent to birth." When we think about caterpillars—those sometimes destructive, crawling creatures—there's nothing much that would attract us to them. However, when a caterpillar experiences metamorphosis, and emerges at last from the chrysalis, totally transformed, we stand in awe and admiration of this exquisite creation.

In the early Christian era, the butterfly was used as a symbol for resurrection—the death of the old and the birth of the new. It was thought that just as the caterpillar's nature is changed through metamorphosis, so those who emerge into a life with Christ will be changed. And also like the butterfly, transformation in our life is a process. It begins with an awakening deep in our spirit that eventually sweeps over our entire being, until we are no longer satisfied with the old. We understand and accept that something must end. Trying to improve our lives any other way only results in frustration, draining us of the very strength, energy, and peace of mind we are seeking.

Change and endings seem to be inherent in nature, in people. We've all had some loss and suffering in our lives. No one escapes it. Even though we don't welcome endings, when they're forced upon us, *consciously choosing change is something that puts us back in control of our lives.*

We can't make the past go away. We can't alter what's happened. But we can make the deliberate decision either to cut our ties from the past, take flight, and break through to new ways, or to allow former trials and tragedies to negatively determine the direction of the rest of our lives. A triumphant life is a choice only we can make. By bursting through our chrysalis, we can move from trials to triumphs.

For your life to improve, it's important to understand that (1) things must change; (2) you must do the changing—the world's not going to change for you; and (3) you have the potential to change—you have more hidden and unrealized talent lying dormant than perhaps you've ever imagined.

Ask yourself what must be different within you in order to love the process of change and actually welcome it. Are there disabling attitudes, self-sabotaging behaviors, or counterproductive beliefs? If so, change them. You have the ability. You are in control of what goes on inside you. If you're acting in a way that doesn't support your highest goals and values, do something else.

LEARNING TO LOVE CHANGE

1. *Get accustomed to transformation slowly.* Start by breaking with the familiar in some small way each day. For example, change your morning routine, rearrange the furniture, drive a new route to work, or wear your watch on the opposite wrist. Archie Bunker, from an old television program, was annoyed with his son-in-law, Michael, because of the way he put on his shoes and socks. He said the whole world puts on two socks, then follows up with two shoes, but not Michael. Archie couldn't understand why he had to put on one sock and shoe, then the other sock and shoe. Michael just liked to be different. It's not only okay to do some everyday things differently, it's preferable if you want to be able to deal positively with those changes that come into your life uninvited.

2. *Look for opportunities to do things differently.* Try folding the towels in half instead of thirds, or putting the toilet paper roll on the other way. Get out of bed on the opposite side or unplug the television set for a week. Decide to go somewhere by another mode of transportation—the train, bus, or subway, if those aren't your normal methods. Order some unusual foods in a restaurant or add something new to a familiar recipe just for fun.

3. *Change your perspective.* It's amazing how a new vantage point will alter the way you see things. For instance, if you go for a daily walk, try reversing your regular route. Or if you're in the habit of jogging first thing in the morning, try going at sunset. Turn your desk so it faces the opposite direction. You'll be surprised at how fresh even the most familiar things will appear.

4. *Don't get stuck in a rut.* Do something different. If you've always enjoyed listening to classical music, try jazz or country. Perhaps you read nothing but business-related and professional books. Then choose a good novel. Or, if novels are your favorite, try a biography. Even dressing differently is refreshing. Switch from classical, traditional styles or basic colors to those that are more flamboyant. Or if loose-fitting, brightly colored fashions have always been your first choice, select something more conservative, fitted, and tailored next season.

5. *Go somewhere new.* If you've never thought you'd enjoy the ballet or live theater, you may be pleasantly surprised. Maybe it's been a long while since you've spent an afternoon in the library. Take a walk through an amusement park, to the end of a pier, or even around your own block. Explore remote, out-of-the-way places with a friend, or get away for a weekend retreat.

6. *Learn something new.* Start a hobby. Sign up for a class or night course. Attend workshops, seminars, and lectures. Join a sports team or take tennis lessons. When you read and come across a new word, make the effort to look up its meaning in the dictionary and try to use it in conversation as soon as you get the chance.

7. *Get to know interesting people.* Be curious about other people's professions, career goals, hobbies, and personal convictions. Being open to their ideas and opinions doesn't mean that you must adopt them as

your own. It does mean to accept them without prejudice while at the same time questioning them and doing your own research to test their truth and validity. Don't forget to include children. Ask about their dreams and goals and they will introduce a new dimension to the concept of change. Listen to their opinions, thoughts, and ideas and they will energize you with their fresh, untainted ways of seeing things. The elderly, too, will be thrilled to talk about their lives and past adventures. Not only can we can gain valuable insight and counsel from their experiences, but it can be fun and enjoyable to hear of times gone by.

8. *Leave the status quo behind.* I remember visiting my grandmother in the hospital shortly before she passed away. My children were pretending to interview Nana about her growing-up years, including life on the farm and learning to play the piano. Although we had all known that she had been a piano teacher for most of her adult life, we were surprised to find out that as a young woman she had played in a band, on the radio, live every Friday evening! This was an exceptional thing for a woman to be doing in those days. She certainly was a pioneer in escaping typical stereotypes with her willingness to do things differently.

Start to cherish life and see it as an adventure. Break away from the routine of everyday living. Leave old ideas and viewpoints behind for awhile and you will soon find that you are more flexible when unexpected change does happen to you. And it will. That's a guarantee. Your life can either be a nightmare or a dream, a living hell or heaven on earth! You make it so by the way you deal with changes and endings as they occur.

The purpose of change is to grow. The purpose of growth is to become better. To change and grow and become better demands that things are different—that we are different. It insists that we burst out of our old safe natures and throw away self-limiting behaviors and beliefs. It means becoming agents of change, taking on unfamiliar roles, and choosing new maps for our futures.

TRANSFORMED—FROM VICTIM TO VICTOR

As little girls growing up, we were often encouraged to be satisfied with what life has given us. No one had to come out and say it. We got society's message—don't expect too much from life or yourself. That way you won't be disappointed. Is it any wonder so many women shy away from change? Be satisfied, we're told, so often that we begin to believe it. Well, I had believed it. Years ago, in what seems now to be another lifetime, I had learned to accept my life just the way it was. This was not good news.

When I was a teenager I was tall and slender and somehow got the idea that I was "gawky" and unattractive. I wasn't part of the "in" group, so I believed I was uninteresting and undesirable, even though I made friends easily and had many opportunities to date. I always did well in school but never thought of myself as intelligent. I was talented in music, art, and dressmaking and other crafts, but I believed I was just "lucky" when it came to those things.

Like many women who lack confidence in themselves and their abilities, I made choices based on my distorted self-image. I thought I was fortunate when, at sixteen, someone older was in love with me and needed me, so in spite of his fluctuating moods and extreme temper, I decided I would build a relationship with him. I got married right out of high school and became a mother a little more than a year later. But I knew from the beginning of the marriage that I had made a mistake. I gave up on the idea of furthering my education because I thought I wasn't smart enough. I married because I mistook my dependency on him for love. Besides, I believed that no one else would ever want me anyway. I was wrong on all counts. Sadly, it took me many years to find that out.

From an outsider's viewpoint, though, my life would have appeared to be a wonderful one. An exciting career made it look as though I was living a dream—modeling professionally, wearing beautiful fashions, attending elegant functions and gala events, and earning more in an hour than I used to earn in a day.

Many women may have envied this life that seemed so glamorous. What most of them wouldn't have known was what was happening behind closed doors. I was a battered wife. My marriage had become a blur of police sirens, hospital visits, doctor's reports, and family-court appearances. I'm sure most people would have been shocked if they had seen the bruises, black eyes, and swollen lips I was usually able to conceal under artistically applied cosmetics. A face and body that was often black and blue, and an occasional fractured bone, had become a routine part of my life.

Although I tried my best to keep it hidden from practically all outsiders, this secret life was destroying me—mentally, physically, emotionally, and spiritually. For eleven stormy years I lived with only the hope that someday there would be an end to this nightmare.

This was an appalling and frightful predicament but, at the same time, one I was familiar with. Abuse had become a pattern in that former marriage and, eventually, I came to the point where I really didn't expect anything different. Besides, the thought of change was frightening. Sometimes it's easier to go on coping with the way things are because we are accustomed to them than to even think about breaking away to start over. When faced with a decision between two pains, often the pain of the familiar is easier to bear than that of the unknown. "Better the devil you know than the devil you don't" we hear. Choosing "the lesser of two evils" seemed to be the only choice I had during that devastating time in my life. Change was not something I was good at. I opted for security even though it meant constant heartache and even though my very life may have been in danger.

Sadly, my story is not unusual. More and more, studies are showing that self-defeating choices are epidemic among women who have fundamental feelings of inadequacy. Low self-esteem is at the root of many problems women have, from overeating to alcoholism, from tolerating abuse to accepting and staying in jobs for which we are overskilled, from lethargy to burnout and ill health. With a poor self-concept, we get what we *think* we deserve, constricting our own lives, our happiness with others, and our future potential.

The great thing about human nature, though, is that we're only satisfied with *coping* or *getting by* for a time, until one day we begin to stretch our wings. We're fed up with merely surviving and we say, "Enough is enough!" We get to a place where we are willing to make new choices, regardless of the cost. It's then that we know, with absolute certainty, that it's time to take charge of the situation, time for a change, and time to fly out into the mysterious future. When we finally reach that stage, the unknown seems to be the lesser of the two evils.

You may or may not be in the depths of despair that I was in, but we all have barriers to overcome. Maybe you've had enough of being discouraged over unrealized dreams and you want to begin to fly in a new direction. Perhaps you're sick and tired of feeling *sick and tired* and know it's time to start a vigorous fitness program or take a serious look at the type of food fuel you are providing for your body. You might want to leave an unfulfilling job in exchange for a more satisfying one or to start your own business. Perhaps you are fed up with feeling bad over past mistakes and failures and you want to move on with your life. Maybe you're being victimized with verbal put-downs or insults, or by being manipulated or controlled by someone. Whatever it is, you know it's time to get serious about finding a way out of your personal dilemma. If you are, you're prepared to sell out, abandon all your excuses, and burn your bridges. "There is in every woman's heart a spark of heavenly fire, which lies dormant in the broad daylight of prosperity; but which kindles up, and beams and blazes in the dark hour of adversity" (Washington Irving).

I'll never forget the day I got to that point. Fed up with my lifestyle and what was happening, I got desperate for some answers. The first step was to decide not to play the role of a victim of circumstance any longer, believing that other people or situations had more control over what was happening in my life than I did. The second was to face the facts. I'd been spending my energy denying the reality of my state of affairs. Acknowledging the problem was a big step toward freedom. Thirdly, I had to accept full responsibility for my future life and my happiness. Waiting and hoping to be rescued had left me feeling powerless.

So many times we fall into the trap of accepting inappropriate advice from well-meaning friends or even some trained professionals—advice that can often make us feel even worse about our situation, leaving us with a sense of hopelessness. However, those counselors and personal advisors who do help us let us know that there is *always* hope once we take responsibility for finding the way out of our confusion. Instead of waiting for others to change, or for someone to rescue us, we can begin to make the choices that will set us free.

Somehow women are getting the message that we're not capable. Nagging feelings of incompetence and inability cause us to believe if we were smarter, or more educated, experienced, or talented, then perhaps we could make ourselves acceptable. And then we start out on a never-ending course of self-improvement, hoping to finally win the approval we think we need in order to feel confident and at peace with our decisions.

When we are without wings, the world can be a big, scary place. Until we get our wings, we can't make a difference in even our own lives, let alone the lives of others. One reason why we might not have our wings already is that we search for them in all the wrong places—in our men, careers, families, friends, material possessions, financial status, or hobbies. None of these can provide what we need to get us up and flying. As long as we continue to look to outside sources to give us our power, we'll stay weak. We must stop looking to the world to attain our sense of value and inner strength, our peace and happiness. The answer is a spark hidden in our own hearts, planted there by almighty God, and even others cannot help us reach our full potential until we recognize it in ourselves.

Once we have our wings, however, nothing can keep us from soaring to heights unknown. It's then we are able to offer our energy, wisdom, and encouragement to others. It's then we are able to transcend the circumstances of the outside world and be truly free to learn, live, and love.

I believe, because you are reading this book, you're ready to break through the barriers that have imprisoned you long enough. Perhaps you have felt a nudging to end some period of your life that was waiting to be ended, close some door that was ready to be closed. Maybe your cocoon is already breaking open. The layers are falling away. You want to leave your chrysalis behind and fly, free from the weights that have held you back. You're ready for your personal metamorphosis. Certainly, endings can be traumatic, but every exit is an entrance to a new place.

It's time for us to leave the status quo behind and make some powerful, positive choices for ourselves. What will they be for you? For me, it meant leaving a devastating relationship; starting some new habits of physical, mental, and spiritual health; and getting my life in balance—body, mind, and soul. It meant choosing to work hard and raise my children alone. More than anything, it meant really getting to know myself and having a clear understanding of the things I valued in my life. To end the old life, I knew I must assume full responsibility for myself and my choices, as well as my successes and my failures.

It wasn't long before I began to experience new levels of self-respect and faith in my abilities. I felt like a different person, but what really happened was that I discovered an inner strength that I had all along. *And through that new awareness, I had grown my wings!* "Then sunshine kissed my chrysalis—and I stood up—and lived" (Emily Dickinson).

YOU HOLD THE KEY!

There is nothing worse for a woman than a sense of powerlessness. Yet, we'll always feel out of control if we continue to look to others to satisfy our needs. When we believe that outer circumstances have more control over our lives than we do, we have a tendency to give up, and lose touch with our ability to make the necessary changes. We base decisions on our emotions and end up making poor choices. At the same time, in our culture, we've been encouraged to give our power away. We've been discouraged from trusting our own judgment and taking our own counsel.

Feeling in control is certainly an important human element, one that is crucial to our success. Understanding how this control factor affects us enables us to deal more effectively with change when it happens. How does it work? I believe that the following illustration provides an excellent explanation.

In a well-known experiment, two groups of adults were put in separate rooms and given extremely difficult puzzles to solve. To make the task even more challenging, two elements were added. The groups were given a time frame in which to complete the puzzles and they had to listen to very loud, distracting background noises on audiocassette during the entire experiment. These were sounds like traffic noises, bells ringing, people speaking foreign languages, babies crying, and children chattering. Can you put yourself in their place? It sounds so much like life in general, doesn't it? There is a problem to solve, with time pressure and distractions. The only difference between the two groups was that one group was given a device with which they could shut off all the noise. However, there was a catch. The device was to be used only if it became absolutely imperative. If the group members felt pushed to the brink, then and only then were they to use this device.

At the end of the experiment, the results were very interesting. The group that did not have the device failed completely. Not only did they not solve the puzzle within the time frame, they didn't solve it at all. They said it simply was not possible, with all the background distractions. The other group solved the puzzle perfectly, within the time frame, and you can probably imagine the most interesting part of the experiment. Right—they did not have to use the device to get rid of the noises. Simply knowing they had complete control was all that was necessary for them to buckle down and tackle the task at hand.

In order to overcome the barriers you and I face, we need to experience that sensation of being in control. In the real world, we don't often get to control our situations, our circumstances, or the people we live, work, or deal with. But there is one thing over which each of us has been given total control. That is our power to choose.

CHOICE: THE FORCE THAT SHAPES YOUR FUTURE

Every day, all day long, you are making choices and those choices are determining the direction of your life. In fact, the life you are living right now is a sum total of all your past choices. Your decisions, rather than fate, determine your future. Abundant life is provided for you but you must choose it.

If it is to be, it is up to me. It has been suggested that these are the ten most powerful two-lettered words in the English language. The more you take responsibility for what happens in your life, the more control you will have in creating a happy, prosperous, and rewarding life-style for yourself. You have the potential to change your life's direction. But the only way to do this is to accept 100 percent responsibility for the outcomes you're experiencing, both good and bad.

There was a time when I rejected this concept. As I sat in a seminar, much like the programs I now present, the speaker made this statement: "You chose who you are and where you are today. Right now, your life is the result of all your past choices. If you want things to change, you must change your choices!"

At that time in my life, considering the situation I was in, the speaker's statement seemed more like an accusation than a promise of hope. It even made me angry to think that someone would imply that I was responsible for the terrible circumstances in my life, that I had somehow brought about a home life of constant disappointments and abuse. I had gone to this program feeling extremely depressed. I left holding back tears and feeling even more desperate, asking over and over, "How could anyone think I *chose* what's happening in my life right now?"

Yet, I couldn't get those words to stop playing in my mind. "You are the result of all your past choices. You chose who and where you are today." Suddenly, I became aware of the power of that comment. If I had somehow created the state I was in with all my past choices, couldn't I change my life by changing my choices? It was becoming clear that this was good news, and not bad after all.

We think that because of our heredity, environment, society, finances, or other people, we are victims of circumstance and that leaves us feeling trapped. You don't have to be a victim of life. You can rise up; take control of your thoughts, feelings, and choices; and get on with life. Taking full responsibility for your decisions and their outcomes is not always an easy thing to do, but it is the only way to make changes in your life. Accepting that everything in life is a choice puts you in control again. Once you know there are other possibilities, you no longer feel victimized, even if you should choose to stay where you are.

Are there a lot of things in your life that you feel have been forced upon you? You might think that you are in a situation that offers no other choices. It might be a desperate situation like mine or something as trivial as trying to get off the telephone with a chatty person. What are your choices in that case? You can explain that you are glad the person called but that you have only three or four minutes to talk, or you can say that you were in the middle of something else and ask if you could return the call later. If all else fails, you could simply hang up! But if you decide to stay on the line, at least recognize that it was a choice.

The truth is that you don't *have* to do anything. This may sound a bit extreme, but it's a fact. You don't have to go to work every day. You could sleep in if you wanted to, and eventually be unemployed! But it is an alternative. You don't have to raise your children. There are government agencies that will take them for you. You don't have to pay income taxes, but of course, jail is the other option. You don't have to work overtime, but then you may not achieve a particular financial goal or have the doors opened to a promotion you want. There are always other choices, and that's the key. It's only when we think and believe there aren't that our situation becomes a trap.

Instead of saying, "I'm broke" or "I can't afford that" say instead, "I've chosen to spend my money in this area; that's why I have none left over for that." You can choose to spend your money on the rent and groceries, and that's why you won't be shopping for a new wardrobe this month. It's not that you can't afford new clothes; it's simply that you've made a wise choice for spending your money this month! Rather than saying, "I never have enough time for . . . ," say instead, "The reason I haven't time for that is because I've chosen to spend my time elsewhere."

Your motive behind choosing to do something is that, of all the other choices available to you, that one happens to be the best choice according to what you value most. You decide to go to work, raise your children, leave or stay in a relationship, or continue at your job because it's the most advantageous way of moving toward your highest values, goals, and purpose in life, not because you've been forced into it without any other options.

When you use terms such as "have to," "must," or "can't," your brain accepts them as reality. In a sense, you're creating your own limitations by giving your control away and allowing outside circumstances or other people to direct your life. Without personal responsibility there's no true freedom. Without self-reliance, we're like robots, being operated and manipulated by external forces.

When we don't exert control over our lives, we tend to live in the world of "if only." We say things such as: "If only things were different." "If only I had that new job, car, promotion, house, or vacation, then I'd be happy!" "If only I had her spouse. Anybody could be happy with a husband like that!" "If only I had more time, more money, more friends, more education" . . . and the list goes on!

The *victim mentality* means you can only be happy if outer circumstances improve. It's the belief that your life is being governed by something outside your control, that your effectiveness is limited by situations or the behavior of other people. It's the feeling that you are not free to choose your own actions.

In many ways, we've been encouraged to trust others' advice more than our own judgment for some of our most important life decisions, from career counselors to health experts, whether it's legal, medical, or financial advice. From childhood, we've been led to believe that others are more knowledgeable than we are and, because they have more experience, we should follow their advice. This belief creates an *illusion* of security. We choose to rely on others rather than taking our own counsel. Then, because we've turned over authority to others, it's no wonder we begin to feel trapped and victimized.

Take some time right now to identify the reasons why you feel that you cannot or do not have your ideal life. Write these in your note pad. Now, go back over your list and check any items over which you have full control. Make a decision from now on to focus only on those. Ask yourself, "What one thing could I be doing that would enable me to make the changes I want to make?" See if there are ways you could *bloom where you're planted*. Personal responsibility means choosing to make the best use of what we have and where we are, in spite of the situation. It means taking control of our choices.

You and I have the wonderful privilege of choosing our attitudes, perceptions, and actions in every situation, which in turn determine our results. Today, I can say that I am a positive, take-charge person, although that hasn't always been true. I have learned to be a victor instead of a victim. I have discovered that developing a healthy mental outlook and positive goals for the future, in spite of apparent circumstances, is always a choice. Still, I have to remind myself time and time again of this truth. It doesn't come naturally and it's easy to fall back into old patterns.

Stress experts tell us that it is not so much an event itself that causes our stress, but how we perceive that event. The perceptions you choose about each circumstance have a direct impact on your emotions—whether you feel good or bad, positive or negative, confident or apprehensive, optimistic or pessimistic. Those emotions then determine your response and eventually the actions you will take.

Consider this **CPRR** "life-saving" formula for winning back control of your life:

Circumstance → Perception → Response → Result

When an event happens in your life, you form an opinion or make a judgment. You see the circumstance as either good or bad. You *explain* it to yourself. This is your perception or your personal view of the situation. That perception, or explanation, determines your response and creates a particular mood. This leads to your behavior or the action you decide to take and eventually the end result.

Normally, we cannot control the circumstance. It may be another person, a job layoff, an illness, an accident, a death, or any situation we cannot change. But we can always alter our perception, which in turn shifts our emotions and the end result. As women, we often believe we are governed by our emotions. Instead, we don't have to be ruled by them but have been given the wonderful power to choose what we focus on and, by doing so, create any state of mind we want. I can think of two incidents in my life where this concept made a difference in how I felt about my circumstances. The first one still makes me laugh when I think of it.

A few years ago, shortly after I had remarried, my husband and I decided to go for a ride on an old steam-engine train. It was one of the last trips this train would take and there was quite a celebration happening. With so many people aboard, my husband and I got separated as we tried to make our way down the narrow, crowded aisles to the food car during the trip. I was glad when he finally caught up with me. I knew he was there without even looking because he started to pinch me teasingly from behind. Laughing, I played right along, knowing that with all the crowds, no one would ever guess what was going on between the two of us. When I turned to say something to him, I was horrified to find that I had been playfully responding to a stranger's advances!

Of course, within seconds, my response had changed. The result had changed. My attitude, physical demeanor, and stress level had been altered, and all because my perception of what was going on had changed. While I perceived it to be something between my husband and me, it was fun. But when my perception had changed, and rightly so, that same situation disgusted me. The circumstance itself had not changed. The events were the same. What had changed was my reaction as a result of my perception.

On a more serious note, the second incident happened when I was on a business trip. I was driving a rental car from one speaking engagement to another. Because I needed to send some information to a client in a hurry, I stopped my car at a small variety store that had a sign in front advertising a fax service. What I discovered when I entered the store, however, was that there was only one person who could serve me, and she was on the telephone. To make matters worse, when she saw me, she turned her back to me so she could obviously have a more private conversation. This annoyed me and I started to pace the floor and go through all the nonverbal signals to let her know I was in a hurry—stretching out my arm in an exaggerated manner as if to check my watch, tapping my toe, drumming my fingers on the countertop, jingling the keys in my pocket. Nothing seemed to work. She continued with her private conversation.

Finally, she put the receiver down and turned around very slowly. As she did, I noticed tears running down her cheeks. She apologized and then went on to say with a rather shaky voice that she had been talking to her mother, who had called to let her know that her father had been rushed to the emergency room. Apparently, he was close to death and they were not even sure if he would live long enough for her to make the drive to the hospital. As you can imagine, my perception of the situation was totally changed. Now, tears welled up in *my* eyes as I felt this woman's distress and heartache. Suddenly my priorities were different. Perhaps I should stay and watch the store so she could go to the hospital. Or maybe we could lock up the store together and I could drive her to be with her family. Everything had changed, yet nothing had changed. I still needed to get this information to my client. I still had a schedule to keep. But I realized I had a choice. I could continue to be upset with the way my plans had been delayed, or I could change how I feel by experiencing her sorrow along with her. Again, because my perception changed, my response and the end result were different. Being behind schedule seemed so insignificant now that I understood her actions, and sensed her pain.

Both of these were valuable lessons in my life. What I had learned was that sometimes a simple change in our perception is all that is needed to put an entirely new slant on a situation.

Now I attempt to use this technique in everyday occurrences. For instance, it works when I'm driving my car and someone suddenly cuts in front of me in heavy traffic. Instead of getting agitated as I once might have, honking my horn and muttering to myself, I choose to change my perception. I *choose* to believe that the driver didn't pull out in front of me to torment me. The truth is, I will probably never know his real intent anyway. So, instead, I use my imagination and tell myself that this may be someone's elderly grandfather, out for a drive, savoring this last opportunity to enjoy his freedom before he must surrender his license and rely on others for transportation. Then, I feel compassion for this driver, whomever it might be. Even though I don't know for sure that it is an elderly person, I am free to let it go. Amazing things begin to happen to us when we merely change our perceptions.

I can almost hear someone saying, "What a Pollyanna way of looking at life!" While it's true that optimists and idealists are often accused of seeing life through rose-colored glasses, this technique is based on reality—the truth that life has its challenges and, if we want, we can choose to see good in every situation.

The benefits are many. When an incident occurs and we perceive

it to be a positive one, we respond with understanding and gratitude. We celebrate it with joy and excitement. The result is one of
acceptance and we move *with* the event, rather than *against* it. This
type of acceptance, when trials come into our life, creates positive
energy leading to constructive behaviors and a more balanced life.

If we perceive life events as negative, our response is anger, frustration, fear, or anxiety. Our reaction is to resist and the result is negative
energy, otherwise known as stress or tension. This leads to destructive
behaviors and imbalance—mentally, physically, and emotionally.

Circumstances we see as positive become challenges. Those we
perceive as negative become our barriers. The only true freedom we
have is the freedom to choose the way in which we will view every
event. So it seems logical always to make the choice that will serve
us the best.

Since there are many forces affecting our lives over which we
have *no* control, it's not surprising that we get caught in the trap of
feeling "victimized" and believe that our lives are being controlled
by outside circumstances. For instance, we didn't choose our
appearance, personality, physique, or parents. We didn't decide
when or where we were born. We cannot choose our height, intelligence, or coloring. Other than voting, we may be in no position to
influence most government decisions, taxes, or high prices. We
don't have power over death, war, recession, or other people's personalities, opinions, and actions.

When we continue to focus on these things, we tend to see them
as being responsible for our lack of success or happiness. We say
things like, "If it wasn't for my boss, my husband, my mother-in-law,
these kids, God, the company, the government, or the full moon,
I'd have a better life." It's easy to blame politics, society, external
events, or our families for the way we act.

In an experiment, women who believed that their dysfunctional
upbringing was one of the major reasons why they were not experiencing the success they desired were asked to explain why they
believed so. Some said it was because their parents were too strict or
protective, and so they were never given the freedom to make their
own choices or learn through personal experiences. Interestingly,
an equal number said the opposite—that with parents who were too
lenient, they weren't given the guidance one needs to cope in
today's world. Another group reasoned that it was because they
came from poor families and so were given no opportunities for

education or advancement. Again, just about an equal number stated their parents were so wealthy that they were handed everything, and never knew what it was like to have to strive or work for survival. It's no wonder, they said, that they were having a tough time in the real world. Some said it was because there was no religion in the home; others said there was too much. Some blamed the fact that they were an only child and others complained that they came from large families and lacked individual attention and love.

Whatever our past or present conditions, we can all come up with a reason for not being as successful, well balanced, or happy as we wish we were. *Even though we have a reason to be the way we are, none of us has a reason to stay that way.*

It's understandable we might be tempted to believe we have little control over our own fates. Most people will agree with us when we complain about the things we think are controlling our lives, whether it's the traffic that caused us stress, the boss who made us angry, or the spouse who keeps upsetting us. When we have one trial after another, it's easy to adopt the attitude that life is difficult. When we look around, we see others struggling too. It seems that life really isn't fair. We become convinced that no matter what we do, or how hard we try, things will never change.

Because life has a strange way of giving us what we expect from it, we'll keep getting more of what we don't want as long as we hold that thought. Of course, there are always some circumstances over which we have no control. When they occur, we sometimes feel trapped, saying things like, "Why me? I can't understand why this would happen!" This is not to say that every bad or negative thing that happens to us comes about because we expect it. It does mean that the final outcome of that event, whether we grow and learn from it, or it destroys us, is a result of how we've decided to view the situation. While we don't choose or want accidents, illnesses, bankruptcies, deaths, or any other unpleasant or disturbing events, how we deal with them is something we determine.

Without even realizing it, we can give away our control. We can allow other people to determine our attitudes. For example, we can listen to the doom and gloom presented through the media. When we pay attention to the news, we hear that crime is up, education is down, unemployment is on the rise, the planet is being destroyed, natural disasters are getting worse, and the quality of our life is deteriorating. It's no wonder that when researchers monitor people's thoughts, they tell us that more than 80 percent of what we think about on an average day is negative.

Coping with change and uncertainty is one thing we'll all have to do as we move quickly into the next century. But when we *choose* to focus on the negative information we're fed daily, it creates a "poverty mentality." We begin to feel hopeless.

When we're unsure of our future, it destroys the confidence of even the most self-assured individuals. Many of the successful women I've spoken with confide that they feel their success won't last. They fear that they could wake up at any moment to the realization that it's all been taken from them, that they've lost everything. Many women, particularly in the creative professions, suffer with what's been referred to as the *impostor syndrome*—a deep fear that they will be *found out*. In other words, they believe that any success they have achieved is due to the fact that they must have simply been at the right place at the right time, and that it wasn't the result of a particular talent on their part. In a recent interview, a well-known comedienne who has enjoyed a full and distinguished career, international recognition, and tremendous financial success admitted that she has never been secure with her fame or wealth. In fact, she imagines that it was all a mistake, that one day someone will look in her direction, say, "Oh, I didn't mean *her!*" and it will be all over. The truth is, when our accomplishments are built on a combination of universal principles and our innate abilities, we are pretty much guaranteed continued success in any venture. The only limits we'll encounter are self-imposed.

Choose to dwell on success instead of failure, wealth instead of poverty, abundance instead of lack, health instead of sickness. Lack of hope means that, somewhere, you've lost faith in your talents. Somewhere along the way, you've given up on your dreams and the belief that all change introduces unlimited possibilities. Hopelessness is one state of mind that humans cannot survive. I think the following group experiment helps to illustrate this truth.

Several individuals were instructed to hold their hands in buckets of ice water. Some were told the experiment would last for three minutes. Others were given no time frame at all. At the end of the experiment, the group that had been given no time frame couldn't last even three minutes, whereas the first group reported that they could have gone on even longer.

When we have hope, it's amazing what we can endure. Our hope can be found in new beginnings but that means having a willingness to change our choices. Here's how.

1. Instead of saying, "I have to," "I must," or "I have no other choice!" say, "I choose to," "I've decided to," or "I prefer."

2. Rather than saying, "If it wasn't for . . . the economy, my bad luck, the stars, or my handicap," remind yourself that "if it is to be, it is up to me."

3. Put an end to blaming and complaining. We waste a lot of time wishing and hoping that circumstances and people would change so that we can be happy. They don't have to change in order for you to have a good life. It's possible to be happy even if you're not in a happy place.

4. Take it upon yourself to do some research regarding your legal or medical matters; health, nutrition, and fitness strategies; and career options before you consult with professionals. You may be able to make some decisions ahead of time. Then you can trust the experts to help you fine tune your plans.

5. Assert your option to choose. You may have been a product of society, the environment, your heredity, or your past, but you don't need to be influenced by these anymore. It's not necessary to be controlled by feelings or conditions. You can choose to make the best use of your abilities and your mind. Start your new life today.

Accepting full responsibility for your life is not always an easy thing to do. Most of us have conditioned ourselves for many years to blame our unhappiness or lack of success on other people's behaviors or events beyond our control. Saying that something or someone has made us happy is just as untrue as saying that something or someone has made us angry. Neither statement is true. In both cases, it is a choice we must make.

Just as I had to acknowledge I was a sum total of all my past choices, so you must realize that you can choose your response in any situation. It's only then that you can experience personal freedom in the midst of difficult circumstances. Only then can you look forward eagerly to the thrill and challenges of life instead of longing for absolute protection and safety. Only then can you be in control.

Aside from empowering us to choose our response to particular circumstances, taking control enables us to get out and make things happen. Don't wait for the time to be right, or hope to be "discovered." Being proactive rather than reactive prepares us to take risks.

POSITIVE RISK TAKING

It's true that sometimes we do feel as though we're being manipulated by outside circumstances, much like being tossed to and fro on a stormy sea, totally out of control. But then we've also had those times when we *have* felt "in control." This usually happens when we've decided to do something risky, something outside our normal personal boundaries. Our most fulfilling and rewarding moments seem to occur when we have chosen to put ourselves into situations where we must stretch to our limit in order to accomplish a worthy and challenging goal.

Those experiences, both scary and exhilarating, give us the sensation of being free at last! These are the cherished moments of utmost fulfillment and contentment that we wish could last forever.

Some people think that those extraordinary moments of perfect satisfaction occur when everything in their lives is in harmony, relaxed, and peaceful. And if somehow they could get their lives to the point where they would stay that way, they would be happy.

The more we strive for happiness, however, the more it eludes us. "Happiness is as a butterfly, which, when pursued, is always just beyond your grasp, but which, if you sit down quietly, may alight upon you" (Nathaniel Hawthorne). Happiness is not something that we can capture and keep in a jar. It happens to us in brief moments here and there. It is a process, a journey, an adventure we must live from day to day. In fact, happiness usually surprises us.

Sometimes we feel that the time we spend on routine activities, whether at work or at home, is robbing us of happiness. We think that if we had enough free time to relax, we could really begin to enjoy life. Sadly, a tremendous amount of free time is spent sitting passively absorbing information from the television set or in some other activity that demands little or no skill. Millions of people spend their evenings watching TV and waiting for happiness to fall in their laps, merely *wishing* for brighter futures. The result is that their lives become either dull or full of meaningless events that make them feel discouraged, apprehensive, and out of control.

We think that time without difficulties or demands will lead to a rewarding, fulfilled life. On the contrary, the rare occasions when we experience a deep sense of satisfaction usually happen when we are fully involved in a challenge that causes endorphins to flow and gets us to extend ourselves.

Children tend to seek out "uncomfortable" situations and explore new opportunities naturally. They find adventure in every seemingly impossible situation. They face challenges with a sense of awe and almost instinctively know that they must at least attempt the impossible in order to grow.

Our three grandchildren are such beautiful teachers of life's lessons. I remember a time when baby Alexandra had been walking for just a few weeks. While I was visiting with her one day, she decided that to get from one side of the room to the other, she should squeeze herself between the chair I was sitting on and the wall behind it.

How much easier it would have been simply to go around in front of my chair. The way was certainly clear for her to do so. But there was no challenge in that! Instead, she pushed and shoved, huffed and puffed, grunted and groaned, and finally made it through the narrow opening. When it was all over, and she had accomplished her goal, she turned and flashed me the biggest grin, her face beaming with a look of smug satisfaction that said, "I did it!" It had been difficult, and she looked so proud of her achievement. It was a triumph that she would have missed if she had taken the easy route, as you and I so often do.

As I watch Kurtis attempt a puzzle designed for children far beyond his age, or Aaron trying to keep up with his older brother, I see that these little people are extending themselves and, in so doing, are gaining a wonderful sense of self-mastery. Not only do most of us, as adults, choose not to put ourselves in these positions, but we go to even greater lengths to avoid them. We seek out the path of least resistance. Yet, we know from experience that it's when we're fully involved with the challenging events of our lives, and conquering the barriers that cross our path, that happiness alights upon us.

Some women have the privilege of spending their workdays involved in only those activities that provide them with this same deep satisfaction. Acting, decorating, sports, music, art, and cooking are a few of the professions that allow people to get so involved in an activity that they are oblivious to what's going on around them. They are so caught up in the moment that nothing else matters. Even if you are not privileged to have such a career, there are many ways to enjoy this same sensation.

Positive risk taking is the key to stretching yourself. When you expose yourself to the possibility of loss or failure, you expand your mind and spirit. It takes courage to open yourself up to demanding projects and stimulating activities. By expanding your horizons, you begin to discover new and better ways to deal with life's ups and downs. You become more confident and flexible. You begin to make more positive choices. So many women stay in jobs that they dislike, hold on to relationships that are destructive, or continue to follow traditions that they're not even devoted to simply because of the "illusion of security" they offer.

WHAT EXACTLY IS RISK?

When was the last time you attempted something exciting that actually took your breath away? In which activities can you become so involved that you lose all track of time? When was the last occasion you willingly endeavored to do something that you knew would take courage?

The Greek word for "risk" translates: "To sail around a cliff; venturing out from a safe harbor to the open sea." So, risking essentially means moving from security to the unknown. Risking is daring to take a chance and allowing yourself to be vulnerable—to potential loss and potential reward. Isn't it interesting that we normally focus on what we think we'll lose rather than what we might gain? This may come from confusing risk with gambling.

There's a big difference between risking and gambling. Gambling might be described as trying your luck at something hazardous or as mere speculation, blind faith, a leap in the dark, or taking a random shot in an uncertain enterprise. True risking is calculated. It means that you are aware of the consequences, have weighed the pros and cons, have considered all your options, and are ready to make a logical, reasonable decision.

When you've done your homework, considered your options and the possible outcomes, and determined that the rewards are positive and clear-cut, then you're ready to develop your strategies and methods.

When you think of it, everyday living and functioning involve some risk. Whether it's backing your car out of your driveway, crossing a busy street, or even getting out of bed in the morning, you're taking a chance!

It's when you eagerly choose to risk, to dare, to take chances and move out of old ruts and comfort zones, that your self-respect grows and confidence levels blossom. It's when you choose to develop a new skill, build a new relationship, apply for a different job or position, or go back to school that you begin to grow your wings!

We find ourselves wishing we could have had our wings when we started out on this journey through life. Young women in their teens and twenties so often feel misunderstood and insecure, with terrifying thoughts of what the future might have in store. But it's there, in those years, when they're struggling to break through their cocoons of self-limiting beliefs and negative past conditioning, that they grow and strengthen their wings.

True risk taking is both scary and exhilarating. Think of the times when you have done something that, had you allowed it, could have scared you enough to hold you back, and yet the promise of the thrill spurred you on in spite of the fear.

Women who win see risk as a stimulating, positive opportunity. Women who hold back view risk as negative—a dangerous, frightening choice. It's only natural that taking risks would make us feel uncertain and apprehensive, and can, in some cases, even be dangerous. In fact, if it's not scary to some degree, perhaps it's not really worthy of being called a risk at all! But when you become comfortable with fewer and fewer new experiences, you lose your motivation to choose risk. And this is the surest way to miss out on all that life has to offer you. "Far better it is to dare mighty things, to win glorious triumphs, though checkered by failure, than to take rank with those poor spirits who neither enjoy much, nor suffer much, because they live in that gray twilight that knows neither victory nor defeat" (Theodore Roosevelt).

The greatest risk, therefore, is to take no risks! When you never test your potential, you are in danger of losing your resiliency. You find it more and more difficult to bounce back after adversity strikes.

CHOOSING RISK OVER SECURITY

Safety is certainly a significant human value and choosing

absolute security and assurance is appropriate if it allows you to achieve what you desire most in life. It's when you are feeling dissatisfied with your career, personal life, or relationships and friendships that it's necessary to consider risk taking. In fact, you can't grow without risking. It's a crucial step in breaking out of old ruts and moving forward.

In my international travels, I've discovered that more than 80 percent of all women in my audiences are unhappy or dissatisfied with their lives but are not sure how to go about changing. Risking allows us to improve the quality of our lives by taking us beyond mediocrity and the mundane; by pushing us beyond indifference and pettiness; by freeing us from ordinary, commonplace concerns and day-to-day stresses.

We hear a lot about "entrepreneurial spirit" these days, yet there really is nothing new under the sun. Women who have overcome barriers over the years, since the beginning of time, have had this spirit. These women are the pioneers, the trailblazers. They are the problem solvers in life, with the ability to look ahead and create solutions for their own and others' success. Not only do they have a burning desire to move ahead, make positive changes, and con-tribute to the world, they are willing to go the extra mile to do it! They are the movers and the shakers, living life to the fullest and always ready for a challenge.

BARRIERS TO RISK TAKING

Here are some of the reasons why we hold back from taking risks. They're not the only reasons, but they seem to be the most common barriers that women have to conquer. Understanding them will be a start to empowering yourself to leave your comfort areas—to do more, be more, and experience more. As you read through them, think about the things you would label "risks" in your life, and deter-mine which of these barriers are preventing you from moving ahead.

1. *We fail to recognize our potential to deal with the challenges that accom-pany risk.*

Often, we don't see ourselves as brimming with potential, yet sci-entists and behavioral experts agree that each of us is using only a small portion of his or her natural abilities—actually less than 10 percent! That means that you have an additional 90 percent potential available to you that you have not even begun to tap into! One of the reasons why we are not using all of our potential is because we don't know it's available. We don't believe we are capable of turning our dreams into realities. Your belief about your potential to deal with challenges is the first key to a life of personal fulfillment.

2. *We have been conditioned to "play it safe" and lead sheltered lives.*

We grow up hearing "better safe than sorry," or "better the devil you know than the devil you don't." With statements such as, "Here, let Dad do that for you," or "Mom will look after everything," we've been given the idea that someone else will take care of us and make everything right in our lives—our parents, the government, a spouse, or the company. This creates an *illusion* of security.

We've also been conditioned to believe that we'll experience disastrous results if we step outside the guidelines that others have set. We've been encouraged to give our power away and not trust our own judgments or internal wisdom in making the right choices for our lives.

In many ways, we see ourselves, our success, and our happiness as being dependent on the men in our lives. This mind-set often promotes the *damsel in distress* syndrome, and leaves us feeling as though we need to be rescued, with men being our rescuers. A number of years ago, an interesting study was conducted in which women attending live theater were observed watching scary murder mysteries, during both the afternoon matinee and the evening performance. When they attended the matinee, women sat through the shocking murder scenes with little or no emotion. However, when they attended the evening performance, with men in the audience, the women displayed terror. Not only did they appear frightened and horrified, but most of them screamed, cried, swooned, or collapsed into their partners' waiting arms!

I become the damsel in distress if my husband is home when a spider arrives on the scene. Without really thinking about it, I call for him to come and "save me." However, if I happen to be home alone, I normally don't have the time to go through the emotions and fool around running for cover, so I just step on the thing, clean up the mess, and get on with my life! We are certainly capable, although somehow we've been conditioned to believe we're not.

A few years ago, I decided to purchase a video recorder. I was proud of myself for taking the initiative, reading various consumer reports, shopping around, and talking with salespeople. I finally made my decision and purchased the one of my choice. I proceeded to read the instruction manual and learned how to operate the camera. However, when it came time to change the cartridge, I happened to be sitting near my son-in-law. I barely caught myself as I almost handed it over to have him figure out how to insert the new one. It seemed the most natural thing to me, even though I am aware of what we, as women, sometimes do to ourselves. What a feeling of competence and confidence I had when I caught myself, took the camera back, read the instruction booklet, and discovered how to do it myself. Now that I understand how it's done, I don't mind passing it on to someone else to handle it. I know I'm doing it for convenience, not because I'm unskilled.

3. We are prone to a "martyr mentality."

Many women in our culture have been programmed to believe that their prime reason for living is to fulfill others' needs and expectations *at the cost of ignoring their own*. While it's certainly desirable and noble to have altruistic goals, the truth is that if you use *all* your life energy making others happy, you'll have no energy left to continue. With a martyr mentality, it's easy to become a "domestic slave," filling your days and evenings doing for others, often feeling as though you've been taken advantage of.

Instead of stretching your own stress level to its limit, arguing with family, or getting to the boiling point, simply stop *doing*. Try leaving the laundry of those family members who are over the age of junior high school. Don't pack lunches. Close the door to that messy room. I agree that it's not easy at first, but I guarantee that the work will get done eventually.

On the other hand, if you truly enjoy doing those things and see yourself as a *willing* martyr, then there's no need to change. Instead, just stop complaining! My mother-in-law is a wonderful example of an agreeable martyr. She is a giving woman who adores her family and finds sheer delight in generally doing for them what they are clearly capable of doing for themselves. It would be like robbing her of inner gratification if we took those opportunities away from her. I also adore my family and am concerned for their well-being, but because of my different life-style, personal values, and the demands of my chosen profession, I recognize that if I value my sanity and health it's better for me to encourage others to look after themselves. When our daughters were still at home, I also saw this as a way of boosting their self-confidence, since they could develop skills they might otherwise not have the opportunity to discover.

An interesting reality about human nature is that when you have looked after your own needs, you're not carrying around a lot of excess emotional baggage. You become more willing and able to give of your time, talents, and energy. Instead of feeling taken advantage of if you do choose to sacrifice, you can do it for the right reasons and in the right spirit. When you learn to nurture yourself, you are set free to be more creative and insightful in helping others.

4. *We feel like victims of circumstance.*

You'll never spread your wings and leave the nest if you believe that outside forces are preventing you from taking action in your life. In the face of the unknown, we often feel that we are not in control. When that happens, it's no wonder that we wander aimlessly. We are, by nature, goal seeking and need targets. It's not until we realize how much control we really do have that we begin to look to the future and set meaningful objectives.

5. *We become paralyzed with fear.*

We worry about what might happen. We imagine all the possible negative outcomes. We focus on the potential loss more than we consider the potential gain. Whether it's fear of failure, success, the unknown, or rejection, fear causes procrastination. It prevents us from developing a plan and taking action. Waiting until all fear goes away is not the answer. True risk taking doesn't happen in the absence of fear. It means advancing in spite of those feelings. We will be dealing in depth with the fears that hold us back in the chapter on goals.

Considering these five areas, what are some of the barriers that have been holding you back from taking risks and accomplishing all you are capable of? Take a moment and jot down those areas that have been affecting your life.

True success begins when we know and understand why we don't choose risk and yet become flexible enough to keep changing and growing until we start to love and look forward to it. Most risk-taking activities do not come naturally. They require us to make an initial effort that we are usually reluctant to make. Your comfort zones are your barriers and they could be holding you back.

POSITIVE ACTION STEPS:

1. *Start by defining your personal limitations.*
What is risk for one woman might be sheer pleasure for another. One may feel uncomfortable eating alone in a restaurant while another might hold back from asking for a raise or promotion; someone else may have a difficult time telling a long-winded or complaining friend that she doesn't want to spend any more time talking on the phone. Bigger challenges might include

- physical risks—white-water rafting, parachuting, or deep-sea diving
- emotional risks—opening up to tell someone your true feelings, learning to trust others, or getting married
- intellectual risks—going back to school, learning to use a computer, or speaking in public
- spiritual risks—living by faith, trusting God, or giving up full control
- financial risks—purchasing your first car, buying a home, or making any large investment
- social risks—entertaining in your home, joining a networking association, or attending a national conference by yourself

Spend some time observing yourself in typical risk situations. Get a good understanding of limits you have set for yourself. You may recognize your comfort boundaries when you catch yourself saying things such as "I could never do that!" or "I wish I had the courage to attempt that." Then pick one of the areas listed above and consciously choose to put yourself in a risky situation!

2. *Choose to do something that at this time makes you feel uncomfortable.*
Tackle this by taking small steps every now and then. For you, it might mean speaking up in a staff meeting, going somewhere alone, or leaving the house without making all the beds. Give yourself a gentle push to keep this up on a regular basis (the small steps, not necessarily the unmade beds!).

3. *Don't put yourself down or compare yourself to anyone.*

If you're trying to get up the courage to join a bowling league, don't compare yourself to a woman who's going skydiving. If saying no to someone is risky for you, it doesn't make sense to compare yourself to someone whose goal is to ask for a promotion to the position of VP of sales and marketing. We all have different tolerance levels for the self-doubt that accompanies risk, so comparison really isn't fair.

To Risk

To laugh is to risk appearing the fool.
To weep is to risk appearing sentimental.
To reach out for another is to risk involvement.
To expose feelings is to risk exposing your true self.
To place your ideas and dreams before the crowd is to risk their loss.
To love is to risk not being loved in return.
To live is to risk dying.
To hope is to risk despair.
To try is to risk failure.
But risks must be taken, because the greatest hazard in life
is to risk nothing.
The person who risks nothing . . . has nothing . . . is nothing.
People may avoid suffering and sorrow, but they simply cannot learn,
feel, change, grow, love . . . and live!
Chained by their certitudes, they are slaves and have
forfeited their freedom.
Only those who risk are truly free.

Author Unknown

FREEDOM CHARACTERISTICS

What is it that enables some women to take risks and to continue taking action in spite of barriers? There are many factors, and that's what we'll be discovering in the following chapters. But here are two of the basic traits that these women have developed within themselves in preparation for their wings.

Characteristic 1: A Sense of Adventure

So many people lead lives of quiet desperation, simply observing life as it passes them by. They are cautious and hesitant, always choosing safe routines over daring opportunities. But women who are unafraid to take positive risks *seek* excitement. They see a challenge in every obstacle. They thrive on overcoming the problems that go along with attaining success. It's their childlike sense of wonder that sets their actions apart from others'—not *childish,* but *childlike.* Just as children have an inborn curiosity, these women see life as a breathless voyage of discovery. They're filled with boundless expectations!

Make it a point to spend "adventure" time with the children in your life. They will shed new light on the meaning of risk. Grant yourself permission to see the world through the eyes of a child. Dare to splash in the puddles and roll down grassy hillsides. And don't ever let your eagerness give way to complacency, sarcasm, or complaining. A daring, inquisitive nature is the spark that ignites your true potential.

Characteristic 2: An Attitude of Positive Expectation

Life has a strange way of giving you everything you expect from it. As Job said in the Bible, "That which I greatly feared has come upon me." Everything that happens *to* you first happens *within* you. What you expect to happen is most likely what will happen in your life. There's a universal law that says that you will always reap what you sow. Your expectations are like seeds you plant every day. "As within, so without," the saying goes. If you don't like what's happening in your life, try planting something new.

This is also known as the Law of Cause and Effect. For every cause, there will be an equivalent effect. If you start your day expecting things to go wrong, chances are it's going to be one of those days. If you expect to get sick with the flu just because it's going around, chances are, you will. If you expect that other people are going to ruin your mood, you'll probably be right. Instead, say, "I have decided not to allow anyone or anything to determine my attitude today!" Write that phrase out on an index card and place it where you can see it first thing every day.

Over the next few days, experiment by planting seeds such as these.
- Each morning, practice saying, "This is a great day. I'm expecting wonderful things to happen to me and everyone I come into contact with."

- When you need a parking spot, expect to get one just where you need it.
- If you're going shopping for something special, expect to find exactly what you want, at a price you are prepared to pay.
- When it looks as if you're in for another bad day, say something like, "Things generally go well for me. I'm always at the right place at the right time."
- Expect the best from family members, friends, and business associates.
- Regardless of your job description or title, whether you work in or out of your home, expect that everyone you deal with will respond favorably to you and your ideas.

In other words, expect that there is a conspiracy and the whole world wants to add to your success in one way or another. Say these two words silently to yourself, over and over: "health, prosperity."

An attitude of positive expectation is pure and simple optimism. Being optimistic doesn't mean denying reality. It doesn't mean merely having a positive mental attitude while ignoring the facts and hoping that things will turn out all right. It's possible to be optimistic and realistic at the same time. Being a positive risk taker means that you have considered all the facts and examined the possible outcomes while keeping an optimistic outlook about your ability to develop a constructive solution or alternate choices. It's this positive outlook that builds enthusiasm. It's this optimistic attitude that gives us the courage to overcome the barrier of anxiety. "In quietness and confidence shall be your strength" (Isa. 30:15).

By expecting the best in life, you are building inner confidence. Consider the butterfly. See her quietness. In her every movement, she exudes peacefulness. Even in the face of winds and storms—the turbulent side of life—she has a restfulness and composure that goes beyond our understanding. She has a certain ease and grace about her at all times. And her "imperturbability" is desired by those around her.

Regardless of how you describe success—personal fulfillment, meaningful relationships, career satisfaction, financial independence—it all boils down to inner peace! In fact, the word "prosperity" literally translated means peace. This is what women everywhere are truly seeking. Imagine how your life would be different if you could experience calm in the face of every adversity. What would change if you knew that you could stay impervious to life's tribulations, immune to their stormy effects?

There are certain elements that all human beings need in order to achieve this incredible composure, and the first is affirmation of their value—in other words, belief in their worthiness. How valuable do you consider yourself? How competent do you feel? And how confident are you in your inner ability and potential to cope with the challenges life may put in your way? Let's examine the next step in getting your wings and taking positive risks: building your sense of personal worth.

CHAPTER 2

Worth
I
N
G
S

I am fearfully and wonderfully made. (Ps. 139:4)

IF THERE IS A SECRET to being happier and experiencing true freedom it is to realize what an extraordinary person you are. You are a valuable, competent, and gifted woman. You don't have to strive to become a valuable person. You already are. You are brimming with possibilities and the potential to turn your life into a masterpiece.

I know so many women, and I'm sure you do too, who don't realize they are like incredible butterflies, nature's great works of art. They don't know they have dazzling wings and were created to achieve excellence, glory, and prominence. In the same way that the butterfly's colors shimmer in the sunlight, these women, too, can bring beauty into the world.

ACKNOWLEDGING YOUR VALUE

Think about the butterfly and how precious and rare she is. Her wings are colored in brilliant splendor. They are delicate, but durable at the same time. Like the butterfly, you are exquisite, powerful, and rare. There is no one else quite like you, and there never will be.

I noticed a woman at one of my seminars not long ago. Maybe you've seen her, too. She wore her pants too tight, perhaps in the hopes of appearing a little bit slimmer. Her sweater was wrinkled, her posture poor, and her hair needed washing. That morning, she laid out all her snack foods on the table in front of her, along with a few soft drinks and her latest lottery ticket. When I walked past her, I was filled with compassion and wondered if she knows how valuable she really is. There's a good chance she doesn't. She probably lives with the notion that her life isn't worth much. She may believe that she'll never amount to anything anyway, and spends her days wishing things were better, waiting for life to improve, hoping she'll have the chance to appear on a game show and finally win something. Maybe she doesn't know that she can make a difference, that she is gifted and able to accomplish great things. I wanted to tell her that she can stand tall and refuse to live the rest of her life feeling worthless.

I saw another woman. You know her too—the one who appears to have it all. She may be tall and slender. Or perhaps she's petite and curvaceous. In any case, she has the ideal job, the perfect guy, and the dream home. She drives new cars, takes super vacations, and always looks as though she's just had a make-over. Not only is she talented and intelligent, but she makes friends easily and seems to draw people to her like a magnet. We think she's happy. She should be, we say. But look closely. Look deep into her eyes. There's a certain emptiness, a longing for something even she can't identify. It could be because she's always looked to other people or outside sources for her peace, satisfaction, and assurance. What a pity she doesn't know that true happiness lies within her.

Perhaps you recognize yourself in one of these women. If you do, I hope you will begin to believe that you are bursting with inner potential. Extraordinary possibilities lie dormant inside you. You were not made to fail. You were not designed for defeat. You were created to fly. When you begin to emerge from your cocoon of doubt or suffering, exhaustion or confusion, your life will be transformed from emptiness to joy and fulfillment. You will begin to know and understand that you are worthy and capable of living a terrific life. Refuse to accept anything but the great work of art you were meant to become. You have within your reach all you need to unfold your full, rich, brilliant wings and take flight.

Self-worth doesn't mean self-centeredness. It is not narcissism or arrogance. It doesn't say, "Look at me. Aren't I wonderful?" It is an acceptance of yourself and a belief in your potential. It does say, "I am valuable and worthy of living a meaningful life." God has uniquely gifted each one of us to contribute and be fulfilled.

Nobody's perfect. We all have flaws. We can, however, accept ourselves unconditionally, just as we are, in the knowledge that we are continuously developing. The one thing, more than anything else, that can keep us from prospering is not truly believing, deep down in our hearts, that we are worthy. We don't feel deserving. Of course, you've had failures and made mistakes. It's perfectly natural to have feelings about those experiences and how you have dealt with them in the past. Yes, you may need forgiveness from God and from yourself for your past actions and decisions. But then it's time to move ahead. You are not your past. You are not a composite of your failures and mistakes. You are not your feelings.

When you accept yourself totally, you can begin to accept forgiveness. Trying to suppress your feelings sometimes only makes them stronger, and leads to guilt, the number-one destroyer of self-worth. I've never known a woman who wasn't tormented by guilt—actual or imagined—at one time or another. We all feel guilty at times, about things we've done or not done, or things we feel we should have done. It's too bad that many women haven't developed the ability to distinguish between true and false guilt. They buy into others' opinions of what is right or wrong instead of basing their decision on their own experiences. If you're feeling guilty over something you haven't done, perhaps you have allowed someone else's beliefs to cause the guilt you are experiencing. If it's something you have done, ask for God's forgiveness, accept it, attempt to rectify the situation wherever you can, and proceed with your transformation. Legitimate guilt is essential. It's what prompts us to do the things we know we need to do.

By accepting yourself, mistakes and all, you are acknowledging that you are responsible for your outcomes. This puts you back in control. Then you know that you can feel a certain way and yet still choose your own positive behavior. It's not necessary to be ruled by outside circumstances, to blame anyone or anything. There's a big difference between the person who says, "Everything about my life is a mess" and the one who says, "I know that what's happening in my life right now isn't the greatest, but it doesn't have to stay that way." The difference is a sense of being in control. We can give our control away by expecting others to make everything right in our lives. The interesting thing is that until we see ourselves brimming with potential we'll continue to blame circumstances for our lack of success or look to others for our happiness. The answer is to take full control of our decisions because, guess what—no one's coming to the rescue! Your future depends on your choices.

THE PRINCE CHARMING MYTH

When I was growing up, happiness to me meant getting married, living in my own home, and raising a family. But in my mind, it also meant that someone else would have more control over my life than I would. I grew up in a loving home, with a traditional family, and even though no one ever told me this, I somehow got the idea that I was unworthy of a great life. With my own insecurities, I never really felt deserving of personal success, meaningful relationships, or financial freedom. I didn't even believe I was capable of handling success if I should somehow attain it.

What I did expect was that, by the time I was eighteen, Prince Charming would come along to rescue me from all my teenage woes and make my dreams come true. Well, a prince did show up, but with my own low sense of self-worth, I had attracted someone into my life who had about the same poor self-esteem that I had. My feelings of insecurity combined with a deep need to be wanted led me to believe that his needing me was enough to base a relationship on. In spite of our common problems, I still imagined that, after our small wedding, we would live happily ever after in a cottage on a hill with rose gardens and a white picket fence. Of course, it didn't turn out like that. It wasn't long after the wedding that the physical abuse began. Not only was my body being destroyed, but my heart was bruised, my spirit was crushed, and my dreams were being shattered. I stayed in that distressing situation until I experienced a miracle that enabled me to recognize my value and to make better choices for myself and my children.

All along, though, there was something in me that empowered me to handle what was happening. How did I survive the horror of knowing what was coming night after night? How did I tolerate the despair I felt as I held my two young children in my arms? How did I endure the sadness as I watched family members looking on, knowing what was happening yet feeling so helpless because I insisted on staying, the eternal optimist always hoping that things would get better?

In spite of my circumstances, an extraordinary sense of hopefulness always seemed to well up inside me. It was not so much positive thinking as it was a special type of faith developing. I was continuously expecting the miraculous and believing that an end was in sight. I had an inner knowledge that better days were in store. Somewhere, I heard a simple phrase that I wrote out on a card and carried with me everywhere I went. I kept it with me for years. All it said was: "Miracles have a habit of happening to those who believe in them." It comforted me, so I kept believing.

That optimism brought with it a special sense of determination. Some might have called it stubbornness. But whatever it was, it not only kept me *in* that dreadful place, it prevented me from giving in to depression and fear. There were times when that fighting spirit was all that kept me hanging on.

I had heard that survival is like riding a bicycle. You don't usually fall off until you stop pedaling. Together, the optimism and the determination created a powerful inner energy. This is what *fueled* me to bounce back after each episode of mental and physical victimization. What I didn't know at the time was that I had the potential even then to create a different tomorrow. Thankfully, I eventually came to believe that my own God-given strength was bigger than any adversity I would encounter in doing so. I learned that there wasn't going to be any fairy godmother. There are no knights in shining armor. (Even if there were, we'd probably spend the rest of our lives cleaning up after a horse!) Instead, I discovered that the only one who could change things was me. We are not rescued by another person, but in looking to God. When we realize this, we can fly free, away from limiting childhood beliefs and fables.

The turning point in my life came when someone introduced me to this very powerful principle. All growth begins with recognizing that we are created with exceptional capabilities. You are a remarkable human being. If there's something wrong in your life, one of the most significant forces in reshaping your future is knowing that answers are available to you. You have an abundance of potential. You are capable and worthy.

A little boy once asked his grandmother what year she was born. She told him, "Nineteen twenty-four." He exclaimed, "Wow! If you were a baseball card, you'd be worth a lot!" It's a cute story, but your value is not determined by your material or financial worth. It's also not governed by your skin color, birthplace, or intelligence. Likewise, your education, profession, age, or sex are not measures of your worthiness. You are unique just because you're you. If you don't truly believe in that, then meaningful relationships, a wonderful spouse, a great job, financial independence, regular vacations, a lovely home, or any form of personal satisfaction will always elude you. Even if you can say that you truly don't *want* some of those things, in order to fulfill your life's purpose you must be able to say, "I am valuable and capable."

Belief in your own significance and abilities is one of the most important keys to achieving excellence in your life, and yet holding ourselves in high regard is often considered egotistical. We're not normally encouraged to think highly of ourselves. In our society in general, self-esteem is often linked with a feeling of smug self-importance. When it's lumped together with words such as pride, conceit, and boastfulness, then naturally we reject it. Self-esteem does not mean trying to get ahead by building yourself up or putting others down, spending a lot of time talking about your accomplishments, or showing off your authority. The word "esteem" simply means to respect and cherish someone or something.

Certainly, modesty is a desirable virtue and essential if we are to achieve true excellence, but being humble doesn't mean self-effacing. If we don't respect ourselves, if we continue to belittle our inborn characteristics and talents, and if we loathe what we see in the mirror, will we ever truly make the effort to fulfill our purposes here on earth?

It amazes me that we can stand in awe of God's wondrous creations and yet, at the same time, tear down and degrade ourselves. We revere the beauty of nature, whether it's found in the brilliant explosion of color in autumn leaves, the intensity of a glorious sunset, or the many shades of a rainbow. We delight in the scent of a rose garden or the exquisite pattern in a butterfly's wings. We are amazed by the power of a waterfall and the immensity of a mountain range. Yet all along, we fail to marvel at the most wondrous creation of all—ourselves.

We must begin to develop that type of solemn respect for our own extraordinary qualities. The same Creator made us, and we are the most significant and remarkable creation of all. We alone can reason, think, plan, organize, mastermind, engineer changes in our circumstances, experience feelings, laugh, and love! Unlike other animals, human beings have the ability to leave behind a heritage, learning from past generations and broadening that knowledge to pass on to our children. Add to that the unique characteristics that you alone have, and you begin to realize what an extraordinary individual you are.

Perhaps we undervalue ourselves because we have not yet discovered how to tap into and release our attributes. Experiencing true self-worth also includes having faith in our ability to face struggles with optimism. It's in the fight that we gain the strength to soar high above the barriers. And yet, we somehow wish we could bypass that part. We long to have someone come along and break open our cocoon for us, freeing us from the pain of the conflict that we believe will leave us weak, limp, and exhausted.

Struggle is an ingenious scheme through which nature compels us to develop and expand. It's when we become reconciled with the circumstances that force us to struggle and then go on to finish the battle by breaking through the barrier that something startling takes place. Beautiful wings unfold. We are brand new, glistening and sparkling. We're strong and ready to forge ahead. By running to embrace the struggle, we have given birth to our freedom.

WORTHINESS: THREE INGREDIENTS THAT MAKE A DIFFERENCE

There are three basic ingredients that make up your sense of self-worth.

Value

You are one of a kind with much to offer this world. A full, rich life is in store for you. The problem isn't so much in *getting* success as it is *receiving* it. One of the problems women seem to share is we have difficulty giving ourselves permission to accept and take pleasure in achievement. Doubts about our true value cast a giant shadow over any success we do attain and block us from experiencing the joy that should be ours.

Competence

You are able to take charge of your life. Instead of simply waiting for things to change or for the right time, believe in your abilities, which enables you to be proactive and assertive. Competence means you know what you want to happen and believe you are able to do almost anything. When you feel competent, you don't rely on others to make your dreams come true. You just go out and take action.

Confidence

You believe in your ability to deal with the adversities life puts in your path, as well as your capacity to handle success once you attain it. Self-reliance and boldness empower you to seek out positive risks and new opportunities actively. With faith in your potential, you are certain about your decisions and actions. Confidence also allows you to admit that you don't know everything, and as strange as it may seem, this brings you trust and respect from others.

Your sense of self-worth is so important because

value says, "You have much to offer!"

competence says, "You've got what it takes!"

confidence says, "Now go for the gusto!"

With a sense of self-worth, you know you can do the following:

1. Take control of your life.
2. Make your own decisions.
3. Be prosperous and healthy.
4. Have your own opinions.
5. Leave the status quo behind.
6. Quit following the leader and be willing to go against the crowd when necessary.
7. Take some time off every now and then.
8. Nurture and pamper yourself once in awhile.
9. Communicate your feelings.
10. Enjoy great relationships.
11. Have the support of those who share your goals.
12. Dream big, and see those dreams become realities.
13. Break free from the pressures of a stress-filled life-style.
14. Move ahead with confidence.
15. Be recharged.
16. Determine what success means to you.
17. Be free from guilt, fear, worry, and doubt.
18. Say no when it's appropriate.
19. Experience vitality.
20. Live every day with enthusiasm.

YOU ARE IMPORTANT!

There are no great and small. We fancy others greater than ourselves because they light the divine spark given them, and we do not. It is because we minimize ourselves that we do not accomplish. We do not realize the power of the positions in which we are placed. (Ralph Waldo Emerson)

One of the greatest challenges in life is to accept ourselves unconditionally. It's not easy to take a hard look at ourselves in a nonjudgmental manner, yet it is a major step in getting our wings. There is no freedom like the liberty we enjoy when we finally take off our masks, give up the pretenses, and become willing just to be ourselves. One of the great tragedies in this life happens when people make themselves miserable by trying to be people they are not. This is the high cost of low self-worth and it is often the result of comparison.

Comparing ourselves to others is a trap we can fall into, and if we are not careful, it can keep us from using the potential we were born with. It happens when we consistently esteem everyone else more than ourselves and, in doing so, fail to recognize our own abilities. We have a tendency to compare our very worst attribute with others' very best. Then, feelings of inferiority lead to a host of other negative emotions including jealousy, self-doubt, anger, frustration, and fear.

Comparison can be a major cause of misery and despair. There was a time when I wrote the words *Comparison Equals Depression* on a cue card, and posted it where I could see it as a daily reminder to myself. It wasn't until I learned to conquer my feelings of inadequacy and forget comparisons that I could relax and find joy in simply being me. During my time as a professional model, I saw some of the most disheartened women, and men, for that matter—people who were working at a career you might think would help them feel positive about themselves. Yet, comparison in that business is a way of life and it has the same detrimental effect as it would for anyone.

Think of the many ways we compare ourselves to others on a regular basis: our appearance, including height, weight, hair type, body build, skin coloring, and facial features; finances and material possessions; life-styles and relationships; hobbies, skills, and education. Many of these are things we cannot completely control and some we cannot control at all.

When we compare ourselves with others, one of two things can happen. Concentrating on others' accomplishments and rewards can deflate us or it can excite us. When it discourages us it's because we see something of value in them that we do not see in ourselves. Their success seems so far from what we can even imagine for our own lives that we are left with a sense of hopelessness, and a "why try anyway" or "what's the use" attitude. We almost believe, subconsciously at least, that someone else's success limits our own chances, as though there's not enough success to go around. We end up being cynical and overly critical. Whenever we find ourselves finding fault with another woman, we should ask ourselves if it's really her, or are we dissatisfied with our own lives. When we compare, we think that if we could have what others have, we could also enjoy a great life. We say, "This will make me happy, worthy, or whole." Then, because we can't imagine it ever happening, it often becomes our reason for not even trying.

On the other hand, if someone else's success excites us, it's because we feel challenged by his or her actions to do something in our own lives that requires some stretching. We feel encouraged to tap into our personal potential, and seem to have the belief that if it's possible for that person to accomplish greatness, then why not us?

Depending on where we are in our own development, whether we see ourselves as being valuable and capable or not, we either throw in the towel and think, "It'll never be that way for me," or we're inspired by the other person's achievements, and feel challenged by the possibilities in our own lives. So, there is a positive side to comparison. But the choice of a negative or positive reaction is always yours.

How would you recognize the trait of self-worth? Think of women you know and describe in your note pad the traits and recognizable behaviors of healthy self-worth in one column and low self-worth in the other.

Now compare the two columns. Where do you stand? We tend to feel good about ourselves when the distance between the way we see ourselves and the way we want to be is the shortest. The longer the line between where we believe we are and where we think we should be, the more discontented we are with ourselves and our lives.

Your Life ⟵——————————————————⟶ *Ideal Life*

WHO DO YOU THINK YOU ARE?

While this might sound like a superficial question, it's a significant one because who you think you are is who you will always be. You will never achieve more than you think you can. You can never fly higher than you aim, and your aim will always be determined by what you believe about yourself. You'll always act in a manner that is in direct proportion to the picture you have in your own mind of who you are. *If you believe that you can accomplish great things, you will. If you believe that you cannot, you won't!*

To determine your self-concept, write in your note pad *I see myself as* and then leave ten numbered blank lines. Fill in each blank by describing in detail who you are. Consider both the external aspects (your various roles, background, education, sports, hobbies, and accomplishments) and the internal aspects (your fears, desires, ideas, beliefs, doubts, values, feelings, and ambitions).

The statements you choose will indicate your present concept of yourself. This is your self-image—inside and out. You may have described yourself as a wife, mother, friend, bank manager, fashion designer, or sales representative. Or perhaps you referred to your appearance, such as height, hair color, or weight. Your description probably included some strengths as well as some weaknesses. Did you see yourself as being persistent, organized, optimistic, and humorous, or clumsy, shy, forgetful, and always late?

According to your statements, do you feel that you really deserve inner peace and prosperity? How confident and willing are you to take calculated risks? Do you feel competent to handle greater achievements should you attain them?

Go back over your list and ask yourself if these statements and beliefs are based on fact. They may not provide a truly accurate description of who you are, but may merely be someone else's opinion. What data is there to support or dispute these interpretations? If you have bought into others' descriptions of you, you may be acting in accordance and then using those preconceptions to explain your behaviors. There is much truth in the term "self-fulfilling prophecy." We predict our actions, act accordingly, and reinforce our self-concept by saying, "See, that's just the way I am!"

Your belief systems will determine the answers. One good measure of your beliefs about yourself is the way in which you accept or reject compliments. Women who don't see themselves as valuable will belittle themselves when others speak highly of them. Before they know it, the admirable quality of *humility* slowly turns into *self-humiliation*. Without wings, women tend either to undermine their own worth or repudiate the one giving the compliment, often believing this is a form of modesty.

Consider Brenda, who believes she doesn't deserve a compliment, because someone else's favorable opinion doesn't echo her own opinion of herself. She typically responds to compliments by saying something like the following:

"This old dress? I was thinking of giving it away to a worthy charity but just thought I'd wear it one last time. Besides, it's got a spot that won't come out. I really have a much better dress at home. I was just thinking I wish I'd worn that other one!"

"My hair? Gosh, I really should have washed it. And it needs a trim. It's got so many split ends. You can't see them? Well, if you look real close, I'm sure you will."

"My presentation at the staff meeting? I guess it was okay. It must have been my lucky day." Or, "You probably noticed that I really messed up right there in the middle. I can't seem to do anything right."

When we attack the compliment giver, we are not only destroying our own self-confidence, but we are, in a sense, attacking his or her judgment, intelligence, taste, or fashion sense. It could be construed as an insult or put-down. The end result is that others will stop giving us compliments and they may even start to hold the same poor opinion of ourselves.

Then there's Cynthia, who fears that the compliment giver will eventually come to know the *real* truth about her, so she decides to get it out right at the beginning. She usually responds to a compliment this way: "You might think it's great spending time with me, but you've never seen me on my down days. Just wait until you really get to know me."

She thinks that if she attacks herself first, then it doesn't matter what you say about her later. Cynthia feels certain that the truth about her "real self" will come out eventually, and you'll most likely be disappointed in her or find some reason to criticize her.

It seems that when we don't value ourselves, and when we lack self-confidence, these responses are automatic. They come out of our own negative inner programming. They're usually not based on truth or past experiences. For instance, chances are no one has ever come right out and asked you, "Hey, have you ever thought maybe it's time to give that dress away?" or "You seem nice on the surface, but I bet when you're having a rough day, you're really mean!"

With wings, and a healthy sense of self-worth, you simply respond with a "thank you," which says that you're accepting the value paid to you by others. Almost without exception, the truly effective women I've spoken with, whether we're referring to business, sports, hobbies, or relationships, have come to know and accept themselves. They feel comfortable with who they are and don't mind others knowing them just as they are. These women, because of their own acceptance, seem to magnetize friends and the support of others naturally.

Self-acceptance is powerful but it is not a substitute for change and personal development. Rather it's the first step in altering our behavior. It's unfortunate that many self-esteem programs and motivational seminars promote self-acceptance *in place of* change. It would be much easier if we could leave it at that. Usually, altering our behavior is a tough thing to do. It takes time, patience, commitment, and a lot of effort. But without changing our actions and attitudes, self-help programs cannot possibly provide lasting results. What self-acceptance really says is that even though you are striving for continuous improvement, you're still able to appreciate and believe in yourself just as you are at the moment.

We've all felt like flops at one time or another or had intervals when our lives were in a muddle. We've all made mistakes or poor choices. We've all had weak moments and failures. The problem is we tend to internalize these events and define ourselves by them. We use them as labels, and we end up feeling discontented. But your past is not you, nor does it determine who you'll be in the future.

The best way to accept your mistakes and setbacks is to see them as pathways to doing things in new and better ways. Handling failure positively means being able to remain poised while devising new ways of doing things. We can only experience this type of composure after we accept who we are, where we are, and that we are capable of changing. The truth is that we get what we think we deserve. With wings, we believe we deserve the chance to experience a new beginning.

SELF-IMAGE: THE KEY TO UNLOCK YOUR POTENTIAL

Much of your sense of worth—the value you place on yourself—and faith in your competence comes from your self-image. Since we all think in pictures, you have an image in your mind right now of who you are: what you are worthy of, and capable of handling at this stage in your life. This picture or self-concept is a powerful instrument. It could possibly be one of the most important tools you will have the opportunity to work with in your lifetime. Researchers now believe that the discovery of the self-image and the impact it has on one's life is one of the most important psychological discoveries of our century.

The self-image is at the core of your being and determines almost everything else about you. For instance, to some degree, it determines your looks—your outward appearance. Think about someone you know who has come through a low period in her life, emotionally or mentally. Perhaps you've noticed how her appearance has actually changed now that she's regained a positive sense of her worth as a human being. Because of this changed image of herself, there is probably a different look in her eyes, a freshness about her facial expressions, or a bounce in her step. In fact, her whole demeanor—walk, stance, bearing, and manner of dress—may project a brand-new, overall transformation.

The self-image also affects our health and energy levels. On days when you are feeling poorly about yourself you don't bound out of bed, go straight for the kitchen, and have a bowl of oat bran and half a grapefruit for breakfast. Instead, your choice might be a chocolate doughnut, last night's leftover dessert, ice cream right out of the carton, or coffee and a Danish on the way to work.

In the same light, when our image is at an all-time low we don't choose to go to the gym and work out in one of those great-looking little suits, in front of others who all appear to have super bodies (the ones who don't even know the meaning of cellulite!). The truth is, we probably can't even drag ourselves outdoors to go for a ten-minute walk around the block. The most exercise we'll probably get is lifting the remote control while lying on the couch watching an aerobics class on television. What tremendous power the self-image has.

Another aspect of our lives affected by the self-image is our ability to build and maintain long-term, loving relationships. We cannot give away what we don't own. In order to give love—full, rich, unconditional love—it's imperative to love ourselves and appreciate our own worth. We are encouraged to "love your neighbor as yourself." I know some people I wouldn't want to love me as they love themselves. It's quite obvious that there is no love there. How many of your friends would appreciate being treated the way you treat yourself? *Loving ourselves is not selfish. Instead, it's one of the nicest things we can do for those we truly care about.*

The self-image also determines our success on the job, in sports, and in hobbies; how likely we are to take risks; how well we deal with stress and cope with change; and even how quickly we show our age. If you want to change your life, start by changing your self-concept.

HOW THE SELF-IMAGE DETERMINES YOUR OUTCOMES

The Process

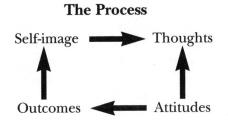

Your self-image, made up of those beliefs you have about your abilities, personality traits, and worthiness, determines to a great degree what you think about during the day. Those thoughts then control your attitudes and emotions, which in turn determine your actions. Each action or outcome then goes back around to form a new self-image, either a more positive one or a more negative one, depending on the results you've just experienced.

So many of us are constrained by false beliefs about ourselves that we've developed over the years. These beliefs have been stored in our memories as though they were the truth, regardless of their validity. Because our nervous systems cannot differentiate between real experiences and imagined ones, it accepts those beliefs as being true. It sees them as inborn traits that cannot be changed, even though they might be mere figments of our imagination, brought on by internal or external influences. Then, like sieves, our brains take in and remember only those things that fit our prior conceptions of ourselves—good or bad, right or wrong, positive or negative. Anything else is filtered out. Our lives are then governed by these self-imposed beliefs and self-limiting barriers. Since this inner image works much like a computer, it follows the instructions that have been programmed. Then we act or react to situations based on that information. It's this ongoing pattern of beliefs that keeps us from breaking though false barriers.

Consider this example. A butterfly, captured and put in a jar with the lid fastened, will only attempt to get free for so long. Eventually, it resigns itself to the fact that there is no way out, and no hope. Accepting the limitation, it finally gives up. At that stage, even if the lid were removed, it still may not try to escape. Because of this powerful past conditioning, it doesn't even consider the possibility. Even with former barriers removed, it doesn't know that it is truly free.

So many women are living out their lives this way, constrained by the same type of preconditioning and self-limiting beliefs developed over the years. They could easily fly free but think that some force is preventing them from doing it. In reality, like the lid on the jar, it may not be there anymore. Once something is accepted by the subconscious mind, though, it is believed and we then act accordingly. Our behavior, success level, and personality will always be linked with our self-image. If, in our self-concept, we cannot possibly see ourselves achieving a goal or conquering a barrier, we truly will not be able to do it.

I've discovered that the self-image works in much the same way as cruise control works in your car. If you've ever used it, you know that once you've determined the setting at the speed you've chosen, that mechanism has a job to do. Its role is to maintain the level you have selected, regardless of external circumstances. So, if you are going uphill, and things are a bit tough, by rights you should slow down. The situation should hold you back. But because you are using cruise control, nothing can fluster you. You've set it at a certain level so you will keep traveling at a constant speed. It may slow you down temporarily, but before long you'll be up to speed again. Likewise, when you are going down a hill, meaning things are going smoothly, you would think you would pick up speed. But when you are using cruise control, it can't happen. Again, this mechanism has a job to do, and that job is to maintain the level you have preset. So it seeks out a way to bring you back down to where you were. Certainly, you may speed up for a short time, but it won't last. With a low self-image "setting," even if things start going your way, and you somehow manage to be at the right place at the right time, before you know it, you'll begin to sabotage your own success.

Teresa was involved in a wonderful relationship for the first time in a long while. In fact, most of the time she felt surprised that it was going so well! But with her poor self-image, the belief that she was a person who didn't deserve such happiness and intimacy, she started to undermine the relationship. She subconsciously began to act in ways that did not support or enhance it. She was either nagging her boyfriend, canceling dates at the last minute, or picking arguments for no apparent reason. She became especially moody, and suspicious as well. She hated herself for acting in such an inappropriate manner, but couldn't seem to stop herself. Her self-image control was set at low and she soon found herself alone again.

Then there was Sharon, who had inherited her grandfather's estate when he passed away. She, too, suffered with a low self-image, feeling deep down inside that she wasn't worthy of the life-style that this money could provide for her. Within one year, she had squandered most of the inheritance and found herself back where she started. She tried to tell herself, and everyone else, that she had enjoyed spending it all and had some great times, and nothing else counted. But she knows now that, had she invested it properly, she may have been financially set for life.

Both of these women sabotaged their own happy futures because of feelings of unworthiness. With their image settings on low, they couldn't possibly succeed.

Whether our self-images are good or bad, we all tend to be like magnets, attracting into our lives the people, circumstances, and situations that will back up the pictures and make them reality. If it's a negative image, we attract negative situations. If it's a positive one, that's the type of people and events we magnetize.

Teresa and Sharon had attracted into their lives everything necessary to create their own realities. Because of their low setting on their *cruise control* image, false beliefs kept them from attaining higher levels of success in their individual circumstances.

Likewise, if we choose a high setting, regardless of our present situation, the image has a job to do. Its job is to bring us up to match that level. Again, like magnets, we will attract into our lives all that we need to fulfill our new images of health and wealth. We'll bounce back quickly from trials, mistakes, and failures. We'll deliberately place ourselves at the right place at the right time. Things will start falling into place. The people we come in contact with will feel encouraged to assist us.

SUCCESS CONDITIONING AND POSITIVE PROGRAMMING

How Your Self-image Is Formed

Your self-image is actually a collection of ideas you have about yourself that you believe to be true, even if they are not. These ideas begin in early childhood with impressions given to us by the significant people in our lives as well as other outside sources. These opinions become our first standard for measuring and establishing our personal worth. We continue to receive messages regarding our value from our families, friends, teachers, and, eventually, the media. These beliefs become very powerful in conditioning our attitudes and behaviors. By defying our false beliefs and creating new, healthy ones, we can begin to release some of the potential we have hidden within us.

A woman in one of my programs shared this story with the group. After beginning the climb up Dunns River Falls in Jamaica, Marisa wondered why she had agreed to it. She started telling herself she was foolish to have thought she could do this. The powerful rush of the water seemed to be fighting her every step of the way. Fear set in and she began to panic, all the while backing her feelings with negative, limiting statements such as: "I never should have attempted this"; "My legs are getting weak and I'm going to slip"; "I'm really not the outdoors type."

Fortunately, she realized what she was doing and stopped herself in time. She had attended some programs in which she was introduced to the theory of the power of our belief systems. Deliberately, she started to program in new, supportive beliefs: "I am strong and steady"; "I am calm and confident, and make this climb with comfort and ease." By changing her beliefs, she was able to finish the climb and actually enjoy the process.

The beliefs we have about our abilities determine our self-image. Many of our daily decisions are based on information about ourselves that we have accepted as true. Since we will always act in a manner that is in direct proportion to our self-image, we can change what's happening in our lives by changing the picture. First, let's find out how the self-concept is formed.

What others told you. One of the major barriers women face is believing they are just not meant to enjoy or even experience success. Because our belief patterns stand in the way of creating the lives we want, we must overcome the negative conditioning we received from others. Here are some of the typical remarks we heard that encouraged us to accept defeat and failure as natural:

"Life just isn't fair if you're a woman."
"You made your bed. Now lie in it."
"Be satisfied with what you have."
"What will other people think?"
"Money is the root of all evil."
"You can't teach an old dog new tricks."
"Being born into this family means you'll be doomed to a life of misery and poverty."

It's not surprising that we don't feel entitled to a successful life when these false assumptions have been presented to us as though they were inherent truths.

Aside from being given these messages, during our growing-up years most of us were told what to do and what not to do. We were often bombarded with negative remarks and continually reminded of our mistakes, failures, and shortcomings. Because faults were emphasized, they became magnified in our minds, and now we wear them like labels. Eventually, we act them out and they do indeed become our realities.

During the first few years of your life, your sense of self-worth was formed almost entirely by your family. As a child, you depended on others to affirm your abilities and value. You looked to your parents to have your achievements recognized. By the time you were four or five years old, you had formed assumptions regarding how well you measured up to others, including your siblings and peers; how successful you would likely be; whether you'd achieve your goals; your potential for making and keeping friends; and what you would be good at or not so good at. Your image continued to develop, based not only on the messages you received from others, but what you chose to *believe* about their comments.

A little girl hears, "You are so much like your aunt Margaret. You look, talk, and act like her." If all the while she is very aware that her aunt is an alcoholic and has never made anything of her life, she may grow up expecting pretty much the same life-style. No one will be surprised when it happens.

Another young girl hears, "You always start projects and never finish them." She accepts this as an inherent negative trait, and feels bad most of her life about her tendency to always want to try something new. As she moves up the ladder in her sales career, she continually changes companies; welcomes the introduction of new products, adding them to the lines she already represents; and eventually starts a number of small businesses, all of which are successful. The problem is that she is constantly haunted by the false belief that the need for change is a negative quality. What she fails to realize is that what others consider her "problem" is simply the ability to take positive risks. She thrives on change and challenges. And she has enough wisdom and insight to know when to leave one venture behind and begin another that would be more lucrative. She is never *stuck in a rut* and could be enjoying her life so much more if she would let go of her past self-image.

If you heard often enough that, because you are just like your mother or father, it's no wonder you're not good at a certain sport, hobby, or subject at school, you could be holding yourself back from using your full potential today. We tend to buy into those old limiting beliefs without questioning them. Yet, if we take a critical look at them, we will find that they are no longer valid. When we investigate them seriously, we see that they have no more power over us unless we choose to accept them as the truth.

Did you hear some of these messages as you were growing up?

"Why can't you be quiet like your sister?"
"You're such a lazy slob."
"Why don't you play quietly like all the other little girls?"
"How can you believe such nonsense? No one else does."
"Do you have to talk so much?"
"Who do you think you are—the queen of England?"
"You only think about yourself."
"You'll never amount to anything."
"Why don't you try using your brain?"
"You don't have what it takes to go to college, start your own business, etc."

Add to that all the labels we've picked up over the years that are difficult to shed today. For instance, if we were introverted, we were labeled "shy"; if we were outgoing, we were called "loud" or "gabby." A woman who thinks of herself as "tubby" or "chunky," the nicknames she heard as a young girl, may have long outgrown that outward appearance, but still carries around the inner image. You may have picked up labels such as clumsy, boring, lazy, or dumb.

Chances are that what you heard growing up was even stronger than these examples. I'm convinced our parents were doing the best they could with the tools they had available to them at the time. They were attempting to provide a proper upbringing and were not out to destroy us. But we built our self-image on what was available to us. Now, we have the opportunity to overcome the barrier of negative programming. We have come to understand that what we put in is what we will get out, just like the expression "GIGO" in computer language, which stands for "garbage in, garbage out."

Handling criticism. As you were growing up, if criticism was combined with anger or the threat of abandonment, you may have more of a difficult time tuning out those old messages. How others spoke to you and treated you did play a crucial role in developing your self-concept, but an even greater impact came from the conclusions you drew as a result of that treatment.

Believing that your worth is dependent on others' opinions can lead you to take criticism to heart, whether or not it's deserved. Many women have an innate need to please everyone all the time. Even though we know it isn't possible to do, this belief seems to constrain even the most confident women. It helps to understand that those who are doing the criticizing sometimes suffer from their own insecurities or the false belief that someone else's success limits their own chances for achievement. They are somehow convinced that they must pull you back from your accomplishments to boost their self-esteem or make room for their own opportunities. The truth is that there is room enough for us all to succeed, but as long as we adhere to these destructive, toxic beliefs, we will not only hold other women back, we will pay the price, too.

By refusing to be swayed by others' distorted opinions, you will liberate yourself to break through the cloud banks that would keep you down. You'll no longer be affected by other people's disapproval. It's a false assumption that you need authorization from others to succeed. In reality, you don't need to win the support or friendship of fault-finding people.

No matter what you do, someone will always be critical. "Criticism is something we can avoid easily—by saying nothing, doing nothing, and being nothing" (Aristotle).

When you are criticized, here are a few ways to respond. First of all, consider the source. Is the person qualified to give this feedback? Is it someone whose opinion you value? In either case, be brave and investigate further. Be curious about what you may learn from the comment. If you are not sure of the motive, try asking just what the other person expects you to do with this information or what she is hoping to accomplish—not in a "how dare you" tone of voice, but in the genuine spirit of seeking more information. Ask yourself if there is any merit to the feedback. This eliminates defensiveness on your part, which allows you to take back control. If you discover that there is any truth to it at all, it gives you a fresh perspective and you can use this valuable input to make progress with the problem.

Finally, don't make rash decisions based on another's criticism of you. I remember a time I was criticized for not having an open mind about a certain new business venture that had been offered to me, when the truth was I simply did not have a good feeling about going ahead with it. Only much later did I find out that the person who criticized me had decided not to become involved either after doing some extensive research and having his lawyer investigate the proposed opportunity more intensely.

There are times when you must turn away from those who would hold you back, attempting to invalidate who you are, what you are worthy of, and what you are capable of achieving. Growing strong, healthy wings is challenging and there are parts of your life that you must leave behind. There is always a cost when breaking through your chrysalis.

When you do break through to the other side, however, you'll meet with others who have grown their wings as well. So, choose to associate with supportive people. Align yourself with those who will bolster you in your vision of greatness. Spend your time with people who encourage you in your dreams and understand your ambitions. You cannot afford to spend your time with anyone other than those who elevate you and rejoice proudly over your accomplishments. To do so would be to invite defeat.

Messages you get from society. Through the media, we are constantly being bombarded with unrealistic standards by which we measure our own worth, happiness, and success. On television and in the movies, we are presented with images of the "good life" and are encouraged to live according to the status quo. Images of "superwoman" lure us into attempting to do too much and then feeling like failures when we discover we are not able to accomplish every goal. Women with wings know that superwoman doesn't exist. If she does, she's usually driven to perform. If she's you, let her off the hook!

Negative conditioning also comes from society in the form of subliminal messages through advertising about our physical image. We live in an extremely body-conscious age in which women are still valued most for what they look like. Our culture programs us with false illusions and we start to doubt that we could have genuine worth because we don't conform to current trends and criteria of outward beauty. Yet, it would be nearly impossible to consistently attain the standard of female beauty we are presented with in fashion magazines—a toned yet curvaceous body with long legs, slender hips, a full bust, broad shoulders, perfect hair, flawless skin, and gorgeous fingernails. Even so, we insist on trying. Or if we don't, we spend valuable energy and time feeling disappointed in ourselves for not managing to look like a photograph that often has undergone extensive computer touchups or some airbrushing. It looks right to us, and others look wrong. In many cases, the *right one* is an illusory image and not one we could attain anyway.

One of the biggest causes of low self-image in our young girls is this distorted body image. Even though self-esteem also drops in boys when they reach adolescence, the drop is much more drastic and rapid in adolescent girls. This is not surprising when we recognize the perfect-body fallacy and impossible standards they are being continually bombarded with.

Men view their bodies in a different way. In general, they tend to be more realistic. When we ask men to describe their appearance, they simply give us the facts. They refer to their height, weight, hair color, or facial hair. They evaluate their bodies in a different way than women, too. A man rates his body according to what he can do with it. He may not feel he is the most attractive man, but has a more positive image of himself because he hunts, jogs, swims, or lifts weights. A woman, however, usually rates herself according to appearance. When asked to describe her body, a woman is quick to point out the flaws: hips that are too big, a chest that is too small, ugly knees, or flabby thighs. Women see themselves as being too tall or short, too fat or thin. They sometimes perceive their bodies as much heavier than they are and this is often connected with how they are feeling emotionally.

Janice is a woman who shared her experience with me after attending one of my programs. She says her family and friends describe her size in a remarkably different way than she does. Whenever they compliment her on how good she looks or how trim she is, she has difficulty accepting their comments. She also notices that she can feel extremely larger or smaller from day to day—heavier on days when she's unhappy with her life and thinner when she feels good about the way things are going. In fact, even throughout the same day, her concept of her body can drastically change, going from one extreme to another if something upsetting happens. Even if she's been feeling fine concerning her appearance, once she becomes emotionally distraught she suddenly feels overweight and ugly.

We know that realistically our bodies can't change that quickly, yet somehow we feel as though they have. This is one of the pitfalls of unconsciously using someone else's criterion as a gauge for what is acceptable.

Most women agree that, if it were possible, they would change at least one thing about their appearance. Some admit that they would rather have a complete overhaul! In fact, billions of dollars are spent each year on diet programs and products, as well as cosmetic surgeries, all in the hopes that somehow we will begin to love our bodies and feel satisfied with our appearance. Here are some less drastic measures that will produce amazing results.

1. Thank your body for the many functions it performs each day—for eyes to see, ears to hear, legs to take you where you want to go. You'll be more apt to nurture your body with an attitude of love toward it. We don't normally nourish something we hate.

2. Learn about your body shape and proportions. Start with a full-length mirror, preferably three way. Wear a bathing suit or your underwear and view yourself analytically, not critically. My friend says she has to put a paper bag over her head with eye holes cut out in order to do this exercise! What you'll be looking for is proportion, which means the size and shape of your body parts in

relationship to each other. You may be short legged regardless of how tall or short you are. You may look small waisted regardless of how much you weigh, yet your hips may be wide in spite of how thin you get. Armed with this information, you can choose silhouettes, fabrics, colors, and designs that emphasize the best and camouflage the rest! It's possible to hide figure flaws by tricking the eye. Decide what you want to be noticed and make that your focal point.

3. Focus on how your body *feels* rather than *looks*. Change your goals from "I wish I were thinner or prettier" to "I want to have more vitality or flexibility." Create affirmations that proclaim how you'd like to feel and express them in the present tense, as though they were factual. For example: "I love and appreciate my body just as it is"; "My body is toned and limber"; "I am graceful and poised." Then, put your words into action by moving, standing, and walking the way you would if those statements were true.

4. View yourself as a whole being, not just body parts. Beauty advertisements and fashion magazines make this difficult to do. There are limitless articles instructing how to tighten your derriere, slenderize your hips, firm your thighs and build your bust. After awhile, it's easy to start seeing yourself as an assortment of disjointed parts rather than a whole person. But you are not your body. Ask yourself what you can do to make the most of what you have. Then, once you've done that, work on developing your intellectual, spiritual, and emotional self. Strive to become an interesting person. When people are asked what they look for in a mate, they certainly place attractiveness high on the list, but most add they are looking for someone who is fun to be with, interesting, and has high morals.

5. Choose your clothing with comfort in mind. If you have red marks and indentations on your body when you get undressed at night, it's my guess that you haven't been too comfortable all day! Undergarments that are too tight or waistbands that pinch are constant reminders that your body's not perfect. The aggravation you're enduring will eventually show—in your facial expressions and demeanor.

6. Change your posture. Not only will your clothing hang better, but when you stand straight and tall, you feel more confident and

positive about yourself. Your breathing will improve and you'll feel healthier.

7. Start an exercise program. Just the act of doing something good for your body increases your sense of self-worth and confidence. Women who exercise regularly report results in many areas of their lives. They sleep better and feel more rested, they begin craving foods that are good for them, and their natural thirst returns. They are more productive and efficient on the job and more relaxed when they're at home. Because they have a new appreciation for their own bodies, they tend to enjoy their intimate relationships more. They seem able to maintain their ideal weight without starving themselves and they have more energy and enthusiasm for life in general.

Ultimately, we are responsible for the way we view ourselves and our bodies, in spite of the unrealistic images we are presented with in our culture. With wings, we know that our true worth is internal and real beauty is an inner radiance. We refuse to be manipulated by external forces. Women with wings no longer have a need to be validated by worldly standards.

Messages you receive through stereotypes. Although we don't usually pay attention to them consciously, we are besieged by stereotypes on a subconscious level. When we hear them often enough, it's not long before we begin to accept and believe the messages.

Consider some of the traditional categories and assumed gender differences that have influenced our thinking over the years: Women are the weaker sex. Who can understand them? Women are all alike; are poor drivers; are not good at math; talk too much; like to gossip; are overly sensitive and emotional; are not mechanically inclined! A woman's place is in the home.

Traditional stereotypes and presumed gender roles are not fair. Don't believe them or accept them, for your life or anyone else's.

What you tell yourself. Every moment of your life you are talking to yourself. It might be in the form of spoken words, or thoughts, or even feelings about some emotional experience. In many ways you surround yourself with subliminal messages whether you are aware of it or not. This information is fed into your memory bank and stays there.

Notice which books and magazines you have on your shelves. It's been said that we can tell a lot about a person by his or her library! What quotes do you have hanging on your walls? What are the sayings on your T-shirts or your favorite coffee mug? While these are usually just seen as "fun" messages, they are still messages. Not only are they telling others a lot about how you see yourself and your life, but they're planting seeds in your subconscious mind regarding your beliefs about yourself. Perhaps you've been programming yourself to fail without realizing it.

Over the last few years, neuroscientists have concluded that the human brain works very much like a personal computer, although it is many times more powerful. Your bio-computer is waiting for a program and your words act as that program. Anything you say to yourself is programmed into your brain and accepted as though it were reality.

This information forms an image and becomes your personal "sieve," straining out any data that does not line up with your prior beliefs about yourself. You continue to attract and allow in only those ideas and thoughts that prove what you already believe to be true about yourself. Then you act in accordance with those beliefs and constantly reinforce that image. Any new information will initially be rejected. This is why negative beliefs are self-limiting and why the self-image is so hard to change.

Most of us are not even aware that we use self-talk and very few of us are aware that it is one of the most powerful forms of programming for our bio-computer. While some of our self-talk is positive and useful, most of it is harmful, limiting, and even self-defeating.

As I travel, I often overhear women programming themselves with negative self-talk. Here are some examples of the casual statements I've heard. See if any of them sound familiar.

> "I'm such a klutz!"
> "How could I be so stupid?"
> "I have no talent."
> "I can't even boil water."
> "I'm not very creative."
> "No one likes me."
> "I guess I'll always be in debt."
> "I'm a born loser."
> "Nothing ever goes right for me."
> "Nothing good ever happens to me."

"I'm so disorganized."
"I'm always late."
"I must be getting old."
"I'm no good until I've had my morning coffee."
"I dread change."
"I always make a fool of myself."
"Lately, I'm always down in the dumps."
"I get the flu this time every year."
"I'm so tired."
"It's going to be another one of those days!"
"I'm an emotional wreck."
"I have a terrible memory."
"I'm so shy."
"I guess I'm not cut out to be in this profession."
"I hate my life."
"I think I'm going crazy!"
"Everything I eat goes straight to my hips!"

Is it any wonder we keep getting more of what we don't want? Your computer is striving to meet the goals you set for it. Its function is to follow instructions regardless of whether the instructions are positive or negative. These self-limiting beliefs cannot be erased. But what we can do is set new limits with our internal programs. Your computer will do exactly as you tell it to do.

It says, "If you want a terrible memory, I can produce that for you!" Then it goes about seeking ways to make your command come true. If you say, "I have great recall," it will go to work to produce that.

In your note pad, list some of the limiting beliefs you have about yourself, based on what others told you, society's messages, traditional stereotypes, or things you told yourself.

One of the great truths of the universe is that thoughts are things. All reality is created by thought. Begin by giving yourself positive thoughts and messages that promote health, wealth, confidence, courage, success, and happiness. Your inner image is a powerful internal programming mechanism that you can use to your advantage. If you want to change what's happening in your life, start by changing your self-image.

How to Change Your Image

The more you tell yourself *about* yourself, the more you will believe it. When you believe it, the subconscious mind takes it as a command to make you into the person you are describing. Since you always act in accordance with your innermost beliefs and feelings about yourself, you will become a self-fulfilling prophecy. The end result will be either negative or positive, depending on what you believe to be true about yourself. Your subconscious mind cannot tell the difference between fantasy and reality. It doesn't evaluate information to determine whether it's good or bad, right or wrong. It treats everything you tell it with indifference and attempts to draw into your life what you need to achieve the results it was programmed to accomplish. Like a computer, it simply puts into action the commands you consistently give it. Restricting beliefs are habits, and habits can be changed by programming in new material.

You have available to you a mechanism that can help you change what you have not been able to in the past. Your self-image is ready to take you to heights you've only dreamed of until now. And it's controlled by your self-talk. The messages that have the most effect on you are the things you say to yourself *about* yourself. One of the most crucial keys to enhancing your self-worth is positive self-talk. Develop the language of winners. "Let the weak say, I am strong" (Joel 3:10).

A number of years ago, when my speaking career was really beginning to take off, I found myself becoming more and more disorganized and feeling totally out of control. When people would ask how my business was going, I'd tell them it was doing great and I was extremely busy, but I was so disorganized that I couldn't imagine ever getting back in control. I probably mentioned it several times each day, either to myself or to others. I also found a cartoon of a woman in an office that looked much like mine—books and file folders falling off the edges of the desk, reams of paper piled high on the floor, stacks of unopened mail, and small loose notes all over the place. Since it reminded me of my own situation, I cut it out and posted it on the bulletin board where I could see it regularly, just as a joke. But the self-image can't take a joke. It accepts thoughts and beliefs as commands and goes about making sure that the image continues as reality. It was saying, "If you want disorganization, you've got it!"

Instead of reaffirming what you don't want to happen in your life, like I was doing, get in the habit of erasing those statements. Each time you catch yourself saying something derogatory or self-defeating, simply say, "Stop" or "Cancel! That's not like me to act this way." Then consciously reprogram your internal success mechanism by replacing the destructive words with more constructive ones. You can counter every negative word of self-talk with a positive word.

When I realized that I had been sabotaging my own success, I took down the picture and changed the things I said to myself. In my case, I started to program in every day, "That's not like me to be so disorganized. Every day, in every way, I am becoming more and more organized."

Although I have to admit that I wasn't becoming more organized at first, I persisted until I got the results I wanted. I began attracting into my life what I needed to gain back control. I happened to spot a book in an airport bookstore on the subject of managing priorities. I met a time-management expert whose job it was to come right into the office and get it organized. I heard about a course on setting and meeting deadlines that was to be held in my area. Soon after, I was introduced to and purchased a new daily planning system that would work well in my line of business. We might be tempted to say that all these came into my life by pure coincidence, except for the law of attraction. We are all like magnets, and our self-talk determines just what we will attract.

POSITIVE ACTION STEPS

Acknowledge

The first thing you need to do is become aware that you *are* talking to yourself and what it is you are saying about yourself on a regular basis. You cannot change something if you don't even know it exists. Over the next few days, take a few moments every now and then to reflect on what you are telling yourself and enter it in a log. Listen to everything you say when you talk to yourself. Are your words providing for your subconscious mind the programs you want to produce?

Take some time now to write down your past self-talk. List in your note pad the ten most significant suggestions you have been giving yourself. This takes a little time but is a revealing exercise. Later, compare this list with what you have recorded in your log.

Assess

As you consciously listen to that small voice within, evaluate each statement. Where did it come from? What purpose are you fulfilling by continuing to say it? Many times our inner voice is simply trying to protect us from getting hurt or feeling rejected. For example, a number of years ago, shortly after I had started a modeling course, an agency sent me to audition for my first potential modeling job. I didn't feel at all prepared, but knew I couldn't afford to turn down the opportunity. During the entire drive to the out-of-town location where the interview was to be held, my inner voice tried to convince me to go back home. From what I can remember, it sounded something like this: "Sue, what are you doing to yourself? Don't you know you are setting yourself up for possible failure, rejection, and disappointment? Why don't you just turn your car around and go home where you are safe and comfortable?" I can tell you that it sounded very appealing at the time! I was almost tempted to give in, but something inside me encouraged me to keep going. Understanding that my inner voice was just trying to help protect me from feeling bad gave me the power to go ahead and take a chance in spite of the possibility of a negative outcome.

Revise

Once you have a clear understanding of what you are telling yourself and why, you can correct your self-talk. Reword it in a way that supports you in your flight toward your highest aspirations.

Instead of "I'll never lose this weight" declare, "I eat right and exercise every day." If you catch yourself saying, "That's just me. I always lose my temper during *that* time of the month!" start pronouncing, "That's not like me to react that way. From now on I control my disposition and reactions." Change the statement "These kids are driving me crazy; I guess I wasn't cut out to be a mother" to "I am gaining new insights daily that help me to be a better mom." When you're getting ready for work, rather than saying, "I just don't know how much longer I can balance all these priorities," try "I feel in complete control of my life and I'm ready to face the world today—I just know something wonderful is going to happen." I hear women declare, "It's no fun being a woman," or "Men get all the breaks." I encourage them to replace those statements with "As a woman, new opportunities are opening up to me all the time—this is a great era to be a woman!"

Providing new, positive programs for your computer is one of the most refreshing things you can do for yourself. Once you overcome the barrier of negative self-talk, positive programming will become a habit and you'll never go back.

Rewrite

You can actually rewrite your self-talk to change habits, alter your temperament, build a winning personality, and attain meaningful goals. The best way to do this is to go beyond revising what you are already telling yourself to actually designing a whole new script for yourself. Here are some examples of the powerful statements that have helped me and so many other women.

I am happy, healthy, and energetic.
I love being a woman.
My life, job, and relationships are getting better every day.
Nothing can hold me back. I am determined, persistent, and committed.
I am in control of the thoughts I choose.
I am free from doubt, anxiety, and anger.
I am calm and in control in stressful situations.
There are no limits in my life; there is no barrier I cannot overcome.
I have an excellent memory.
I always have time to accomplish all that is important to me.
I love and appreciate myself just the way I am.
Everything I need is being provided for me. New opportunities are opening up all the time.
I am brimming with talents, skills, and potential.
In everything I do, I am competent and confident.
I look forward to challenges and deal with them head on.
Everything that happens in my life is serving a special purpose.
I expect the best from myself and others and that's what I get.
Thoughts cannot dwell in my mind unless I give them permission.
I am capable and confident in difficult situations.
I am an extraordinary woman with much to offer the world.
I am incredibly self-motivated to accomplish the goals I have set for myself.

In a special journal, write out these and as many others as you can think of. Then, try reading your list first thing every morning! Can you imagine the boost you will get when you encourage and believe in yourself this way?

Some women say they feel as though they are lying to themselves. Remember, this is not a method of self-deception. Instead, it's a tool for new direction. Your words are mighty instruments available to you to change the outcomes in your life. Use them to your advantage.

Always state what you want rather than what you don't want. For example, instead of "I no longer eat junk food," say, "I now eat only those foods that are good for me." The more positive your words, the more successful the results. Your self-talk should also be in the present tense. Rather than saying, "I wish to . . . " or "I plan to . . . ," express it as though it is already happening. "I am now successful and earn a great living doing what I love to do."

Aside from writing it down and reading it regularly, you can use your new script by saying the affirmations silently to yourself or out loud. When you talk to yourself out loud, you are forcing yourself to put your thoughts into words and your thinking will become clear and more specific.

To alter anything in your life—a habit, problem, or direction—begin by changing your words. The signals you send to your brain will energize you and you will feel better physically, emotionally, and mentally.

Even though you cannot completely get rid of old beliefs and concepts, you can definitely override or modify them with new images of self-assurance, health, courage, and competence. You can condition yourself for success. Then you'll be prepared to go out and put your dreams into action because you will have boosted your confidence.

SELF-CONFIDENCE: THE KEY TO EXCELLENCE

Here are thirty additional steps to improving your self-image, building confidence, and feeling good about yourself.

1. Keep a success journal and record your accomplishments at the end of each day.

2. Recognize your achievements and reward yourself regularly.

3. Surround yourself with "victory" symbols—trophies, awards, diplomas, certificates. We tend to see men doing this more than women; we need reminders, too!

4. Keep a file of congratulatory letters, thank-you cards, and notes of appreciation that you have received and reread them when you need a boost.

5. Save any articles, newspaper clippings, photos, and ribbons that remind you of your past successes.

6. Join a networking organization or positive support group.

7. Associate with confident people who share your goals and can encourage you.

8. Limit your association with those who attempt to undermine your worth.

9. Take inventory of your personal strengths and list the qualities you value most about yourself.

10. Look your best at all times. Wear great-looking clothes, and buy at least one quality outfit per year.

11. Act "as if" you were confident; check your overall bearing.

12. Develop an expertise in something unique.

13. Read a book on communication and increase your vocabulary.

14. Volunteer to give a speech on a topic that's especially meaningful to you.

15. Take a course to learn something new.

16. Attend personal and professional development seminars.

17. Do something special for someone less fortunate.

18. Set goals that require you to take risks and be courageous, even in small ways.

19. Be affirming, agreeable, approving, and accepting of others. Give away what you'd like to receive.

20. Never verbalize that you are lacking confidence, or allow yourself to host "pity parties."

21. Carry a crisp $100 bill in your wallet, not for spending, but for planting seeds of wealth and prosperity in your subconscious mind.

22. Open a "Triumphant, Victorious Bank Account" and deposit anywhere from ten to fifty dollars after every major accomplishment. Eventually, use that money to go out and celebrate your success.

23. Give yourself away—your time, special gifts and talents, energy, or money.

24. Be a coach to someone else.

25. Learn a new hobby or sport.

26. Have at least one confiding friend, someone you trust implicitly.

27. Allow someone to love you. Accept his love in the way he is prepared to show it.

28. Listen to inspiring and motivating messages on audiocassette.

29. Put written reminders and affirmations on cue cards and post them where you can see them regularly.

30. Give credit to and thank all those who have contributed to your success up until now.

With a healthy self-image and a deep sense of your own worth, you will experience the emotional freedom you need for personal fulfillment, the confidence to follow your heart, and the courage to assert yourself.

MASTERING ASSERTIVENESS

Acting assertively will make the difference between being powerful or powerless, being the victor or the victim. You can choose either to influence or be influenced. It's been said so many times, but it's still a fact: You have complete power over only one thing—your choices. The starting point is to know without a doubt that it's not what happens to you in life but your reaction to it that counts. When you become absolutely sure of this, nothing will ever be able to destroy your self-esteem or confidence. When you begin to assert yourself, failures, setbacks, others' opinions of you, embarrassing moments, or any other personal challenge can never devastate you.

With wings, you'll enjoy high levels of dignity and self-respect. When you see yourself as a worthy, capable individual who deserves the best treatment, that's what you'll usually get.

Without wings, women often believe they have only two choices when they feel manipulated by others—to react *passively* or *aggressively*. Neither of these insecure responses is the answer. Attack and defense are poor approaches and hardly ever get the desired results. Most of us have insecure types in our lives whom we must deal with. The first step is to recognize the signs.

Telltale Clues of Insecure Behavior

Low self-esteem characterizes passive and aggressive behavior. The aggressors are often driven to compete. They measure their own worth by comparison, and have a desperate need to win. They try to avoid situations where they might lose, and when they do lose they become resentful. When people exhibit passive signs of low self-esteem, all we can do is help them discover their true worth and inner potential by supporting and encouraging their strengths.

You will notice that insecure people may
- seem resentful and rebellious toward any type of authority
- attempt to take control of situations in an aggressive manner
- try to build themselves up by putting others down

- find fault with others but are unable to take criticism themselves
- have a way of rationalizing their mistakes and failures
- passively try to please everyone, all the time
- be driven to prove themselves
- make big plans but are unable to see them through
- exaggerate in order to make themselves look better

None of these is the answer to improving self-esteem, yet they are the paths so often chosen when insecure people find themselves dealing with situations in which they feel out of control.

There's a truth behind the principle of control and that is that you will feel positive about yourself to the degree that you feel in control of your life. Likewise, you'll feel negative about yourself when you believe you are not in control. Assertiveness is one very powerful key. Self-control means you won't be swayed by others and is the result of having an internal focus. When we have an external focus, we believe that outer circumstances and other people have more control over our reactions and outcomes than we do.

In many ways, we actually teach others how to treat us by what we tolerate or what we won't, and what we anticipate. However, we are not mind readers, nor should we expect other people to read our minds. When we need help, we must ask for it. I would even go so far as to say that when we need a certain *response* from someone, we can and should express that need.

Let me share a personal story with you that shows how this worked for me. As I was writing this book, my husband and I were also renovating a major part of our home. It had been our dream since we bought the house a number of years ago to make two rather small rooms into one big country kitchen. This meant taking down walls, adding on sections, and completely replacing windows, floors, and cabinets.

With my speaking and travel schedule, it wasn't going to be easy to find a time when I would be around to make all the necessary decisions and supervise a project over several months. Because I was going to be home anyway to write the book, I felt that this would be a good time to do the renovations. My husband suggested that I wait for one more year, or at least until the book was finished so that I wouldn't be under any added pressure.

I was so convinced that this was the best time that I went ahead and got things in motion. Even so, I was smart enough to know there would be days when I would be tearing my hair out. And I knew that when I expressed my feelings to my husband, he might be tempted to say, "Well, you just had to go ahead in spite of my advice, didn't you?" (Another version of "I told you so.")

I decided that, in advance, I would ask him for a big favor. I suggested that when I was having *one of those days* he could say instead, "There, there, honey. It's not going to last forever. When it's done, it'll all be worth it!"

He grinned and kind of rolled his eyes, but agreed! We actually rehearsed the whole scenario. Sure enough, the day came. I'd had enough. All I wanted was to be able to snap my fingers and get my old kitchen back. It suddenly didn't seem all that bad to me in the midst of the present mess and dirt.

When I screamed, "I can't live like this anymore!" it seemed for a minute as if I was going to get the old "I told you so." But instead, just as if some mechanism had been activated, my dear hubby responded with just what I needed most to hear. "This is going to be the most beautiful country kitchen there ever was and it's almost over. Hang in there, hon!"

Now, I knew it was rehearsed. I knew it didn't come naturally. But did that matter at that moment? No, because he cared enough to make the effort to give me what would sustain me over the next few weeks. We can either waste a lot of time getting upset about the way others treat us or we can let them know in advance how we need them to respond!

Teaching others how to treat us works in professional settings as well. A friend was commenting recently on the fact that she deals with men from all levels on a regular basis in her business, but she never seems to have to contend with sexual innuendoes, harassment, or any other form of male chauvinist behavior. I had to admit that, even though that's the case with me as well, it wasn't always true. Her comment reminded me of how I learned the valuable lesson that assertiveness was the answer.

I had been hired to speak to a group of sales managers with a motorcycle company, and was forewarned about a particular man who had an especially annoying habit of flirting. He showed no respect and took unfair advantage of almost every woman he came into contact with. Many women, even though they didn't like his behavior, would play along. Although he was basically a bully, in some ways he was a "nice guy," so they were willing to overlook this problem. There was a time when I might have reacted in the same manner, but this time I was ready for the challenge. On my way to the event where I was to speak, I rehearsed what I would do. I made a decision to walk right up to him, energetically extend my hand to shake his, and confidently introduce myself in a "nonvictim" manner. When I did, he responded with the same dignity, and behaved respectfully for the entire evening. It was a simple technique, but I've discovered that it works almost every time.

I have another friend who says that anytime she receives an inappropriate comment from a man, she responds with a simple "Excuse me?" or "I beg your pardon?" Then she waits quietly for him to repeat himself. She says he rarely does.

We can encourage others to treat us with dignity. We get to set the tone. We can actually exude an energy and a message that asserts, "I'll accept nothing less than utmost decency and high regard, and in turn I'll respect you."

Some women settle for less because they want peace at any cost, and others because they want to appear desirable. It's hardly worth the price we all end up paying because of these responses. Of course, there will always be those men who will continue to badger women no matter what we do. But by taking a different approach, we can at the very least encourage them to find new ways to respond to us.

Assertiveness is not for getting rid of anger. Its purpose is not simply to tell others what's on your mind. That's aggressiveness. Instead, assertiveness is always geared to some sort of change. There is no guarantee that you will always get the change you are after. Others have the right to assert their wishes as well. But asking does increase your chances.

Even though we cannot determine another's attitude toward us, we do have the remarkable ability to affect his or her behavior. If we feel strongly about not being manipulated, it's up to us to remind people of how we want to be treated. Let's not leave it up to chance, hoping for the best or complaining when it doesn't happen the way we'd like it to.

On the other hand, if you expect to be upset, then you will most likely not be disappointed. It's almost impossible to victimize someone who simply doesn't expect to be victimized. I am not referring to the victims of our world who have been injured or taken advantage of by some illegal or immoral activity, but rather to those women who have given up their control and spend their lives doing things they'd rather not be doing. Women who feel manipulated into personal sacrifice usually suffer with hidden, or not-so-hidden, resentment. Instead, we can go into every situation refusing to tolerate even the thought of being taken advantage of and expecting to win.

Many women do not speak up for fear of hurting others' feelings. Certainly, we can all have some influence on each other and it's our responsibility to be considerate and use diplomacy, but no one can determine someone else's feelings. That's a choice he or she alone must make.

When we take responsibility for projecting an image of respect and dignity, we can begin to build harmonious, cooperative relationships based on trust rather than threat; warmth, compassion, and openness rather than control.

Anti-Victim Action Steps You Can Take

1. Start by developing the habit of "confident expectation"—expecting to be self-assured and courageous, and to be treated with respect.

2. Reject any thought of being abused, manipulated, or intimidated.

3. When someone wants you to do something you don't want to do, say no without feeling that you have to justify yourself or apologize.

4. When salespeople continue to hound you, whether in person or on the phone, tell them that you are not interested. Refuse to be pressured by sales tactics.

5. When you encounter an uncooperative service professional, leave and deal elsewhere.

6. If you're tempted to do something just because it's always been done, make your own decision and offer no explanation.

7. Refuse to feel guilty about not following someone else's rules when it comes to your well-being.

8. Stay committed to yourself if you've made a decision to eliminate certain foods from your diet, whether for health, weight loss, or religious reasons.

9. If there's someone in your home who constantly criticizes you, remind him that you don't want to put up with this type of badgering. Tell him that you may have to leave the room until he can treat you in a more appropriate manner.

10. When someone insults you, try saying something like, "That sounds like a put-down. Was that really how you meant it?" Then, just wait quietly and let him decide how he'll respond.

11. Ignore obscene remarks, bad language, or dirty jokes. Break eye contact and don't respond. Never allow someone else to determine your emotions and behavior.

12. Don't be manipulated by other people's anger or supposed helplessness. Help them if you can and want to, but set your own limits. Say no when you have to and stick to it.

13. At a social gathering, when someone wants to kiss you and you'd rather not, instead of giving in and feeling abused, refuse and simply extend your hand for a handshake.

14. If you want to attend a special event and your partner doesn't, rather than complaining, tell him you have two tickets and you'd like for him to accompany you, but you understand if he isn't interested. Then, either go with a friend, or go alone and give the other ticket away to someone who otherwise wouldn't have the opportunity to attend.

15. When your partner always wants to control the television remote control, consider buying your own set. Put it in another room and use it when necessary.

16. If someone in the house insists on hollering at you from another room, pretend you don't hear and go about your normal routine. Sooner or later, he'll get the hint and come to where you are.

17. When you have feelings of guilt or inadequacy, ask yourself if they've been handed down from someone else. If they are deserved, then make the necessary corrections, ask for and accept forgiveness, and put the past behind you. If they are not deserved, remind yourself that you can choose to accept or ignore these feelings.

18. Eliminate words like "should" and "ought to" from your vocabulary. When others use them to get you to take action, check them out before you feel obligated. For instance, when someone feels that you "should" discuss a certain matter and you don't agree, respond by stating, "This doesn't seem to be the most opportune time to talk about this. I'm sure it would be more advantageous and productive to cover it some other time."

19. When someone asks you a question you're not comfortable with, don't feel you have to answer. You don't owe anyone explanations for what goes on in your private life. Say something like, "For personal reasons, I've made a decision never to comment on these matters."

20. You are only responsible for half of each of your relationships. Don't allow others to intimidate or coerce you into feeling that you are responsible for their feelings and behaviors. Although you are responsible *to* them—to be the best person you know how to be—you are not responsible *for* their reaction to you. Everyone holds the key to his or her own happiness and success.

All of these steps are choices you can make. Whether you accept or reject them is always a choice. In any case, you're the one who will have to live with the results. And that's reason enough never to have to explain your choices to anyone.

Even though it's best to choose assertiveness in every circumstance, it doesn't mean that you'll never have to compromise. When you disagree passionately with someone you truly care about, being assertive also includes give and take, or finding a middle ground. The key is that the final result can be a double win, satisfying both parties, whereas aggressiveness or passiveness almost always ends up being a win-lose or lose-lose situation.

For instance, even in a thriving relationship, regardless of how much you care about each other, you may not see eye to eye on which restaurant to eat in, which movie or television program to watch, who gets to hold the remote control, which music station to listen to and how loud it should be, where to vacation and for how long, whether the windows are open or shut at night, how much you should tip, who drives the car and how fast, what to do on Saturday evenings, and who pays for what. You will probably never have a job where you agree with everyone you work with on every issue. There will always be differences of values and core beliefs. There will be times when you are asked or expected to give more than you're getting paid for, to go above and beyond your job description.

Women without wings live in a fantasy land where they believe they can have everything just the way they want it, all the time. They believe that with a little effort they can convince the other person that their way really is best. They become convinced that other women's lives are that way, which leads them to have unrealistic expectations about their own lives. When that happens, they have a difficult time appreciating what they do have, and are always longing for what they may never have.

With wings, you'll know that it's human to be a little dissatisfied, and to sometimes wish things were different, but you'll also know the difference between fantasy and reality. Feeling worthy, believing in yourself, and having the courage to be assertive are steps in spreading your wings. These steps aren't always easy. There are many barriers to changing your self-concept and building confidence, and several can be overcome by taking charge of your belief systems. To do this, let's consider the many ways you can develop and use your internal wisdom and guidance system. Insight is the next step in getting your wings.

CHAPTER 3

W
Insight
N
G
S

> I turned my mind to understand, to investigate and to search
> out wisdom. (Eccles. 7:25)

THERE'S A WONDROUS, HIDDEN PART OF YOU that goes beyond that
which is known by your conscious mind. It is the subconscious part,
your perceptive self, that remains unrestricted by logic. It's the part
of you that lies guarded and untouched by your doubts, inhibitions,
fears, and narrow thinking—barriers that can hold you back and
prevent you from enjoying total freedom.

Even though analytical thinking is important and useful, it can
take you only part of the way in your journey to success. A happy
flight comes more quickly to women who are attuned to their
insight.

It's a well-known fact that most of us, over a lifetime, develop only
a small portion of our potential and natural mental capacities.
What's not as well known is that it is relatively easy to draw on these
abilities that lie dormant within. They are just as vital to achievement as logical intelligence, and just as accessible.

Insight is simply a matter of discernment or a keen awareness. It's
that point where one's mind makes a giant leap to a higher plane of
knowing and astute sensitivity. It's a natural function for all of us but
particularly for women. When we begin to trust it, our insight acts
as an accurate personal advisor. The ancient Hebrews had a word
for this type of wisdom. They called it *hackmah,* meaning "the skill
of living." This skill comes in many forms. Let's take a look at three
of them—intuition, imagination, and creativity.

THE GIFT OF INTUITION

Your intuition is an instantaneous perception of your mind before analysis has a chance to take place. I believe that it's the very voice of God, our source of all wisdom, speaking to us in the form of hunches, inner signals, and gut feelings, guiding and prompting us to take action. We all get intuitive thoughts, but women seem to be more in tune with them. Perhaps that's why our sixth sense is sometimes referred to as *feminine radar!*

When we pay attention to this voice within, and develop trust in it, we can always know what's best for us. We will instinctively know how to make the right decisions for ourselves rather than trusting only outside sources. Through intuition, we can ignite our potential to provide answers to our most serious questions, create innovative solutions to challenges, and generate some truly original concepts and ideas to contribute to our world.

You've probably discovered that the information you receive through intuition is remarkably accurate. Yet when you're asked to explain where the knowledge comes from, you can't really say. When we rely on intuition, we tap into information that, until that moment, has not been available to us. We can make judgments based on feelings, yet some more logically minded individuals may find it difficult to have faith in our perceptions without more specific data, such as flow charts or bar graphs! In our culture, it seems we are encouraged to follow more traditional ways of knowing over the nonrational methods.

When our opinions are not acknowledged or even tested, we may lose our confidence in this source of inner knowledge, and eventually stop drawing on it. It's no wonder, then, that few women really have faith in these feelings or even entertain them. How often do we merely brush them aside and think to ourselves, "It's only me. It can't mean anything." Our inability to explain intuitive thoughts in intellectual terms eventually inhibits even our trust in them.

My friend Maryanne and her husband, Hugh, operate their own business and work together on a daily basis. When she has an eerie feeling about a business decision, he now listens. It wasn't always this way. One day after interviewing a rather impressive man who was extremely experienced in their industry, my friend expressed her intuitive concerns to her husband. With all this man had to offer their business, Hugh was surprised when she said she felt hesitant about hiring him. When she couldn't really explain her feelings, Hugh hired him anyway, based on the applicant's apparent knowledge and competency. Before long, valuable clients were lost and huge amounts of merchandise had been stolen from the company. They were both devastated. Needless to say, now, when she says she has a funny feeling about something, he wants to know more!

Although it's a natural function, and there really is nothing mystical about intuition, what it can do is quickly and directly open the way to information without depending on rational thinking methods. If you begin to pay attention to and rely on your voice within, it can present new knowledge in many forms. It will give you the wisdom to know whether things seem right or wrong. It will help you in making good choices and decisions about every aspect of your life. It will provide answers when there seem to be none and clear direction when you need it most.

Learning to trust your inner self isn't easy. But it is something you can master. Like a muscle, the subconscious mind needs to be exercised in order to operate at its maximum potential. What happens is we get so comfortable solving our problems through routine methods that we forget to turn to our creative abilities.

Once we realize that we are spiritual beings by nature, our God-given intuitive abilities can help us triumph in all areas of our lives including learning new skills, enjoying vibrant health, being better spouses or parents, taking calculated risks, capitalizing on new ventures, increasing our earning power, and developing strong, positive relationships.

Trusting this extraordinary source of guidance can also prevent an emergency situation. When Shelly's young son complained of stomach pains, she sent him off to bed and suggested he just lie quietly until the pains went away. Even though he was resting, she was not. Her intuition was acting as an alarm. Her son said he was feeling better, but Shelly had the nagging feeling that there was something more serious to be concerned about. She couldn't explain it. It was just a feeling. The rest of the family thought she was making too much of his condition when she decided to take her son to the emergency room, but trusting her intuition paid off. His appendix was about to rupture and had she not listened to that voice within, the results may have been tragic.

Often, when we're faced with making a decision, we don't have time to do all the fact finding necessary to make a logical choice. Also, we encounter so many challenges in today's world that cannot be handled simply by reasoning. We must apply that internal wisdom.

Our intuitive self is constantly sending us messages. It urges us to stretch and learn. It enables us to recall important information just when we need it. It prompts us to take action or move in another direction. Women know intuitively when our husbands need encouragement or a hug. We wake up naturally just before our babies cry. We think of a friend and the next day she calls or we receive a letter in the mail. Our intuition is clearly one of the most important aspects of our wings that we can develop.

Tapping these amazing intuitive abilities will release hidden strengths that all women can benefit from, but especially those who appear to be working under pressure to thrive or even survive in the professional world. The hearts and minds of these women are often weighed down by unrealistic expectations and obligations. Stress threatens their health and, in some cases, their very lives. Many have compromised their integrity in their attempt to get ahead regardless of the price. Intuition can help them come back to their true selves, become established and secure once again, and guard against self-destructive thoughts and actions.

This intuitive side of your nature is actually your spiritual self—who you were before you developed your other self, the intellect. As babies, even before we communicate verbally, we use an intuitive language. It allows us to enjoy a special bonding with the other people in our lives on an instinctive level. *Perhaps this is what Christ meant when He taught that the Kingdom of Heaven is within. He encouraged us to come to Him in a "childlike" state.* As children, we drew unconditionally on our intuition since we hadn't fully developed our logic. The messages we received intuitively were clear then and we were more apt to take them seriously. Unfortunately, since birth, we are conditioned that if we cannot see, hear, taste, touch, or smell something, it must not really exist.

Even our education system, as good as it is, seems to value logical, linear thinking processes. Because creativity has not always been encouraged, it's not surprising that when as adult women we get intuitive thoughts and feelings, we don't freely trust them. However, the good news is that recently students with artistic talents are being given more support.

I am not talking about new-age philosophy or some form of *mental gymnastics,* but rather age-old truths and universal principles. As children, we are pure and simple spiritual beings, before we are bombarded with society's beliefs about analytical thinking. It's when we learn to communicate with words that we begin to relate our experiences in rational terms. We then become so programmed to use reasoning that we sometimes forget that we have our intuitive, creative inner self to rely on. God gave us the incredible gift of intuition. Let's take it seriously.

INTUITION AND YOUR SPIRITUAL NATURE

As you become more experienced in drawing on your intuition, you'll begin to see that few of your life's experiences are meaningless or accidental. What would have once seemed like a coincidental occurrence will now be seen as a contributing force to the order and direction in your life and your spirituality will be stimulated and heightened. Even when apparently bad or negative events happen, you will know that there is a connection between those incidents and your overall life purpose.

If you have any doubts about this spiritual connection, just consider the role of intuition in traditional Christianity and take a look at the historical use of this gift by women in Scriptures. The women who knew Christ believed in Him because they intuitively recognized His power. It was often the men who questioned. Women relied on reflective knowledge and it became their most powerful gift. They also used the contemplative power of prayer, realizing that this type of insightful searching would uncover a deeper understanding of spiritual truths. Through meditation they were able to combine the spiritual concepts of faith and wisdom to gain a better understanding of deeper spiritual matters.

This wonderful gift is available for all who desire it. It is your intrinsic ability to access truth and direction anytime you require it. What a comforting thought! Countless times, when I have needed knowledge or guidance, I have received it in a special quote or letter or conversation that might have appeared to come to me through sheer chance, but now I know differently. There have been other times when I have received confirmation of an idea I wanted to implement or a decision I was about to make through similar extraordinary sources. During my life, I have experienced numerous such events, and I call them miracles.

THE WONDERS OF PREMONITION AND DIVINE PROTECTION

Sometimes we are allowed a glimpse into the future through our intuitive thoughts, as a forewarning. One of the strangest occurrences I've ever had was a time when I was driving in my car and was just about to round a familiar curve in the country road by my house. Suddenly, I heard the screeching of tires and that awful thud of metal hitting metal, followed by shattering glass. I knew instantly that an accident had just happened up ahead, and slowed my car until I could inch my way around the bend. I wasn't sure what I would find. As I came around the corner, what I saw astounded me. It *was* an accident, involving two cars and a motorcycle, but it had clearly happened some time ago, since the police, an ambulance, and a tow truck were already on the scene. What I had heard was apparently only in my mind. The impact of this whole situation didn't really strike me until some time later that day. Apparently, I had been miraculously spared. Just before I had started out on my long road trip, I had prayed for safety. I believe that I was being protected by hearing the sound of the accident, which slowed me down and prevented me from being part of the whole crash.

Another example of protection is one of the most exciting and reassuring things that occurred when my children and I lived on our own. We had just moved into our small apartment after leaving the abusive relationship of my former marriage. We were having extreme financial difficulties at first, and from time to time would receive checks, sent anonymously, from very special friends. The amount of each check always seemed to meet the need of a specific financial obligation at the time. This was amazing in itself! One particular Friday, though, money that I had earned was to be delivered in the mail but, for some reason, it didn't arrive. After making some inquiries by telephone, I discovered that it would be two more weeks before we would receive it. We desperately needed groceries and I was counting on that paycheck. I knew we could always call on family or friends to help us, but I asked the children not to tell anyone and, instead, we chose to believe that our need would be miraculously met.

Children have such wonderful faith. They were so excited that they actually encouraged me! We could hardly wait to see how this miracle was going to happen. All that was left in our cupboards by then was peanut butter and crackers. So, that's what we ate—for breakfast, lunch, and supper. After attending church on Sunday morning, I was talking with some friends and told the children to go ahead and wait for me in the car. They came running back to me to tell me that our car was full of boxes of groceries, with no note or any type of explanation. We hadn't shared our need with anybody, yet someone had been inspired to do this for us. Months later, we discovered through some friends that a wonderful couple in our church had simply wanted to help a needy family and they had felt a strong urge to put this food in my car that particular Sunday. As you can imagine, we are eternally grateful to that couple, and, beyond that, the whole incident built our faith that our needs would always be met, whatever they may be.

Some women have been benefiting from their intuitive abilities for years, while others may be hesitant at first to open up to this side of their natures. To begin your spiritual journey, start asking for divine direction, and expect to receive an answer. As the Bible says, *"You have not because you ask not."*

Begin to trust that inner voice. For many of us, this is a hard thing to do. Over the years, we have not been given consistent encouragement or accurate guidance and feedback in this area. Consequently, we lack confidence in our insight.

Take time to write down some of the insightful thoughts you have had that may have protected, guided, or informed you in the past.

INSTINCT: OUR SAFETY VALVE FOR HEALTH

Instinct, a facet of intuition, plays an important role in helping us deal with the stress that accompanies challenging events in our lives. Something extremely beneficial that women tend to do instinctively is cry. On average, most women cry four times more often than men—at least once a week. It's unfortunate that our society discourages crying, especially in men and boys. Rather than seeing it as a weakness, we should allow ourselves the comfort of indulging in this natural, healthy form of emotional release and communication.

Research is now shedding fascinating new light on crying and tears. Many psychologists agree that crying provides a type of purification, a powerful cleansing through the release of harmful substances produced during stress.

Can you remember the last time you had a good cry? It probably left you feeling drained yet refreshed and invigorated all at the same time. You may have even felt similar to the way you feel after a good, hearty laugh or making love. In fact, many women cry after experiencing the joy of lovemaking, thereby enjoying double benefits.

Many psychologists agree that weeping is beneficial in a number of ways. If you've been taught that it's not okay to cry, you can relearn this ability. The first step is to understand the results you'll experience.

Feelings created by sad or painful experiences can cause tears to flow freely and automatically. Some researchers believe that emotional distress produces toxic substances in the body and tears help to carry some of these chemicals from the system. Suppressed tears can linger and continue to cause problems for a long time. In an experiment, volunteers were asked to collect emotional tears produced as a result of watching a touching movie, and also biological tears produced when exposed to fresh-cut onions or walking into a smoke-filled room. What they discovered was that the biological type was the same as the tears that are continuously produced beneath the upper eyelid to keep our eyes moist and healthy. Conversely, emotional tears contained a variety of toxic chemicals that have the potential to poison our systems. So, it seems crying is a natural mechanism that can help discharge the harmful substances caused by emotional distress.

Crying is also beneficial because it releases emotional tension. It provides a wonderful relief from pain and pressure. Stress causes an imbalance in our system, and crying restores that balance. It acts as a catharsis. It purifies the body and provides an emotional release for the mind. After we've had a good cry, we often fall into a deep sleep and awake refreshed. Crying is nature's way of helping us to cope. Even though we may not see it as such at the time, it will always leave us strengthened rather than debilitated, uplifted rather than exhausted. So, crying can provide not only a wonderful psychological refuge from stress, but it is also essential in helping to keep our bodies free from disease.

In the next chapter, we will be dealing with how to handle those times when you are close to tears on the job, in a meeting, or anytime you feel that it simply is not appropriate. Crying can be, however, an effective way of communicating in our personal relationships and may at times be a call for help. When Carrie would cry in the middle of an argument with her husband, she perceived it as a sign of her own weakness or surrender. At times, she also secretly wondered if she was subconsciously using it as a form of manipulation in an attempt to gain control. In reality, it was neither of those. Instead, her tears were a signal that she was in pain. She was secretly hoping he would respond to her hurting and sense of frustration, loss, or sadness. She wanted him to attempt to come to her rescue and soothe the pain. Sometimes we need to explain this to our partners ahead of time to be sure our crying won't be construed the wrong way.

Tears are like laughter in that they can have a wonderful bonding effect, connecting the people involved. One couple told me that the first time they experienced *true intimacy and openness* in their relationship was when they cried together over something they both deeply cared about. They say the emotions they shared through tears resulted in a union of understanding and a level of intimacy that far surpassed what words, or even their physical union, had ever brought them.

Crying serves many purposes. By releasing toxic substances that are produced by emotional distress, it restores a sense of balance in our lives. So, for your health's sake, go ahead and enjoy a good sob once in awhile.

Groaning is another healthy release. We groan instinctively when we yawn and stretch, when we lift something heavy, and when we've eaten a terrific meal. We moan when we're enjoying a great back rub and in moments of passion or intense lovemaking.

In many instances, it's been proven that groaning very definitely has therapeutic qualities. In childbirth, women groan spontaneously. Patients emerging from surgery find that moaning helps to alleviate their suffering. As amazing as it seems, I have found that after one of those exasperating experiences of stubbing my toe, or banging my knee against an open desk drawer, if I yell loud enough and long enough, I not only scare the wits out of the cat, but the normal physical effects that you might expect to occur, including long-term pain and bruising, are minimized.

Since the beginning of time, people have believed that groaning eases emotional pain as well. A time I will never forget is the day my father passed away. We knew he was seriously ill and near death, and the entire family had been able to gather for one last visit with him in the hospital. It shouldn't have been a complete shock when my mom called early the next morning to say that he was gone. But it seems that we are never fully prepared for the loss of a loved one, regardless of the circumstances.

As I stood in the shower that morning, before going to be with my family, I was almost overwhelmed. My body seemed to take over and the moaning began instinctively. I stayed under the warm, gentle stream of water and allowed the groaning to continue until I felt complete relief. Later, when I was alone in my car, it started again, and once more I granted myself permission to give in to that form of release. I believe that being set free from the pain in that way was one reason why I was able to endure the physical and emotional stress of the next few days and weeks and even now am able to continue to mourn the loss of my father in a healthy way.

It's too bad that our culture generally discourages this beneficial response. Our family members and even well-meaning professionals may quiet us, telling us groaning is disruptive. We tell ourselves that it's a negative reaction and try hard to hold it back. We need to see that groaning is actually an effective, simple, and natural way to get relief from pressures of all kinds.

Physically, these *primal moans* help you in a number of ways. By involving the entire body in gentle, rhythmic activity, you'll feel more relaxed. Because they require deep, diaphragmatic breathing, there is an increase in the oxygen supply to all parts of your body. Groaning also provides a type of *inner massage* by producing strong vibrations within your body.

All of this really made sense to me when a young mother told me of the time she asked her small child, "I know you're feeling ill, but do you have to make so much noise?" and the little one replied, "It just feels better when I groan!" Isn't that the truth?

One major barrier to enjoying the benefits of this type of therapy is the personal embarrassment! You may want to follow these few tips.

- Practice this technique where it will not disturb others, when you are home alone, or if you can get out into nature.
- If you can't be alone, warn others in advance, so they won't think you're in trouble and calling for help.
- When you are in your car, keep your windows rolled up.
- If you're at home, put the cat out!

One of the most amazing facts about human nature is that we can take advantage of some of the things we do instinctively, yet we are not controlled by our instincts. Unlike other species, who only respond to inherent drives, you and I always have a choice. We can continue to tap those instinctive resources that are beneficial to our overall being and take control over those that are not.

RELEASING YOUR HIDDEN POTENTIAL

Faith *can* move mountains! Trusting in your natural insight can empower you to make decisions—quick decisions and the right ones. You can know what's right for you and what's not. You have probably already discovered the power of prayer in enabling you to find lost items, avoid unnecessary mistakes and setbacks, and overcome fear. You'll only fully reap the benefits if you're aware of your internal wisdom, have faith in your potential, and practice using these gifts regularly.

I couldn't begin to count the number of times over the years that I have needed an answer to a problem or a new idea for a project I've been working on, and have been directed to the exact source for that solution—whether it was through a book in a store, getting in touch with an old friend, or even coming across a lost item in my own home.

Not long ago, I misplaced a photo album that was extremely valuable to me for sentimental reasons. I was starting to wonder if I had thrown it away by accident. I decided to ask for an answer and then just let it go for a few days. One evening, my cat clawed open the door of a dining-room cupboard that was seldom used and she climbed inside. I could hear her moving around and went to see what mischief she was getting into. As I reached in to pull her out, my lost photo album fell on the floor. In all my searching, I hadn't thought to look there. Our answers come to us in many mysterious ways.

Often when I need to fill a certain spot in my calendar with speaking engagements, I pray for guidance and find I'm prompted to call a particular client. I'm no longer surprised when I hear that client say, "You've called at the perfect time. We are just putting our program together and getting ready to select our speakers." Those occurrences encourage me to keep following my inner urges!

Start developing the habit of asking for new ideas or solutions to problems. Good times to do this are just before falling asleep at night, when you're going for a walk, or whenever you're alone in your car. Just remember to expect an answer.

When you're sitting in a seminar listening to a good speaker who stimulates your creative juices, notice how thoughts and suggestions simply seem to come to you. Anytime you are away from the pressures of daily living, your mind can work freely and you will be amazed at the concepts that surface. Always make sure you have paper and a pen handy, especially upon awakening in the morning or from a nap. I have developed the habit of carrying a micro cassette recorder with me everywhere I go, to capture my thoughts. I even keep one in the bathroom, just outside the shower within easy reach. That's one place new ideas really start to flow.

Your subconscious mind is like a huge memory bank and remembers everything you have ever heard, seen, read, or done. Why not draw on some of that information to help you devise solutions to your current problems? You will be amazed at how many valuable ideas will come bursting through!

Listening to your body as well as to your inner voice plays a crucial role in learning to use your intuition. There is a large network of nerves located behind the stomach called the solar plexus. This is also known as the center of emotion. It enables us to have a very precise response to situations. That's why we call them *gut feelings*. Begin to pay attention to the signals your body is sending.

A number of years ago, I had been diagnosed as having a rare blood disease even though my doctors really couldn't put a name to it. I had never been so sick in my entire life and when I was eventually sent home, being told that there was nothing more they could do for me, I truly felt close to death. I actually had no fear of dying but what I did fear was leaving my two small daughters without their mother. I wept openly for them and decided to believe I would get an answer. I truly needed a miracle, and for the first time in my life, I prayed for and expected to receive one.

Shortly after that, I started to listen to the signals my body was sending. I began to crave foods that were entirely different from what I had been eating until then. My diet had been atrocious and consisted mainly of caffeine, sugar, and starchy foods. It turned out that my health problems were almost entirely diet related. Believing I was being divinely guided, I began to come across all types of reading material regarding natural healing, health foods, the benefits of various herbs and nutrients, as well as information on how to lead a balanced life-style. Gradually, I got myself on track; stabilized mentally, physically, and spiritually; and experienced an incredible recovery. My doctors were amazed. What happened was I had asked for a miracle and trusted I would receive one. By tapping our insight and then listening for an answer, our bodies will tell us, in one way or another, exactly what they require. We need only to hear and then to take action.

Have you checked in with yourself lately? One of the barriers to a balanced life-style is being out of touch with the *real* you. We get accustomed to seeing ourselves as the "outer image," the competent, logical, in-charge person that the world around us sees. But what about your true feelings, beliefs, perceptions, and ideas?

TRUSTING OR GULLIBLE?

There are many reasons why we ignore our hunches. For instance, when others ask us to trust them, in either our personal or professional lives, we may have a gut-level feeling that we should hold back. But if it's our nature to want to trust, we may not pay attention or even recognize it as a warning from our inner consciousness. Later we find ourselves remembering the *sirens and flashing lights* and wondering why we didn't heed the signals. There's a difference between being intuitively trusting and simply being gullible. We need to learn to separate emotional false alarms from true hunches and gut feelings.

When we ignore our impulses, it could be because we wonder if it's just fear holding us back from tackling a frightening situation head on. Often, when we want to move forward quickly in a new venture, we're aware that fear of failure, rejection, or making mistakes might come to us disguised as an instinct. If we are not experienced enough in listening to those inner messages, we may not be able to tell the difference. Then, out of a sense of dedication to our plans and ideas, we forge ahead in spite of the warning signals. We believe it's only fear of the unknown and are determined to conquer it. It isn't until later, when we are paying the price for our mistake, that we realize it really was our internal wisdom attempting to protect us, and we should have listened.

This happened to me a number of years ago when my speaking career was beginning to take off. I became involved with someone who wanted to promote one of my most popular programs in the form of public seminars. This person seemed to have a tremendous amount of knowledge and expertise in the seminar business, and after we discussed the many exciting ways this program could make a difference in the lives of so many women, my trust had been won. The main drawback was the request for quite a large retainer to cover costs during the organization of the project. While this seemed understandable and logical, my intuition was sending signals, warning me to back away from the entire venture.

Like many women, I wondered if it was simply fear holding me back, and chose to ignore the hunches. I went ahead in spite of them. Within a few weeks, I knew I had made a very costly mistake. The hotel was never booked, the bills incurred had not been paid, and eventually the entire program had to be canceled. Not only was it an embarrassment and an expensive lesson, it could have jeopardized my reputation as an aspiring professional speaker.

While being overly cautious could hold us back from taking advantage of new opportunities, being overly trusting could bring about unnecessary loss or hardship. We need to learn how to distinguish between false alarms induced by fear and real alarms based on accurate gut responses. How do we really know if what we are feeling is simply fear to be overcome or insight warning us so we can avoid a costly mistake?

One solution is to practice turning within to ask and listen for answers regularly. Like any skill, *hackmah,* or wisdom, has to be developed. Journal entries or talking things out with a trusted friend will help you to build on your natural discernment and better assess what's going on in your mind. Perhaps you're distorting a situation or overlooking some critical details. The important thing is to get your thoughts out in the open. Unchallenged, they begin to have an unhealthy power over you. If you hold them in, they can misdirect you, work you into a frenzy, or frighten you needlessly.

Another way to tell the difference between unfounded fear and wise caution is to weigh seriously the pros and cons, and be totally aware of all the possible outcomes of each decision. This is a good time to check with professionals to get their expert advice. Discuss the situation with several other people whose opinions you trust. Know exactly what you will lose if you decide to go ahead and then determine in your own mind if you are willing and able to risk that amount. If not, then it usually is not a good idea to risk.

Optimism is a marvelous quality but there are times when

pessimism pays off. For instance, if the price of a failure or setback is too great, you may want to choose pessimism. It would be foolish, for instance, to be optimistic and trusting if the cost of failure was illness, death, imprisonment, the loss of a fortune, or a broken relationship.

With wings, you will

- have faith that you can trust your inner voice
- listen to your body for accurate gut-level reactions to situations
- conquer your fear of the unknown
- distinguish between real obstacles and imaginary ones
- not hesitate to gather professional advice when making important decisions
- be willing to take risks in exchange for possible gain

IMAGINATION: EXPANDING OUR INNER RESOURCES

"Imagination is the highest kite one can fly" (Lauren Bacall).

Everything created on earth was first a thought. It's been said that the imagination is the workshop of the mind. It's also probably one of the most underused capabilities we have available to us. Women are finding that one sure way to strengthen their wings and connect with their internal wisdom is to examine and reclaim their imaginative spirit. In our minds, we can create *new* flight patterns for ourselves rather than spending valuable energy trying to change existing ones.

Using creative imagination requires whole-brain thinking. The brain is like two minds in one. The left brain thinks in terms of logic. We use it for judgment, analyzing, processing, comparing, and linking ideas together. Current scientific brain research has revealed that men more than women tend to be governed by the left hemisphere of the brain. Our right brain is the source of feelings and it serves us in visualizing, remembering, and developing patterns.

The rational left brain considers details and makes the rules. It is predictable, sequential, and cautious. The right brain produces novel, fresh ideas, and breaks all the rules. It is playful, curious, and takes risks. If we could get both sides operating in harmony, flashes of insight and new ideas could be put into action in conjunction with the tools of logic, words and symbols. What a mighty combination!

When we study the thought processes of people in highly creative professions, such as advertising, design, music, writing, and other arts, we find that they rely heavily on the intuitive right part of their brain. They get new ideas not from logic or analyzing, but through the flow of their creative imagination.

Years of conditioning lead us to believe that using our brains refers only to the left brain. Education also favors left-brain types, since degrees and certification are awarded to those individuals who use predictable patterns of rational thinking. Scientific research and mathematical logic are almost devoid of any right-brain concepts.

Yet imagination is our inner fountain of personal fulfillment and success. It is not hampered by logical past conditioning or self-limiting beliefs and programs. This could be one of our most powerful female mental attributes, a capability that lies at the very heart of creative achievement.

CREATIVITY AWAKENED

There really is nothing mystical about creativity. It's not some unexplained secret power, available to a select few. If you can think, you can imagine. If you can imagine, you can create new ideas.

In order to thrive or even survive in the world today, you need to use your imagination. Your prosperity depends on your ability to generate innovative solutions to the problems we all face. With our busy, fast-paced life-style, it usually seems easier to follow routines rather than to be visionaries and blaze new trails. Being creative doesn't have to be time consuming or difficult. It can happen in an atmosphere of playfulness!

Creativity comes from many sources. For instance, a great deal of it comes out of necessity. I remember that some of the best meals we ever enjoyed as children happened on what we dubbed "clean-out-the-fridge day." It was usually the day before grocery shopping was to be done. The leftovers from each evening of that previous week were brought out onto the counter and the creation began. Foods were mixed and tossed, reheated and rehashed. Wonderful aromas floated from the kitchen throughout the house. We never knew exactly what to call these creations, but whatever they turned into, they were always delicious and memorable. By adding some fresh-baked biscuits and a tossed salad, we enjoyed the finest meal you could imagine. And it only happened out of necessity—cleaning out the old, making room for the new, and not wanting to waste an ounce.

During the years that my children and I lived on our own, we were usually suffering from *malnutrition of the bank account!* I remember a time when, after paying all the bills, we had $12.50 left over to go grocery shopping for the week. Together, we got out the cookbooks for menu ideas, then pored over the various flyers we had received in the mail, noting each item on special and adding up the prices as we very carefully planned our meals for the week. If we needed two carrots, or one onion, that's what we priced. We came up with some very interesting meal ideas as we went along. Between the sale items and the prices we were already familiar with, we were able to make up our list and amazingly figure it right down to the penny. I'll never forget the excitement of watching the girls go ahead of me, up and down the aisles, discovering that one more item was on sale, something we hadn't counted on! They were delighted, since now we had thirty-five cents or forty-nine cents more to splurge on the other things. If it hadn't been for tough times, they would never have known the thrill of *creative shopping.* And perhaps they wouldn't be as grateful as they are today for even the simplest blessings in life. "It is better to create than to be learned; creating is the true essence of life" (Reinhold Neibuhr).

Lynn, a fashion designer, has just opened her own business, something she has dreamed of doing for many years. The front half of her home is her storefront and, because funds are limited, she has had to use her imagination and creativity to decorate. She receives so many compliments on her exceptional display ideas because they are original and uncommon. Lynn admits that if she had the money to pay someone else to do it "right," she may not have created a shop that is as unique and interesting as hers.

Minor frustrations can stimulate our imagination, too. Consider the person who got tired of looking for a lost eraser and, out of desperation, finally glued one to the end of a pencil. It solved the problem, and we've been using it ever since!

A woman in one of my seminars told me she became really creative when the garbage collectors in her city went on strike. Each morning, she very carefully wrapped her garbage in some inexpensive gift wrap, added a small bow, and then left it on the front seat of her car with the window rolled down. She says she wasn't the least bit surprised (or disappointed) when she came back later to find her garbage had been *stolen!*

Mary Phelps Jacob, back in 1914, longed for freedom from corsets with their stays and laces, so she stitched together two lace handkerchiefs and added a pink ribbon. What she had done was invent the modern-day "backless" brassiere. And women today are still enjoying the benefits.

Creativity also comes out of trying to cut costs. One of the smaller companies that I consulted with a number of years ago offered a $100 reward for all money-saving ideas that were submitted by employees and could be implemented right away. The first prize was presented to the female employee who came up with the suggestion that in the future the amount of the reward should be cut in half!

Creativity: Adding Spark to Your Relationships

So many of my seminar participants and family members have shared with me the creative ways they have used imagination to improve their personal and family relationships. Here are a few of them.

1. Patty sends her kids on a summer "treasure hunt." Whenever she spots small, inexpensive games, books, toys, crafts, art supplies, and puzzles, she purchases them and then wraps them individually. After hiding them all around the house and yard, she starts the children off with clue number one. Additional clues have been attached to each present. When they've discovered them all, the kids divide their treasures, and spend the rest of the day enjoying them. It does take some planning and effort, but also gives her a solid chunk of time for herself once it's completed.

2. When my sister Lois and her husband, John, planned their first vacation without the children, she tucked a love note under the covers for Lee-Anne and Jenna to find at bedtime on the first night. Then, because they had gone on a seven-day cruise, she left a map showing the route they'd be taking, and one envelope per day telling them where they would be that day, what they'd probably be doing, and that they would miss them. The children felt close to their parents in their absence and felt as though they'd had a part in the trip as well.

3. Our mom made storybook albums of the lives of each of her five grown children. She filled them with personal memorabilia— anything that was really important to each of us, such as photos from childhood right up to the present, any news clippings in which we were featured, ribbons, diplomas and certificates we had earned, report cards, special projects, and pictures of trophies from school, sports events, or work. They made wonderful Christmas gifts one year, gifts that we'll all cherish and enjoy for a lifetime.

4. Sandra, whose children arrive home from school before she returns from work, occasionally posts small notes for them to find, starting on the back door, moving to the counter where they leave their school bags, then to the fridge where they naturally go for a snack, and so on throughout the house! What a wonderful way to let them know she's thinking of them even if she can't always be there.

5. Renee, a computer consultant, used the same idea for her husband the night before she left on a business trip. First thing the next morning, Frank found love notes everywhere, starting in the bathroom on the back of the toilet. Another on the mirror said, "I love your gorgeous face!" and one on the inside of his underwear said, "What a great body!" She says she sometimes leaves chocolates and a rose on his pillow, or sprays her perfume (his favorite) on the sheets. How could he help but think of her and miss her all the while she's gone?

6. Tammy decided to attach a bouquet of balloons to the inside of the front door. Each balloon contained a different love note for her husband. Next to the bouquet, she left a pin attached to a note instructing him that today was his day to "burst her balloons." He then got to read how she felt about him.

7. Once or twice a year, Jacqueline makes all the arrangements to spend a night at a relaxing country inn with her husband, complete with a heart-shaped tub, dinner served in their room, and a romantic movie. She plans it all and then just lets him know when and where to meet her. Jacqueline admits she used to ask herself why it always had to be her and not her mate who did the innovating, until she realized that many men are left-brain thinkers. For them it's logic all the way!

8. Marion's friend had to spend one week in the hospital. She wanted to take her a special gift, so instead of the usual flowers or box of candy, Marion found seven small items that would be appropriate and useful during her stay there—things such as hand cream, a note pad and pen, a bar of fruit-scented soap, a crossword-puzzle book, a magazine. She then wrapped them individually, and labeled them with the names of the days of the week. She attached a note telling her friend that these were "one a day" presents. Apparently, the nurses were as excited as her friend about what was in each package and made sure to remind her to open it first thing each morning. She said it *almost* made her stay enjoyable.

Once you get the creative juices flowing, there's no end to the exciting ideas you'll come up with. Most of these women said their families and friends told them that having someone so thoughtful and creative in their lives made them feel good about themselves. Instead of complaining about others not caring about their needs, these women chose to acknowledge and affirm others. This is the way most people discover how to be creative. They learn by someone else's example. When we have our wings, we can take responsibility for introducing ideas to the people we care most about. By using your imagination, there's no limit to the number of ways you can surprise the special people in your life.

Instead of waiting for others to notice your needs, take the lead. The people in your life have limitless abilities and talents, just waiting to be set free. Before you know it, they'll be responding by flying on their own wings, and showing you how much you mean to them.

Women Are Natural Creative Problem Solvers!

Although times are changing, women through the centuries have not been encouraged to use their creative abilities, being prompted instead to fall into line with traditional roles, whether in the home or the workplace. So many may have thought that, simply because they were women, they lacked creative talent, or that if they did have it, it was of no value in the marketplace. We have assumed that left-brain linear thinking matters most. It's only recently that right-brain thinking and creativity have been recognized as critical factors for success. Studies reveal that women are excellent creative thinkers. In our current society and economic conditions, there are endless ways in which women can now put this ability to use each day.

Creative problem-solving is a great way to strengthen your wings. Whether you've chosen to work in your home or to go out into the corporate world, or both, your job provides many opportunities to exercise your creative thinking abilities. For one woman, it might mean coming up with innovative ways to keep an active toddler occupied while she diapers the new baby. For another, it may be figuring the new budget or planning future growth strategies for her company. Whatever your challenges, you have the potential to approach them with ingenuity. So take charge of the powers of your mind and awaken your own creativity. Determine to do more than just "think." Use your imagination. Take action. Turn your ideas into realities!

Kindle Your Creative Abilities

Journal keeping is one of the very best steps in developing your creativity. During the process of reflecting and listening, journalizing on a regular basis is a valuable tool to help you record your thoughts throughout this procedure. Then, when creative insights do come, you will have a vehicle for expressing them, one that is familiar to you and easy to use. Otherwise, those precious ideas and concepts float across our minds for but a moment and then hastily disappear, just as a bubble bursts and vanishes into the atmosphere. By journalizing, we can capture our inspirations quickly and accurately.

Quite often, journal entries will express thoughts or concepts that we have never before been able to put into words. By documenting these ideas, we can review, develop, and draw on them for years to come. Be sure to record anything that you want to remember, ponder, or analyze later on.

There are many beautiful, bound books filled with blank pages available today, or you may choose a simple spiral-bound notebook or sketchbook. Whichever you decide to use, stay away from note paper and always use a pen. Loose pages and pencil writing won't last through the years. Even though you'll most likely be the only one to read them, you want your thoughts to endure.

Using a typewriter or computer to express yourself would

naturally be faster, but I find I am more likely to be inspired and think deeply when I make entries in longhand. For example, I chose to write many segments of this book in longhand for that very reason and only entered them in the computer later on for easier editing.

Put your journals in a private place where others won't be tempted to take a peek. However, if you so choose, journals are also a wonderful, intimate way to leave a part of your life behind for your family and future generations. They will enjoy getting to know you from a different perspective and may learn from your experiences. What you don't want is to have to carefully edit or scrutinize your entries wondering if someone will read them, so decide ahead of time which type of journal you will keep.

If you feel the need, share your entries with only a few carefully selected people whom you fully trust. Not everyone will have the discernment, comprehension, or personal experience necessary to contribute positive or helpful input. For the most part, your journalizing will be a private matter.

Because one of the goals of journal keeping is free expression, don't spend time being concerned about accuracy, proper grammar, spelling, or perfectly formed sentences. Don't erase, correct, or change anything you write. Just keep your pen moving and the creative flow going. This is not about flawlessness or intellect. It's about what helps you to feel free and uninhibited. This experience is for you alone, so let go of any fears you have about writing. Immerse yourself in the adventure of self-discovery.

Set apart a special time of day and make your entries on a regular basis until it becomes a habit. If you do miss a day, week, month, or even year, don't be hard on yourself. Just begin again and celebrate the fact that you have a chance to start over.

Record your personal ideas, challenges, and struggles as well as the insights, answers, and creative solutions you receive in your spirit. Every now and then, glance through previous entries and you will be amazed at the incredible growth you've been experiencing.

Next to journal keeping, the best way to develop your imagination is to exercise it. Challenge yourself on a regular basis. Master a new language. Do crossword puzzles, brain teasers, and other word games that provoke creativity. In our home, we often have a jigsaw puzzle in progress, and taking a break to work on it for even a few minutes seems to provide the stimulus I need to get a surge of imagination flowing again.

Self-reliance is another key to unlocking your potential. If you want your imagination and intuition to flourish and work for you, take full responsibility for creating your ideal life. You may be surprised to find that the more you depend on your own abilities, the more proficient you'll become at tapping your potential to control the direction of your life. If you always rely on others for answers to your problems or solutions to your challenges, your own creative abilities will eventually dry up.

For instance, instead of depending entirely on your doctor's advice for your health care, do some studying on your own. Research the best way to get nutrition to work for you, discover which nutrients feed which parts of your body, and learn how to maintain peak levels of energy through natural methods. When you do have a health problem, investigate briefly some of the probable causes and cures for such an ailment, and *then* see the doctor. When you want to remodel your home or landscape your property, instead of relying on the architect or designer totally for guidance, why not design the layout, floor plan, or other details yourself first? Then present these ideas to the person best suited to carry out your plans. Take charge of your finances and formulate your own budget, savings plan, and retirement options before you spend time with a financial consultant.

Women who take back control of their lives in this way report feelings of exuberance and freedom and an increase in their imaginative skills. Although experts, consultants, and advisors can always play a role in your success, they should be working in cooperation with your thoughts and ideas and not as absolute authorities in your affairs. They should be viewed as partners, working side by side to create with you your desired outcome. Besides, when you do decide to consult an expert, you can make his job easier by having done a lot of the research. You'll save yourself money and time. In some cases, you may discover that you don't need the advice after all.

Whenever your creativity is stymied, or you find yourself procrastinating, take time out. Play hooky for an hour or so. Get outdoors. Do something different. When I find myself muddling through my day, I can get inspired with new, intuitive solutions if I make the effort to get away from my normal surroundings. It's usually those days when I think I *can't* afford the time that I benefit the most from taking a break. I've learned to go for a walk near the lake, explore my own backyard, or simply visit the market down the road to admire the colorful displays of fresh fruits and vegetables. Sometimes just making a trip to the bakery, to delight in the scents of coffee brewing and bread fresh from the oven, invigorates my creative juices.

I have a friend in the advertising business who says taking time out to jog several miles provides her with some of her best insights and ideas. Another friend, an artist, goes for a walk through a near-by neighborhood where homeowners have grown exceptional gardens complete with country walkways, picket fences, and bird feeders. The beauty of nature has a wondrous therapeutic effect on her, aside from helping her to see things from a new slant.

If you can't get away from your desk, try reading some fiction or listening to jazz or classical music for five or ten minutes. Glance through a favorite photo album or read something funny. Get out some fluorescent markers, colored pencils, or crayons and sketch something. Or close your eyes and doodle, letting all your emotions flow through your pen or marker. Keep a glue stick, glitter, ribbons, construction paper, yarn, scissors, paints, and brushes together in a basket and store it nearby for times when you need to stimulate your talents. Make fanciful images from your artist's supplies, or create collages by combining photographs, old greeting cards, or pictures clipped from magazines. Having fun like this not only invigorates your senses and arouses your creativity, but it will make you feel warm and peaceful, leaving you with a sense of joy and well-being.

Some women find that noise, rather than quiet, helps to block outside disturbances and interruptions and makes it easier to concentrate. I happen to be one of those people. When I was growing up, I liked to study or do homework with loud music in the background, and no one seemed to understand my unusual inclination. While I agree it does seem peculiar, today I benefit by using what I knew intuitively all along. My husband has a very noisy hobby: quarter-mile drag racing. I often go to the races with him on weekends, and purposely take along my briefcase filled with work. The background noise blocks out some of the incessant chatter that often goes on in my head, and enables me to stay entirely centered on the project I'm working on. I feel more creative and I usually get so much more done than I would in my office, with all the interruptions and distractions.

So many women today work in tense, demanding situations. Along with the great strides we've taken to live as equals with men, we've also paid the price. Even though we've gained ground in the battle for women's rights and equality, somewhere along the way we seem to have lost our ability to tune into our spiritual source of wisdom.

A woman's natural tendency was always to see magic and potential in everything and everyone. Now, we must relearn those ways. We must begin tapping our intuition and using our imagination, in our homes and in the workplace, in our communities and in the world. It's when we are refreshed and relaxed that we are able to see new opportunities for creative expression all around us.

With wings, you will

- associate with creative people, especially children
- travel to different places and meet new people
- play group games such as charades and word games
- start a new hobby or take up a craft or sport
- try some form of art; for instance, drawing, painting, sculpting, woodworking, sewing, or needlework
- do something technical such as repair your car or learn a new program on the computer
- read biographies, success stories, self-help books, do-it-yourself manuals, nature stories, or humorous novels
- practice writing daily in a diary or journal
- pay attention to hunches and premonitions
- view life from a fresh perspective

Creativity and boundless imagination are available to every woman. Within each one of us lies a great source of wisdom—our spirit. What we must do is discover how to manage it and nourish it if we are to be fully alive. The next step in growing our wings is to nurture that spirit.

CHAPTER 4

W
I
Nurturing
G
S

> Choose your emotional sanctuary—reading, writing, playing a musical instrument, painting, gardening, running, or daydreaming. The retreat you choose is not important; only that you do it and that, in doing, you renew your spirit.

WHEN WE HAVE a healthy sense of self-worth and value ourselves as creative, insightful beings, we begin to appreciate the need for self-nurturing, the next step in developing our wings. Self-care plays a vital role in our ability to achieve happiness. Nurturing ourselves is not only a "nice" thing to do, but it is essential if we want to thrive, or even simply survive in this hectic, demanding world. When we learn that it is our responsibility to nurture ourselves, we cease looking to others to uphold us.

Self-care is a critical ingredient in retaining our youth and vitality, experiencing inner peace, and enjoying healthy relationships. It's crucial if we sincerely want to continue caring for others out of a bountiful supply of love.

We are so good at nurturing others. It's a woman's inherent trait. Yet how often do we care for ourselves in the same way? Synonyms for *nurture* include *nourish, strengthen, feed, sustain, maintain, support,* and even *keep alive!* The word *nourish* comes from the Latin, *nutrire,* meaning to breast feed, and it also gives us the words *nutrition* and *nurse.*

Perhaps it's time for us to be nurse to ourselves. The memories I have of nurses caring for me as a young person during one very lengthy stay in the hospital are comforting. They conjure thoughts of warmth, contentment, and protection. Nurses provide a type of freedom, as brief as it may be, from distress—emotionally as well as physically. When we become *constructively selfish,* we begin to take time to reward, comfort, and love ourselves. What is best for us is usually best for everyone concerned.

HEALTHY SELFISHNESS:
OVERCOMING THE GUILT TRAP

Women with wings are easy to spot. They are the ones who practice healthy selfishness. They know the benefits of granting themselves time out, whether it's for fun get-togethers with friends, family times, leisure activities, attending seminars and workshops, or simply personal quiet time. They are the ones having the occasional manicure, pedicure, or massage. You'll see them buying good books and wearing nice clothes. They give themselves permission to be pampered in a variety of ways. These are the women who truly believe in their own value. It's not necessarily that they have more money or time. It isn't that they don't understand the value of self-denial or delayed gratification in its proper place. It's really not about those things. It is about treating themselves now and then, in big ways or small ways, just because they recognize and understand the benefits of investing in their own well-being.

To nurture yourself simply means to take care of yourself—mentally, physically, spiritually, and emotionally. It means devoting time to living your life with healthy self-respect.

When something is of value to us, we show our love for it by spending time with it, nurturing it, and looking after it. I enjoy observing people and the ways they nurture those things they care for. Grandparents study and cherish the grandchildren they adore. They always seem able to give their time and attention to them. I watch my husband with his race car, as he polishes, repairs, and regularly tunes it. He always finds the time and the money he needs. In a similar way, as a bird lover, he makes a point of buying seeds and filling the feeders all year round. Animal lovers make the effort to put out some nuts and other food for the squirrels and raccoons. People make the effort to walk, groom, and play with their pets.

When we love something, we respond in a gentle, thoughtful, caring way. Even when we perceive a need for a change or correction, we are willing to take the necessary steps to make modifications. Yet many of us deny ourselves this same loving care.

Women are well known for nurturing others, often at the expense of their own well-being. We are givers by nature and we know intuitively that caring for others is an important element of a balanced life. In the core of our beings, we understand that a great part of the joy of flying is generosity to others. Yet how can we give freely and completely when we're feeling empty? Somehow we continue to give, but then we feel taken advantage of. Instead of reaping the rewards of giving from a full, rich heart, and feeling refreshed, we feel used. We continue to tell ourselves that a "good woman" keeps giving until there's nothing left to give. But when *we* suffer, those we are nurturing somehow sense our emptiness and they, too, suffer from guilt for having needed us to care for them in the first place. It's not until we are feeling fulfilled that we can give from an abundance.

We know this but we still somehow see nurturing ourselves as a self-centered act. Perhaps we received messages as we were growing up that we were selfish, that taking care of our own needs was self-indulgent. *Now we feel guilty about wanting to feel good.*

So many of us have become proficient at coping with our challenges and barriers—sometimes too proficient. We've learned to be adept at merely *putting up with* the stresses of life. Where do we begin when we are feeling overwhelmed by turbulence, which comes in the form of too many things to do, places to go, people to see, and other responsibilities?

We'll enjoy a smooth flight in spite of the storms and turbulence when we have the courage to pay attention to our mental, physical, and spiritual needs. That's when we are able to use our wings to our best advantage.

SLOW DOWN

Today, quiet intervals for self-reflection and renewal don't seem to come to us naturally. Yet they are vital if we are to fortify ourselves for the perpetual struggles we all face. They are essential if we are to stretch our wings, reach our objectives, and fulfill our purpose in life. It's those times of refuge that empower us to tune into our gifts, hear our inner voice, and restore what we have given away.

Until this century, because of the very nature of our feminine roles, we had opportunities to experience those moments of stillness and seclusion. We spent time baking apple pies and doing needlework. We planted gardens. We visited with friends, tried new recipes, and played with our children. While hanging clothes on the line in the backyard, we could be inspired by gentle breezes, the warmth of the sunshine, and a bird's song. We ironed, we read, we prepared a great meal, and we talked to God. We felt composed, and had an inner stillness that showed itself on the outside. The peacefulness we exuded also had the potential to soothe those we cared for.

Recently I received a letter from a woman vice-president in a large sales and marketing corporation. Her impressive title suggests she is living a glamorous and exciting life. What it really means is she is responsible for a staff of over one hundred, works overtime almost every day, attends one meeting after another, and feels she hasn't enough time to think her own thoughts. She writes:

> I remember those days as a young mother when my house was full of the scents of floors freshly waxed and laundry just folded, a pie cooling in the open window, and supper simmering on the back burner. My life had a sense of order and calmness that I rarely, if ever, feel today. Certainly, I am grateful for all the opportunities I have as a corporate executive, but at the same time, I long to experience once again the peace that has escaped me.

I'm sure she is not suggesting she would want to give up the conveniences and achievements she enjoys today to go back to those times. We know that in days gone by, there were other disturbances and distractions that caused mental, emotional, and physical exhaustion. However, in our hectic, fast-paced world today, we need to consciously make the effort to nurture our spirits so we can replenish our insightful natures and regain some of the serenity we have lost. We need to listen to our hearts so we can avoid burnout. In addition, we must take care of ourselves first so we can continue nurturing others, which seems to be our greatest calling.

In the process of winning our freedom to live as equals with men, many of us have inherited something we didn't want. The tradeoff for our newfound liberty is that we are now prone to many stress-related illnesses and often suffer from inner conflict and agitation. The very freedom we sought and won has the potential to harm us and keep us from experiencing the contentment we yearn for.

Many of us have been working hard to resolve the problems that have been brought about by our own supposed "success." We're searching for ways to slow down. The day needs to come when we make some space for ourselves to mend our damaged spirits and our broken wings.

A life of magnificent possibilities requires tranquillity. Flying up and over any obstacle is smoother when we're experiencing inner harmony and composure. In today's fast-paced life-style, it's easy to get caught in the trap of believing we need to speed up in order to get where we're going. It's a myth that those who fly the highest are always hurried or flustered, in some type of whirlwind. If we were victorious in the true sense of the word we would have time for the most important aspects of our lives, what we value most.

Even though I am aware of the tremendous benefits, I don't always triumph in my quest to live out my highest values and priorities by slowing down. The frantic inner voice urging me to do more, be more, and give more isn't easy to calm. I continue to have days that are more chaotic than I would like. But overall, I am learning to take time for those areas of my life that really matter to me— spending unplanned time with my husband by spontaneously accompanying him to pick up car parts when he asks me to "go along for the ride"; taking extra time to talk with my daughters when they call or stop by with a concern about mothering, home-making, or relationships; spending a special day with our grand-children, listening to their stories, laughing, and playing with them; or going to see a good play with a relative or close friend. Sometimes the beds don't get made because I've decided to write a letter to a long-lost friend, or my desk remains piled with unfinished work while I enjoy a few uplifting moments playing the piano.

There are many days when I have to fight the urge to put people or my favorite things off because there are seemingly more important things to do. When I give in to the "busyness" of life, I find my soul longing once again for a simpler, unhurried existence, and the inner stillness that I know will come when I get serious about nourishing myself.

Most of us feel uneasy looking after our own needs. Even if we know how crucial it is, we still feel guilty for investing the time or money to nourish ourselves. With our "martyr mentality," we feel uncomfortable about wanting to join an exercise class, take a night course, attend a women's meeting, or just get away for the day. In desperation, we lock ourselves in the bathroom to do some reading, because, at least there, we have a legitimate reason for closing the door and spending time alone! We make excuses whenever we want to do something good for ourselves. We have a hard time, for instance, simply saying that we're going to be gone for an occasional evening and that the family's supper is coming from the local takeout restaurant. We spend much of our time apologizing and asking others not to be angry with us for deserting them. Then, out of guilt, we overcompensate for it in our giving when we get back home.

Men don't seem to have the same concerns when it comes to looking after their personal needs and this is something constructive we can learn from them. They don't need and often don't even ask for our approval when they want to get away from it all by going hunting, golfing, or fishing with their friends. They don't apologize for reading the newspaper during breakfast or watching television for an evening as a means of relaxation or temporary escape from the world. They don't feel they must explain the money they spend on the equipment they need to nurture themselves with their sports and hobbies. They know how and when to do things just for themselves. When they do enjoy these activities, moderately and in balance with their other obligations, they don't see themselves as *abandoning their responsibilities,* yet most women would. Is it any wonder so many women spend their days feeling drained and lethargic, and the mere thought of taking time for themselves sounds like something from a romance novel?

Slowing down is not only a *nice thing to do.* It is essential. We must stop speeding through life. Our flight is not a race. It is a tender journey to be savored each moment of the way. Some of us dart around so quickly we forget where we have been and lose sight of where we are going.

Sometimes it's our inner life that needs quieting. Research has shown that our brains can process thoughts four times faster than we speak. What we do is fill up that extra time with a lot of mumbo jumbo. We remind ourselves of things we believe we have to accomplish, process various thoughts about our daily activities, replay unsettling events that have occurred in our recent past, and have ongoing miniconversations with ourselves.

When our self-talk becomes chaotic, it's a signal that we need to gain some sense of focus. Every now and then, when I really have a lot on my mind and I'm staring off into the distance, my husband waves his hands frantically in front of my face to get my attention. It makes me laugh but it also helps me to realize I'm not really accomplishing anything while I'm on *overload*. When he brings me back to reality, I can then consciously slow my thoughts, choose some positive self-talk, and quiet the clamor within.

The best way to muster the power to take flight again is to learn to catch ourselves *before* we become paralyzed. One way to do this is by monitoring our thoughts. We strengthen the inner woman when we substitute positive, practical thoughts for the negative, erratic ones. Focus on what is right about your life. Dwell on the good things and think about what you can be thankful for.

UNDERSTANDING YOUR BODY-MIND CONNECTION

The universal principle of sowing and reaping is constantly at work in both your body and your mind. There's an old, familiar saying that expresses how this law affects your health: "What the mind harbors, the body expresses." We become what we think about.

On one hand, that could mean that, if you insist on harboring negative thoughts and destructive emotions, your body will eventually manifest some form of disease. And it's true, our negative thoughts do have a detrimental effect on our bodily functions. On the other hand, it also means that entertaining positive thoughts and constructive emotions can promote wellness and vitality.

Research has proven that, even with casually spoken words, we can raise or lower our body temperature or blood pressure, tense or relax muscles, and expand or constrict arteries, which, if continued over long periods of time, would eventually result in either improved health or some form of illness. Even in our dreams, the body interprets a frightening event as reality, and responds with an increased heartbeat. Since it cannot tell the difference between fantasy and reality, the body accepts the messages we give it.

Chances are, you have experienced waking up before the alarm clock goes off. This is one example of how the mind can deliberately program the body, and the body responds. Why don't we take advantage of this wondrous inner power in our everyday lives? The next time you're sprawled across your desk at three o'clock in the afternoon, totally drained and convinced you cannot make it through the rest of the day, try programming into your mind thoughts of dynamism. When you feel lethargic first thing in the morning, remind yourself that you are brimming with fresh possibilities! If you're in a situation that you find boring, plant seeds of enthusiasm. Your beliefs are powerful.

Get into the habit of *harboring* thoughts that can promote radiant health. For this reason, it's probably not a good idea to spend much time reading the medical journals, since you may find yourself becoming convinced that you're suffering with disorders you've never even heard of. When my sister was studying to become a nurse, she told us the students had been forewarned about this phenomenon, and sure enough, many of them mysteriously suffered with symptoms of the various diseases they were analyzing. So, refuse any notion of sickness you or someone else might believe you have. Instead of speaking about your poor health or referring to it as "my heart problem" or "my high blood pressure," say instead, *"My body is continually renewing itself and I am experiencing vibrant health!"* It's always your choice to do so, and your words have power. "Thou shalt decree a thing and it shall be established unto thee; and the light shall shine upon thy ways" (Job 22:28).

I remember hearing of some interesting and unusual results of autopsies that had been performed on seniors who had died apparently of old age. What was discovered in many of the cases was some form of disease that should have taken over these bodies years ago, and the only explanation for the seniors' longevity was their positive attitudes and cheerful personalities. According to the family members, each of these individuals had a special love of life and people. They had optimistic outlooks, always expected the best for themselves and others, and denied any thoughts of illness or bitterness. It wasn't that they had rejected reality. They simply chose to focus their minds on only those thoughts that could benefit and enhance their lives.

The seeds you plant are always your choice, so why not choose seeds of health, peace, and harmony? The universal principle of sowing and reaping applies to your body and your mind, and you will eventually "reap" the healthy harvest of your positive thoughts.

Unfortunately, many women believe that they have no choice but to live their lives under the rule of their feelings. *Most of us think that our emotions are something that just happen to us, and that we must fall under their spell, powerless and vulnerable.* We believe we wake up in either a good mood or a bad mood, or maybe just in neutral until something happens to us that will sway us one way or another. We say things like, "The traffic made me feel frustrated" or "My boss upset me." Neither of these perceptions is true. You always have a choice. You can allow other people or situations to control your feelings, or you can take charge. Perhaps you know instinctively that you have more control over your state of mind and your emotions than you have been using. Now it's time to start taking charge.

When we suffer emotionally, for whatever reason, we sometimes try to change how we're feeling indirectly, through some physical means—either by overeating, smoking, taking drugs, drinking alcohol, or reacting in a physically violent manner. Those methods do indeed change our feelings for a time, but with harmful side effects. A more direct and dynamic approach would be through changing the messages we're sending to our brain. We can do this through our physical demeanor as well our choice of thoughts.

Not only is your mind responsible for programming physical reactions in your body, but your body has the remarkable ability to program your feelings and state of mind. Just as it is impossible to have a change in your emotions without having a corresponding change in your physiology, it would be impossible to change your physiology and not experience a change in your state of mind. Facial expressions and posture set off certain biological responses that alter how we're feeling. Actors use this built-in mechanism all the time. When they must present a certain emotion, such as anger, happiness, fear, worry, or astonishment, they first take on the physiology of someone who would be feeling that way and, very soon after, the emotion follows. You can apply this technique in your personal life when you need to alter your emotional energy.

For example, researchers have found that the facial muscles you use when you smile tend to adjust the blood supply to the brain, and actually change both your physical and emotional states. Your overall bearing can have a similar effect. When you change your posture and begin to sit, stand, or walk with energy and a sense of purpose and zeal, you begin to feel vital.

When you take on the stance of someone who is feeling powerful, positive, and optimistic, it's almost impossible to feel disheartened. When you choose to move with energy and stand tall with a smile on your face, you simply can't feel sluggish. If you find yourself crying uncontrollably, take on the physiology of a person who is feeling calm and in control or any other state you'd rather experience at that time. You'll be able to get yourself to change almost instantaneously.

The same is true with your voice tone, pitch, and rate. If you choose to talk with passion even about something you find rather dull, or with confidence even when you're feeling unsure of yourself, your emotional patterns will soon change. Altering your physical state is a remarkably effective key to transforming your emotional state. Whenever you are overcome with grief, have tears welling up in your eyes during a board meeting, or are feeling frustrated when dealing with a demanding boss or upset spouse, take charge by controlling your state of mind and physical demeanor.

The old adage "If you would be powerful, pretend to be powerful" suggests that we should develop the habit of *acting as if* we were feeling a certain way so that the corresponding emotion will follow. Act *as if* you were feeling energetic, excited, happy, or in control and you will be. This is one of the most powerful tools we have available to us to change our state of mind. In other words, as the familiar adage says, "Fake it until you make it!" When you lack confidence and feel that you can't do something you really want to, choose to behave as if you can. How would you walk, look, and talk if you were happy? If you were emotionally healthy and contented? If you were enthusiastic? When you practice acting as if you were, before long you'll be living it!

I'll never forget how liberating it was for me when I came to the realization that I did not have to be governed by my emotions or give in to depression. We choose our state of mind. Maybe we don't choose to be depressed, but we can choose to help ourselves with new ways of handling those tendencies when they occur.

It's human nature to be vulnerable to negative emotions. Many women battle with feelings of despair at one time or another. As we've learned in this section, our attitude and physiology most definitely play a significant role. Having a high regard for our life is a principal factor in maintaining health and energy. Aside from these factors, our physical well-being is another crucial element.

VIBRANT HEALTH AND VITALITY

Radiant health and boundless energy are your birthright. You were created to enjoy youthful vitality, mental alertness, and emotional balance throughout your entire life. Health is natural. Disease is not. A trap that we fall into is the belief that illness is inevitable.

Illness can be a message, however. Sometimes it is an attempt to get us to see a problem inside ourselves. It is always a reflection of some conflict with our well-being, either mentally, physically, emotionally, or spiritually.

Most of us women, nevertheless, neglect the natural signals our bodies send us when we have a need for rest and rejuvenation. We push ourselves right past the signs of poor concentration, memory problems, listlessness, performance mistakes, and mood swings. At times, we attempt to recharge ourselves with sugar, caffeine, nicotine, alcohol, or other drugs. By continuing to ignore our need for renewal and balance, we are inviting fatigue, stress, and eventually illness.

What we need is a deep understanding of the nature of our Creator's universal laws combined with an awareness of our own unlimited potential. Your body was designed to be completely self-replenishing, self-regenerating, and self-healing. It is rebuilding and renewing itself at every moment. It takes its direction from your mind, so when a physical disorder is sending you signals, see it as a message to look deep inside yourself. Use your intuitive abilities to see what you must do about your thoughts, attitudes, and beliefs to restore balance to your body. Develop the habit of tuning into the constant communication that takes place among the mind, body, and soul.

We often become sick because of our beliefs. Sometimes, illness comes at a time when it fills a need. Either it appears as an inevitable response to certain circumstances, or in some way seems to solve a problem in one's life. For some of us, it's a behavior we've learned to use to get us something we need, or to rescue us from a situation we want to be freed from. Knowing what we're trying to escape is a big step in conquering illness.

When I was younger, I found that I would get sick every time I had said yes to doing something I really didn't feel capable of doing. If I doubted my own potential, illness came as a logical way out. Once I understood why I was getting sick, I could then choose not to allow it to take control of me. I still may have self-doubts but I can choose to handle them in a different way. Instead of giving in to illness, I can either admit my insecurities and select a different route, or I can move ahead in spite of the fear. Whichever way I choose, however, it is a conscious decision and it dissolves the power illness may have had over me.

Our choices do play a crucial role in our health. In addition, our bodies are made up of life energy and will only function efficiently with proper food fuel. In spite of developing positive beliefs, if we don't provide the right nutrients to our brain, nerves, muscles, or organs, we can't expect them to perform adequately.

Food nourishment is vital and affects the performance of every organ in your body. Foods can support the immune system, increase energy, and enhance your performance. Chances are, you won't even have the power to use what you've discovered so far in this book if you are not fueling your body properly. Your body is constantly at work, healing itself, but it is only as strong as what you put into it. Women who care about the way they replenish their bodies are alert and productive, and they enjoy long, physically active lives.

Foods can also be a source of emotional sustenance, promoting a deep sense of consolation and pleasure. Unfortunately, it's often during times of emotional stress that we allow our healthy eating habits to decline. Then we make poor choices, dictated by moods, impulses, or convenience. These are times when it is even more critical to focus on balance and nourishment. Just as the performance of your car's engine depends upon the fuel you provide for it, your body and mind rely on your food choices and eating patterns. *The more efficient your body, the stronger your wings and the higher you'll fly. That's when you'll release your potential to produce outstanding results.*

NATURE'S ENERGY SOURCES

Several years ago, I decided to study nutrition because of my personal illness. What I discovered was that there was a lot more information available regarding sickness than there was concerning optimum health. Any data I did find about nutrition was so contradictory that I decided to do my own study with what I called my "high-energy diet." As a result, the key concepts of healthy eating that I'll share with you have dramatically transformed my life. I now need less sleep yet feel more rested. I have enough energy to lead six-hour seminars for several days in a row, or get on a plane and fly from city to city each evening, and still enjoy great health and energy. I can truly say I feel younger and more vigorous now than I did twenty years ago.

When I began my speaking career, after several days on the road, eating in airplanes and hotel restaurants, I noticed that I wasn't as alert as usual and I often felt lethargic. However, when I made a conscious effort to order special meals minus the salt and sugar, drink lots of spring water, eliminate caffeine, eat more fresh fruits and vegetables, cut back on meat, and increase my supplements of certain vitamins, I noticed an improvement almost immediately.

One basic rule, and a good starting place for increasing your energy and health, is to eat food that is in a form as close as possible to its natural state. Now, that makes perfect sense, doesn't it? Sugar-coated cereals with colored marshmallows don't grow in gardens. Drinks corrupted by caffeine, chemicals, and syrups don't come from lakes and streams. The fields are not full of *fast-cooking* oats or *instant* rice, which should tell us something about the way we are fueling our bodies. I am always saddened when I see what goes into some people's shopping carts.

A nutritionist friend, when stressing the benefits of a vegetarian diet, pointed out to me that we don't normally hunger for a good cut of beef simply because we're driving past a field of grazing cows, whereas we will more likely crave a juicy, ripe pear or apple when we see an orchard full! When we present these nutritional theories to our family members, we're bound to get some resistance if the new ways don't line up with their traditional diets. My husband, for instance, insists that he most definitely does crave a juicy hamburger when he sees cows grazing, and he plans to continue! I remember the day he proved his convictions beyond a doubt. I had been working in my office at home and called him at his workplace. While we were talking, I happened to look out into our front yard to see a most unusual looking creature. When I described it to him as a large dog that looked more like a bird, he concluded that it must be one of the wild turkeys that had been dropped at a nearby conservation area and somehow it had made its way to our yard. When I asked him what I should do, he quickly replied, "First of all, preheat the oven at 325 degrees!" Of course, he was joking, but some of your family members, like mine, really enjoy their meat and always will.

I saw a cartoon recently in which a man was sitting down to a snack of *broccoli ice cream* that his wife was serving him. He was inquiring, "Haven't you carried this nutrition thing just a bit too far?" I know that most of us would just like to enjoy our food and not feel guilty about liking some of the things that are not doing the most for us. To add to the problem, we're getting resistance from our families when we attempt to switch over to the "good stuff." But how you choose to nourish and replenish your body *does* affect your moods, energy levels, memory, and ability to think clearly. When you eat, your body converts the proteins, carbohydrates, fats, vitamins, and minerals into chemicals your brain uses to learn, think, feel, and remember. Once I fully understood the impact of food in these ways, I became dedicated to planning enjoyable meals that include healthy eating, for myself and my family. The message here is a simple one: To be well, eat well. An ancient proverb says that a fool "lives to eat" whereas the wise man "eats to live."

Through the news media, journal articles, various books, and seminars, we have been given an abundance of knowledge about health and nutrition. We also have scientific and medical testimony regarding the results of our eating habits. I don't think we need more data. Rather, we can allow our common sense to guide us. We need to listen to our bodies' messages. Today, there are endless reports of current scientific research and recent medical studies that reveal we should be drinking more water, certain nutrients found in foods can ward off diseases, herbal remedies really do work, and walking is good for our health. This is not necessarily new information, but it is encouraging. Maybe we just need to get back to basics and spend some time contemplating what's healthy and what's not. Fortunately, we often know much of that intuitively. From there, we need to take responsibility for our choices and live (or die) with the consequences.

Apart from craving certain foods and feeling full and content after a good meal, we seldom consider the link between our foods and our physical or mental health. I used to notice that when I attended a play or ballet performance after a big spaghetti dinner, my head would start to nod shortly after the lights went out. I believed it was due to the quantity of food I had consumed. Yet mental alertness and physical energy have more to do with *what* we eat than how much.

Consider Jean when she attends a business luncheon. She forgoes the cream soups, heavy sauces, rolls with butter, and fried foods in favor of a light lunch of broiled fish or chicken with a salad. While others wash their meals down with wine, she enjoys a glass of sparkling water mixed with fruit juice. She's the one who stays alert for the balance of the day, while the others are less responsive, feel sleepy, and have a hard time concentrating.

When you need to make a presentation or are scheduled for an interview during the morning, you can be your best and brightest if you have a breakfast of half a grapefruit, a bowl of whole-grain cereal with skim milk, a slice of whole-wheat toast with unsweetened fruit spread, and a cup of herb tea in place of bacon, eggs, and coffee.

Food also plays a role in regulating our moods. When Stacey has had a grueling day at work and needs to relax and forget about it all, she has comfort foods, such as pasta or pizza, for supper. Sometimes we just need to let ourselves off the hook for a time. In any case, remember that much of life goes in cycles, similar to the ebb and flow of the tide. We all have prime-energy times and down times. Take advantage of the peak-energy days when you are on top of the world and use the others to regroup and reflect, knowing you'll soon bounce back.

THE BODY: SELF-CLEANSING, SELF-HEALING, SELF-RENEWING

With some fundamental changes in the way you fuel and look after your body, you can restore its ability to energize and heal itself. For starters, include in your diet a large percentage of foods that are high in water content. Fluids are essential for cleansing the body. Since our bodies are predominantly made up of water, and we lose so much during the day, it is logical to help replace it through foods that are naturally rich in water—in other words, fruits and vegetables, preferably fresh and raw, or their freshly squeezed juices. It's the water in your food that helps to transport the nutrients to various parts of the body, as well as flush out your system.

The amount of water you drink will eventually be dictated by your thirst. That way, you never need to be concerned about drinking too much or not enough. At first, though, if you are not in the habit of drinking water regularly, you may have to make a conscious choice to drink more. When you begin to replace tea, coffee, and soft drinks with water, your natural thirst will return. The only time you need to be concerned about how much you drink should be during meals, since fluid is known to dilute the digestive agents in your stomach. When you do begin drinking more water, you'll want to invest in a good purifying unit, for instance, reverse osmosis, which is the method used by scientists when they need water in its purest form. There are many brands of under-the-counter-style units on the market right now. I believe that water purification units will soon be standard appliances in every home, just like stoves, refrigerators, and microwave ovens.

If you crave the feeling of bubbly carbonation in soft drinks when you are really thirsty, switch to a mixture of fruit juice and club soda, or mineral water with a wedge of lemon or lime. It won't be long before you'll be wondering how you ever handled the sugary sweetness of soda drinks.

YANKING YOUR SWEET TOOTH

Researchers over the years have been puzzled by the fact that certain races who existed on diets that consisted mainly of raw meats and animal fats, with very few fruits and vegetables, suffered none of our degenerative diseases. That is until they were introduced to our sugars and starches. Sugar provides *empty calories*. It has little or no nutritional value and is often responsible for many of our health ailments.

Sugar addiction is one of the main culprits of low energy and fatigue. Instantaneous energy surges through the entire body, but too much sugar overworks the adrenal glands, leaving you feeling exhausted and irritable.

Any food has the potential of being addictive, but sugar is high on the list. If you feel compelled to stop at the corner store or donut shop for a gooey, sugary treat, or if your hand is always in the cookie jar, you're probably hooked. Maybe you've gone so far as to hide sweets in various convenient spots around the house or office to make sure there's something handy when you have to have your daily "fix." Some of us have been known to buy a dozen donuts on the way home from work, eat them in the car, and throw the box away so no one will be the wiser. And who has not experienced leaving the groceries in the trunk but bringing the bag of cookies into the front seat? If you're a *sugarholic* and can't pass up sweets, you know how troublesome and complex the habit can be.

Sugar addicts usually don't need to be told how bad it is for them. They not only have to live with the negative effects on their health, but with nagging guilt every time they are reminded of their obsession by their sugar binges. A woman in my seminar admitted to occasionally making a pan of brownies, nibbling on one at a time until they're gone, and finally washing the pan before anyone comes home! The result of guilt is usually craving more sugar and the cycle continues.

Sugar robs our body of important and necessary nutrients. When that happens, we don't cope well under pressure. We can experience violent mood swings. We sleep poorly, feel nervous and cranky, and are prone to headaches and illness. We are eternally exhausted and when we want a quick pick-me-up, we go for the sugar-laden goodies. Then, our blood sugar goes up, reaching its peak very quickly. It's true that we feel energized at the time, but it's all downhill after that. Because the pancreas responds to the sugar surge by rapidly secreting insulin, the blood-sugar level often plummets far below where it was initially. The result is fatigue, lethargy, lightheadedness, mood swings, and varying degrees of depression. Then, what do we want more than anything? More sugar! This is how the violent ups and downs begin.

To break this intense cycle, try to keep your blood-sugar level fairly even. Snack on good foods between your meals, those that are high in B vitamins—the complex carbohydrates, such as whole grains and fresh vegetables. Fruit is good because, aside from satisfying your craving if you're having a sugar attack, it's also a natural thirst quencher, is high in essential nutrients, and makes you feel full longer. Be cautious with exceptionally sweet fruits and juices, because their natural sugars can send your blood-sugar levels just as high as other sweets. If you are sensitive to sugar, it's a good idea to combine fruit with a solid protein or starch food, such as cheese, nuts, seeds, raw vegetables, hard-cooked eggs, crackers with peanut butter, or bread. I have developed the habit of carrying with me a bag of unsalted peanuts mixed with raisins, or a snack pack of crackers and peanut butter or cheese. Now I nibble on those when sugar cravings strike.

Something else you can do when you get a sugar urge is exercise. Whether it's a brisk walk, calisthenics, jumping jacks, or a few minutes on a minitrampoline, exercise can act as a sugar stabilizer and controls the chemical "crazies" produced by blood-sugar swings.

Speaking from experience, I know that it is possible to yank your sweet tooth and adjust your palate to desire less sugar, or even no sugar at all. By cutting back instead of cutting out, you can reduce your cravings without the negative side effects of withdrawal symptoms.

Start by cleaning house. Banish from your cupboards all sugary foods. "Out of sight, out of mind" holds true in this case. Cut back on your use of white and brown sugar, corn syrup, maple syrup, molasses, and even the natural sugar of honey. Make it a habit to read package labels closely. Sugar is one of the most common food additives and can be found in some of the most unlikely places— such as soup, ketchup, mayonnaise, canned foods, pickles, and even toothpaste. If a product lists sugar as one of the first two ingredients, you're better off avoiding it. Instead, stock your kitchen with nourishing snacks like popcorn, yogurt, graham wafers, whole-wheat crackers, salt-free pretzels, nuts and seeds, and fresh fruits and vegetables.

If you've tried all these and you still get those urges, have an occasional binge once a month or so. It won't be life threatening unless, of course, the problem is a medical one and you are hypoglycemic or diabetic. I've found that depriving myself totally often doesn't work. It also helps to consider my upcoming schedule. If I know I am not going to be under any added stress or dealing with a very difficult person within the next twenty-four hours, I go ahead and splurge. So treat yourself on rare occasions, and you may even be surprised to find that it isn't that satisfying anymore!

Sugar is just one of the "white killers." Salt is another, which is also highly addictive. Because it is a natural preservative, it can be found in many prepared foods. The body needs some salt but it is the excess salt intake that causes harmful side effects. Too much can aggravate premenstrual syndrome, promote high blood pressure, and increase emotional irritability.

White flour is something else you may want to watch out for. It has been stripped of most of its nutritional goodness, which is why you'll notice on the labels of some flour products that certain nutrients have been added. It's an attempt to make up for the loss. Opt for whole-grain breads and cereals instead.

Caffeine, aside from its addictive quality, has a drying effect both internally and externally. Additionally, because it destroys B vitamins, those nutrients that help us cope with stress, caffeine can have disturbing side effects that include nervousness, lethargy, exhaustion, and poor mental control. Caffeine is found in cola drinks, coffee, tea, cocoa, and chocolate. Either reduce your intake or the strength of caffeine-laden drinks. Water-decaffeinated coffees and teas can be good, but other methods of decaffeination involve using substances that may be just as harmful to your body as caffeine.

Fats solidifying in your system may be another cause of that draggy feeling. Not only does eating too many fats contribute to excess weight, it can also put extra pressure on the heart, leading to any number of heart diseases. Start cutting back on cream soups, gravies, sauces, pastries, meats, and dairy products. Polyunsaturated fats found in sunflower oil, corn oil, soya oil, nuts, and some fish oils do not raise cholesterol levels in the same way as saturated fats. In fact, they are believed to aid in repairing the daily wear and tear of body cells.

There is truth to the old adage that you are only as good as the food you eat. Make it your goal to switch over to healthy eating for just twenty-one days, and the benefits you will enjoy almost immediately will encourage you to continue.

To combat resistance from the family, try keeping supplies of ready-to-eat nutritious snacks available. Start adding whole grains and fiber to cereals, soups, and casseroles in small amounts. Add a handful of oat bran or wheat germ to soups, stews, meat loaf, meatballs, or the coating for chicken, and to your muffins, whether you bake them from scratch or use a packaged mix. Make muffins even more nutritious with some finely chopped dates, nuts, raisins, or unpeeled apples. Fiber has become the heart of most contemporary diet programs. Vegetables and fruits with edible skins; beans; whole-grain cereals like oatmeal, granola, and shredded wheat; and popcorn (hold the butter and salt!) are great sources of roughage, which has also been referred to as "nature's broom"! Choose healthy snacks. They can be a quick source of energy for the body and mind. For instance, pretzels in place of chips make a good snack because they are baked, rather than deep fried, and can also be purchased salt free. Fresh fruits and vegetables, graham wafers, unsweetened yogurt, fruit health bars, whole-meal muffins, rice cakes, and crackers spread with a little sugar-free jam all make good snacks, too.

NUTRIENTS THAT MAKE A DIFFERENCE

Certain nutrients have been found to help specific parts of the body and mind function at optimum levels. For your muscles and internal organs to work at peak efficiency, certain vital nutrients are necessary on a daily basis. The same is true for your mind and memory power. While eating these nutrients will not by itself improve your ability to reason, understand, or have total recall, if your diet is deficient in any of these elements, your brain is most likely working below its full potential.

Ideally, we would get all the vitamins and minerals we need in their original form—our food. These days, it isn't always possible to eat a well-balanced diet for a number of reasons, so many supplements are now marketed purposely as energy and stress supports. Not only are we on the go, with very little time to plan and prepare healthy meals, but practically everything we eat has been altered from its original state by the time we eat it. Either it's been processed before it gets to the store, or we adjust it ourselves by our cooking methods. Many of our prepared foods are in reality a concoction of artificial colorings, flavor enhancers, emulsifiers, additives, preservatives, chemical fertilizers, pesticides, and fungicides, many of which have been found to be harmful to our physical and mental constitution. Through the increasing power of consumer awareness and choice, and thanks to the media, many of our food products now come to us free of some of the harmful additives and preservatives. Yet, in spite of this, the nutrients we might get from our food are continuously being diminished by external poisons and other destructive elements that we are exposed to, such as

- tobacco and its smoke
- alcohol
- sleeping pills, tranquilizers, and other drugs
- air and water pollution
- radiations emitted by common household goods and modern-day conveniences
- emotional stress and illness

All of these elements put extra demands on our bodies and the nutrients we do get from food must work extra hard. That's why I fortify my diet with a number of vitamin and mineral products. I want to emphasize that the following list of nutrients represents only a brief and general introduction to a complex and often very controversial subject. Common sense and eating a well-balanced diet is the first step in supporting your mind and body in their effort to perform at optimum peak levels. In this section, I would like to share with you what I have found helpful in fortifying my well-being. For instance, I supplement my diet with the following:

1. Vitamin C, because it assists every process in the body, including

the immune system, healing of wounds and burns, relief of cold and allergy symptoms, and repairing damage done by smoking, alcohol, and drugs. It also aids in removing toxins from the body, including lead and mercury, which affect the functioning of the brain. Scientists have shown time and time again that one of the major causes of most human afflictions is insufficient vitamin C. In our modern world, the main reason identified for this deficiency is our high levels of stress, which suppress the body's production of vitamin C. One of the things I like best about this vitamin is that it is responsible for producing collagen, which is the "glue" that strengthens our connective tissues and holds us together. So I take it because I look better when I do! People who get lots of vitamin C in their diets simply don't age as quickly. Yet it would be difficult, with our processed diets, to get even our basic daily requirement from the foods we eat. Many nutritionists recommend taking vitamin C supplements. Food sources of vitamin C are fresh fruits and vegetables, especially oranges, grapefruit, broccoli, and green peppers.

2. B complex or folic acid, because it is the vitamin most critical to the nervous system and our ability to fight the effects of stress. It does so much to relieve the emotional and physical symptoms of most of the physical changes in our bodies, including those chemical crazies that occur during premenstrual syndrome, menopause, and pregnancy. In our house, we call them "happy pills"! The number-one enemy of vitamin B is sugar, and because it's so hard to detect the amount of sugar we get in prepared foods, we are probably taking in more than we know. It is destroying our B vitamins, which could be a major cause of much of the tension and emotional anxiety we experience. B vitamins can actually improve brain functioning, are essential for a good memory, and boost mental energy so you can concentrate, hence the nickname "B smart." It is also necessary for the growth and reproduction of all body cells. Foods rich in this vitamin are fish (especially tuna and salmon); organ meats; bananas; dark-green vegetables such as spinach, parsley, and broccoli; root vegetables; oats; and whole-grain cereals and wheat products.

3. Vitamin E, because it keeps us youthful and provides the best possible protection against heart disease. The letter *E* stands for *essential*, because it is essential in reproduction, in both humans and animals, hence its reputation as the fertility vitamin. We might also

say the *E* stands for energy and endurance, which has been proven over and over again with athletes as well as animals. Vitamin E is found in dark-green vegetables, brown rice, wheat germ, vegetable oils, eggs, nuts (especially almonds), and organ meats.

4. Calcium, because every part of our body demands it and every physical process depends on it. It is essential for ache-free joints, healthy bones, nerves, muscles, and blood clotting. In fact, it is so vital that the body will actually eat its own bones to survive if there's not enough supplied in your diet. That's why, as we mature, we are more prone to osteoporosis and broken bones. Calcium helps to transmit messages to the muscles and organs. It has also been referred to as "nature's tranquilizer" as it calms the nerves. Food sources of calcium are yogurt and other dairy products, bone meal, apples, cabbage, soy products, and seafood.

5. Lecithin, because it contains choline, which makes us more physically and mentally alert and is used in the treatment of diseases affecting the memory. It is an important component of the myelin sheath, a covering that shelters our nerves and plays a role in our ability to deal with stress. It also aids in the digestion and absorption of fats and acts as a solvent for cholesterol. It's available naturally in soybeans, corn, and egg yolk, the richest known source of choline.

6. Garlic, because it acts as nature's antibiotic, inhibiting the bacteria responsible for staph and strep infections and disease-related yeast.

7. Alfalfa, because it provides much of the protein we need, especially if we follow a vegetarian diet. And the protein produced by alfalfa sprouts is in its most complete, digestible form.

8. Zinc, because it's one of the most versatile of all nutrients. It's used by more parts of the body than any other, with the exception of iron. It is vital to the integration of vitamins, proteins, and enzymes in our system and plays a role in healthy hair, strong nails, a clear complexion, resistance to disease, wound healing, emotional control, sexual health, and vitality. Like calcium, it's a natural tranquilizer and critical to healthy nerves. Food sources include liver, seafood, spinach, gingerroot, mushrooms, and some varieties of nuts.

Even though I make every attempt to get my nutrients from food sources, I take some supplements because they make me feel better, I have more energy and I can work more effectively and productively. They protect me from disease, and keep me calm. They are easily accessible and their effects are long term. Of course, the best advice is to strive to get as many of your required nutrients as possible from a varied, well-balanced, and natural diet.

Aside from these nutrients, herb remedies are another source of abundant vitality. Herbs have been used for centuries. They have provided natural antidotes over the years and are often referred to in the Bible: "Even in the green herb have I given you all things" (Gen. 9:3).

Only since the twentieth century have natural herb remedies been replaced with high-tech synthetic drugs prepared in laboratories. Today, we are seeing a resurgence in their use and popularity for a number of valid reasons, mainly because there are very few side effects if any, no evidence of withdrawal symptoms, and they do not encourage dependency. Where modern drugs treat the symptoms of illness, herb preparations get to the heart of the matter and deal with the cause of disease. Herbs don't simply mask the symptoms, they stimulate the body's natural healing mechanisms. Herbs can be used in a number of different forms, such as loose teas, oils, lotions, capsules, and tablets.

Ginseng enhances our ability to handle mental stress and has been called the harmony herb, the root of heaven, and the herb of eternal life. It is grown in certain parts of the world, including China, Korea, and North America. It can be prepared as a tea and is available in most health-food stores. For centuries, it has been acclaimed as a natural revitalizing agent and many feel that it increases their strength and endurance.

Chamomile is an excellent muscle relaxant and nerve soother. When I have a cup of chamomile tea just before bedtime, I immediately drift off into a long and restful sleep. Many women tell me it is an excellent source of relief from premenstrual syndrome and also acts as a cleanser for the body.

Lavender dissolves physical fatigue, mental exhaustion, and emotional stress. It can uplift and stimulate a tired mind, leaving you rejuvenated, or brewed as a tea combined with chamomile, lime blossoms, and lemon or honey, it will help you to sleep well.

Peppermint is a wonderful tonic that will alleviate an upset stomach and indigestion after a meal. It also relieves nausea and constipation. As a tea mixed with chamomile it is effective in soothing tension headaches and migraines. Combined with rosehips and hibiscus, it becomes a refreshing pickup.

Age-old herbal remedies can definitely influence the balance of body, mind, and soul.

I would encourage you to do your own study project and experiment to find out just which nutrients and herbs you would like to add to your diet. Since there is no "average" person, only you will know what you need. Improved health through natural nutrition can mean a life that is free from disease, medication, or anything that would prevent you from doing what you're able to do when you're feeling terrific!

CONQUERING THE BARRIER OF OVERPOWERING EMOTIONS

As women, we are frustrated by our complex, fluctuating, out-of-control moods and feelings, which can set us back in our quest for freedom. They can leave us feeling overwhelmed and distraught, and greatly affect the quality of our lives.

The cause might be one of many things, such as loneliness after the breakup of a relationship or the heartache of losing a loved one to death, sometimes before resolving personal conflicts. Others include having too many priorities or feeling like a walking "to-do" list, bitterness after a harsh argument with a friend, embarrassment following a temper flare-up with your boss, being disappointed after losing a friend or a job, blowing up at the kids and saying things you wish you could take back, feeling misunderstood by your spouse, worrying that the extra weight you've put on makes you less desirable, despising yourself for giving in to temptation and going against your own values, or living in fear of some unforeseen event.

Sometimes instead of nurturing ourselves during these high-stress times, we add to the problem. When memories of our downfalls, mistakes, or setbacks come to haunt us, we accept them, dwell on them, and allow them to take over. These thought distortions build and have a way of tormenting us. They soon rule our attitudes and govern our responses to others. They determine how we perceive ourselves, and eventually the choices we make.

Premenstrual syndrome or PMS is another source of frustration for many women. This is a very real hormonal imbalance that occurs anytime during the two weeks leading up to menstruation and triggers a corresponding mental and emotional imbalance. Those are the times when we tend to do things out of character. When our hormones have gone crazy, we tend to lose it emotionally. Feelings of low self-esteem, tension, sadness, intolerance, mood swings, increased anger, and a general dissatisfaction with life seem to sweep over us like a giant ocean wave. Tears come easily. We are more critical of our appearance. We think nasty thoughts. We blow up and do or say hurtful things. Then we must suffer with the guilt that follows and have doubts about our emotional stability.

Add to that the physical symptoms of fluid retention, bloating, breast tenderness, muscle tension, backaches, and cramps, as well as exhaustion, clumsiness, lethargy, and forgetfulness, and it's no wonder we feel as though we've been transformed into some kind of "monster" woman.

Until very recently, the traditional response from a male-dominated medical profession was to dismiss PMS as an imagined illness—something that was just in the mind. This resulted in many doctors prescribing sedatives. Others recommended hysterectomies or psychiatric treatment for this "mental" condition.

Today, we know it's possible to take charge of this very real condition, understand it, and guard against it by following these few simple steps leading up to our periods.

1. Be aware of your personal cycle by charting the onset, intensity, and duration of your normal symptoms and noting them on a calendar. Don't assume you'll remember your cycle and which days you turn into that "other person." There is usually a regular pattern, which makes it easier to predict what to expect so you can direct your schedule accordingly. The more you know about yourself, the more control you will be able to exert. Once you see a pattern emerge, you'll be able to plan ahead and compensate for the days you'll be unable to respond in a positive way to people and routine activities.

2. Let family members and others in your life know in advance what is happening. State clearly up front that you need an ear to listen to you. That way you're not setting yourself up for disappointment, hoping others will somehow sense your needs. Of course, not everyone will want to listen nor will everyone understand, but chances are, you will be able to solicit more support this way than if you said nothing. Even developing the ability to express what you are feeling will enhance your capacity to cope. By not overloading

yourself with extra responsibilities and by limiting your interaction with others to only the most essential contacts during that time, you'll be able to wait patiently for your positive self to return.

3. Give yourself permission to take time out. If you don't, you can become overwhelmed by what appears to be mental or emotional weakness. Taking a break from routine activities might mean getting extra sleep, taking a nap during the day, or avoiding excessive demands or exhausting confrontations, waiting until your period is over before dealing with some of the really touchy issues that have come across your path. Make it a point to create your personal sanctuary—a private place where you can meditate, write in your journal, or read a good book. Play your favorite music and pamper yourself.

4. Nourish your body by increasing your daily servings of wholesome, fresh foods and reducing your intake of sugar, salt, caffeine, and high-fat dairy products at least ten days prior to your period. You can alleviate or reduce many of your physical and emotional symptoms by eating several small nutritious meals and snacks at regular intervals each day, which helps to stabilize low blood-sugar levels, one of the causes of the violent ups and downs associated with PMS. On the other hand, occasionally bingeing on comfort foods—those familiar childhood treats of macaroni and cheese, chewy peanut-butter cookies, butterscotch ice cream, or French fries with gravy—is not the end of the world. Treating yourself once in awhile can be a deeply nurturing self-care experience. Some foods really do provide an instant solace for our hurting souls, unless we feel guilty and tell ourselves it's unacceptable. Recognize bingeing as a signal that you need more care, not less, and allow yourself to enjoy eating without the barrage of negative self-talk. Use your healthy nurturing voice instead to remind yourself that you are simply taking care of your needs. This may not be the right time to put restrictions on yourself. In time, by giving yourself other choices, you will begin to develop a new attitude toward food and improved, healthy eating habits.

5. Deep breathing can help you to control the anxiety, panic, and sleeplessness associated with PMS. Regular and relaxed diaphragmatic breathing releases muscle tension, soothes nerves, and aids in digestion. Many of us, during high-stress situations, forget to breathe altogether!

6. Develop a gentle exercise program for before, during, and immediately following your period. Bending and stretching, walking, gardening, playing sports, and gentle dancing can be a therapeutic form of exercise during times of premenstrual tension. Women who exercise twenty to thirty minutes per day say it is one of the best self-help remedies, even though they admit it's more of a challenge to get themselves up and doing it at that time.

Some of these strategies will work better than others for you. Choose those that make the most difference in your cycle. Unfortunately, by the time I got a handle on all of this, I was about to enter menopause! The good thing about it, though, is that most of the same techniques and suggestions will work then, too.

Whether it's brought on by PMS, menopause, or any other mental, emotional, or physical imbalance, we all have times when we feel frazzled, defeated, or discouraged. If we lose sight of our basic requirements, we end up with a sense of hopelessness. Even though we cannot change what has happened in the past, we do not have to continue to be governed by our emotions. We can move beyond discouragement and disappointment, work through our anger, worry, jealousy, or doubt, and master our negative thoughts to experience victory. When you find yourself giving in to self-destructive thinking, give yourself permission to enjoy a planned retreat. Here are some ideas for you.

NURTURING RITUALS

We all want to retain our energy and health. It's natural to want to stay youthful and enjoy all those benefits as long as possible. By nurturing your body, mind, and spirit, you'll begin to feel recharged and renewed. You'll experience new levels of contentment. Feeling good is your body's way of saying, "Thank you. You're doing something right. I appreciate you." Here are some self-nurturing steps for body, mind, and spirit, to restore perspective and harmony to your life.

Rejoice in the Wonders of Water

Many of us overlook one of nature's most astounding secrets of health and energy—beautiful, miraculous water! Since the beginning of time, water has had tremendous significance in quenching both physical and emotional thirst. One of the reasons why you may be feeling lethargic or emotionally or physically exhausted could be that you simply are not using enough water. Of course, there are many other contributing factors to feeling eternally sluggish, such as the polluted air we breath, our self-destructive diets, and the ongoing pressures of always having too much to do. But water, with its therapeutic qualities, can help to flush away a lot of our problems, internally and externally. It is nature's most readily available invigorator, always restoring and refreshing.

It seems we are drawn instinctively to water. When my children were little, they would squeal with joy in the bathtub and wouldn't want the experience to end. They seemed happiest when they were wading in a pool, getting sprayed by the hose, playing with water squirt toys, or romping and splashing in puddles. Like magnets, all children are attracted to water and delight in its benefits. Since we began our "life journey" by swimming in our mother's womb, perhaps water is nature's way of drawing us back, encouraging us to stay in touch with our first source of comfort.

Over the years, many water-based therapies have been used and developed. Depending on the temperature, bath water for instance can sedate or stimulate. In either case, it can leave us refreshed and rejuvenated.

In Search of Tranquillity

"I went at noon to bathe, and floating on my back, fell asleep. Water is the easiest bed that can be"(Benjamin Franklin). A calming ritual that I have practiced for a number of years is the bedtime bath. It's an age-old custom that banishes tension and helps us to rebalance and recover a sense of well-being. I like to slip into a tub full of nice sparkling hot water that has been sweetened with soothing oils or scents. Lavender is particularly calming and Epsom salt is known for its muscle-relaxant properties. You can scout out some aroma-therapeutic blends that are designed to ease stress.

Occasionally, for a special candlelight bubble bath, you can add a bit of foaming gel. Then turn off the lights except for the flicker of scented candles that you've placed all around the room and enjoy sitting amidst the iridescent bubbles. Add to that some soothing music and a warm cup of herb tea, and you can soak away all your cares—mental, physical, and emotional.

Holding the warm cup of tea in your hands and feeling the steam rise up from both the cup and the bath can also have a tremendously comforting effect. Sometimes it's a good idea to shut out all the lights. Bathing in complete darkness helps you to close out everything else and simply concentrate on the sheer pleasure of the water. Its warmth and your buoyancy can help your body replenish itself.

And, remember, this is not the time for scrubbing and getting clean. Just lie back on an inflatable pillow, close your eyes, and relax! Because of its temperature-sensitive nerve endings, your skin responds to the soft caresses of warm water. Tight muscles are relaxed and circulation is increased. When you're ready to face the world again, dry off with a fluffy cotton towel and finish by lathering on silky lotion or oil. Dust yourself all over with some scented powder or spray on your favorite perfume. Slip into a soft, satiny robe and rejoice in being calm and comfortable.

This is a time to relax body and soul, wipe your mind clean, and release the exhaustion. Use your imagination and see all the concerns that have accumulated during the day being rinsed away into the comforting, healing water. A wonderful thing begins to happen. Your brain receives this message and, since it believes everything you tell it, like a computer it will immediately go to work to carry out what you've programmed in. You'll start to feel better right away and the results will be long lasting. With your mind cleansed, pleasant thoughts will be able to flow. You'll be relaxed and prepared for a good night's rest.

When it's just not convenient or possible to take a bath, try a hand or foot bath. Fill a basin with hot water and add a few drops of rosemary essential oil or some chamomile tea for a comforting effect. You can also simply massage your hands while holding them under very warm running water. I know several women who do this during their break at work if they're going through a particularly stressful time. It provides immediate results and doesn't take much time. Warm water relaxes; cool revitalizes. You may want to try both, one after the other. Finish off by massaging your hands briskly with a towel and applying some lotion.

Alive, Awake, and Alert!

When you need to be rejuvenated and reenergized, or when you're *sick and tired of feeling sick and tired,* use water to reclaim your vitality. When you're dissatisfied with yourself, your life, and the world around you, try taking a shower. There's energy in moving, rushing water. Water has a rejuvenating effect on all living things. Trees and flowers perk up after a rain shower. Plants seem to sparkle when they've been watered. And we do too.

First thing each morning, spend some time consciously appreciating the benefits of this marvelous stimulator. As you let warm water cascade down upon your body, revel in it. Feel the blood rushing to all your organs and cells. Water vigorously pounding down and bouncing off your skin wakes up your whole body. And if you really want to stimulate the nerves, try turning on the cold water— gradually, of course. You don't want to shock your system, but by going slowly from very warm to very cool, your entire body literally comes alive. And don't just stand there! Use a loofah or bathing brush and scrub your body. Then, start jumping and moving, and keep moving. It's the next best thing to plunging into a cool lake for a swim. You'll feel exhilarated and delightfully energized. It's a habit I started a number of years ago when the idea was first introduced to me. Now, my family enjoys the benefits as well. In our house, you can always tell when someone in the shower has just turned from hot water to cold, with all the dancing, yelping, and jumping going on! As you towel dry, continue the benefits by rubbing your skin briskly and thoroughly. Smooth on some body lotion and tell each part of your body you love it and appreciate it. When you get in the habit of starting each day this way, you'll feel better, look better, and have a happier, healthier outlook.

Aside from baths and showers, there are many ways to enjoy water. Anytime you can be near running water, you'll notice an enhanced sense of well-being! Thundershowers in summertime dancing on your roof, a waterfall splashing in the woods, a fountain in the park—all have a rejuvenating effect. The fine spray coming from the seashore touches your skin and you breathe it in. Even the sound of waves as they bounce off the rocky beach or slap up against the shore is comforting. Spend some time around rushing, moving water, and experience for yourself the many wondrous benefits.

We have a screened-in porch at the back of our home, looking out into the woods. I love to sit in my wicker rocking chair during warm summer showers and just enjoy being surrounded by the balmy mist, with the rain beating a gentle rhythm on the roof. There's a magical tranquillity that slowly takes over and I feel it washing away all the anxiety—mentally, physically, and emotionally. Even a few minutes provide a wonderful source of well-being and energy.

Water on the Inside

Water is the great purifier of life—without and within. Internally, there are many benefits from drinking pure water, but not just a glass now and then, and not simply beverages or liquids that are water based. Tea, coffee, sodas, and alcoholic drinks actually put an added burden on our systems because they are so adulterated by chemicals, sugar, or caffeine.

If your body is low on water, it will call out for help. When you get these signals, you may be tempted to go for the coffee or cola, but the caffeine in these beverages has a drying effect. Instead, drink a glass of water first, to restore essential fluids; then enjoy a comforting cup of herb tea or drink of your choice if you wish. Chances are, if you have water each time your body calls out for a drink, you won't need nearly as much of the other drinks you've been having during the day. One strategy that has worked for me is to keep a jug of water on my desk in front of me along with a glass that I continue to refill. Not only does it serve as a reminder, but it's more convenient than other drinks that I might be tempted to choose. If you haven't been a water drinker, you'll be surprised at how quickly your natural thirst returns.

Water is absolutely essential for most bodily functions, including blood building, proper functioning of the digestive system, and purifying through the kidneys and sweat glands. When the body gets the water it needs to perform optimally, here are some of the additional benefits you'll experience.

Water also
- acts as a magnet, attracting impurities and flushing out wastes
- transports oxygen, hydrogen, and nutrients through the blood
- provides an additional source of minerals, like calcium, magnesium, and iron
- aids in weight loss, as it metabolizes fat cells and improves muscle tone

Incredible as it may seem, water is possibly the single most important element in maintaining your ideal weight. Not only does it suppress the appetite, but it actually helps to reduce fat deposits. More water is also the best treatment for water retention. When your body receives less water, this is perceived as a threat to its very survival and it begins to hold on to any water it has stored. Because it's being stored in spaces outside the cells, it shows itself in swollen hands, feet, and legs. Instead of relying on diuretics—a temporary solution because the condition quickly returns—you should provide the body with enough water to take away the threat. Only then can stored water be released.

If you think that drinking eight eight-ounce glasses of water each day will make you spend most of your spare time in the washroom, you'll be glad to know that your bladder will adjust within a few weeks. Before long, you'll be experiencing benefits like a feeling of youthful bounce, pep and sheer vitality, resilient skin, and a glowing complexion. You'll be ready to face life feeling renewed and revitalized.

Laughter

"A cheerful heart does good like a medicine" (Prov. 17:22 TLB). Ever notice how you feel the morning after? After an evening of laughter and fun, that is? Can you remember the last time you had a hearty laugh, when your sides ached till you thought they'd split and your face hurt? You probably had tears rolling down your cheeks while you held your stomach and gasped for air. Maybe it was a good joke, a funny movie, an embarrassing moment, a humorous book, a get-together with friends, or fun and games with family. When it was all over, you probably felt energized and ready to tackle the world.

"He who laughs . . . lasts!" Whatever the cause, laughter has many benefits. First of all, humor is known to have mood-altering effects. It is healing, calming, and soothing to your soul! As muscles tighten, relax, and tighten again and again, tension is released. It's almost like providing a "massage" for your internal organs and muscles. When you laugh, your brain releases endorphins and a lot of other biochemicals and powerful antidepressant elements that contribute to an overall sense of well-being and comfort. Along with deep breathing and healthy air exchange, laughter actually creates the same type of "high" as exercise. In fact, just a few seconds of hearty laughing are equivalent to several minutes of aerobic exercise. It's a lot like giving your cardiovascular and respiratory systems a good workout. And the best part is that it doesn't require any spiffy little exercise outfits, special shoes, elaborate equipment, or definite scheduling. It's affordable and accessible!

You can actually *plan* to integrate laughter and humor into your life. Start by organizing dates and special times, either alone, for your own enjoyment, or with other people. These laughter dates can include such activities as family times and group games, comedy theater, musicals, or movies. You'll find that laughter has an amazing bonding effect as well. When I watch a funny movie while on an airplane, I notice that during the really hilarious scenes, people turn to look at someone across the aisle, even though they have had no contact up to that point. It's as though our enjoyment of the humor is multiplied when we can share it with someone else!

For those times when you're alone, put together your own "humor first-aid kit"—a special bag filled with funny literature, comics, cartoons, humorous video- or audiocassettes, and anything else that will start you laughing. Keep it handy for days when fun seems to be missing from your life. Go to the gift shop and start a collection of funny greeting cards. Make your own scrapbook of cartoons clipped from the newspaper or magazines. My grandparents had a book like this, and I remember as a kid going to visit and spending hours flipping through the pages. Some were sidesplitters and some just brought a chuckle, but the book provided a temporary escape from the world. Making a conscious attempt to bring laughter into your life will help you to develop your own unique sense of humor and heighten your awareness of the funny side of everyday situations.

There are several reasons why we don't laugh as often as we could. Aside from simply not taking the time to work it into our lives, we sometimes fear ridicule, embarrassment, or criticism. There's almost an anxiety about letting ourselves go. Is it any wonder we might hold back from having a good laugh, when we think of some of the things we heard as children?

"When are you going to grow up?"
(Hidden message: Laughter is not appropriate for adults.)

"Wipe that smile off your face!"
(Hidden message: If you're smiling, you're not taking me seriously. I'm not laughing so you don't have the right to laugh.)

"Settle down!"
(Hidden message: You're acting like a child.)

Maybe acting "childlike" once in awhile isn't a bad idea. It's estimated that children laugh up to five hundred times a day, whereas adults laugh only fifteen times maximum! Go ahead and give yourself an internal workout. Don't wait for it to happen. Plan it. "Laughter is like jogging on the inside."

There are other reasons why we don't laugh. It's difficult even to want to laugh when sorrow comes into our lives. Katie was only thirty-four years old and the mother of two small children when she became very ill. When her doctor gave her the news that she had only a few years to live, that wasn't the worst part. It was the pain she knew she would have to endure. Suffering is not funny. But she considered the limited number of choices she had and determined to face this adversity with a little humor. After the initial shock had subsided, she and her family rented some comedy movies. She began to read the work of a number of humorists at bedtime and listen to laugh tracks during the day. Family and friends began to send Katie anything that might make her chuckle—comics, cartoons, and funny greeting cards. Although it's not getting rid of the disease, laughter eases the pain and even some of the symptoms. Now, her friends say that when they visit Katie, her laughter is so infectious that they can't help but join in! She doesn't take herself or her illness too seriously anymore. She knows what it takes to get through a day. She knows that everyone struggles with something, and that life will come to an end for all of us one day. She's trusting God to look after the details and continues to have a good laugh now and again.

Friendships

"I didn't find my friends; the good God gave them to me" (Ralph Waldo Emerson). Our female friendships are essential today more than ever before. We are able to provide for each other in many ways. Friends are our best buffers in times of stress, our best supporters in times of loneliness or doubt, and our best encouragers in times of change. Yet how many of us spend time consciously thinking about our friendships or have a truly thought-out plan for developing and reinforcing those relationships?

Discovering our kindred spirits and deepening the bonds we hold dear doesn't generally happen without a deliberate attempt and some old-fashioned hard work. There is an ancient proverb that says, "He who wants friends must show himself friendly." Friendship is a two-way street. It normally takes an intentional effort to cultivate the types of friendships that provide companionship and satisfy our need for closeness.

Ideally, we will nurture our primary friendships first—those with our husbands, children, and other family members. Yet friendships outside our family relationships can provide an extra outlet for intimacy and take away the pressure that comes from wishing family members could always relate to our emotional needs. Because those special people in our lives cannot be everything for us, it's a good idea to cultivate other relationships that will counterbalance or fill the vacuum.

I've heard it said that a true friend is someone who knows everything about you and likes you anyway! When you share your strengths and weaknesses, this friend provides love and acceptance. She is one who sticks by you in your dating years when your knight in shining armor turns out to be the star of your worst nightmare. She is the one who listens patiently when you fantasize about changing your name, dyeing your hair, and running away to a deserted island because you can't face what's happening in your life any longer. She is there through the hormonal crazies of pregnancy, PMS, and menopause. She is someone you can trust with your thoughts, concerns, and feelings. With her, you can know you'll be understood.

Building new friendships is risky business. It takes courage to open up and allow ourselves to be seen for who we truly are. There is the very real fear of rejection when we are contemplating sharing with another our deepest hopes, fears, and doubts. Yet the only way to connect on an emotional level is to take away the masks, discard our acting skills, stop hiding behind protective walls, and become crystal clear. What a relief it is to share our feelings openly with a compassionate friend, to receive only reassurance without condemnation.

We need our friends as confidantes and supporters. They know what it's like to be a woman, so we have no need to explain ourselves or why we think and behave the way we do. We can depend on them for in-depth understanding. Those who have our best interests at heart will hold us accountable, confront us when we are wrong, and help us to grow. With wisdom gained through their own experience, they can challenge us to reach out and be our best.

If you look back over your life and examine some of your most memorable friendships, you may see a pattern. You will probably notice that each one appeared at just the right time and had a special role to play. These friends came along to teach you, with love and patience, something important about yourself or your life that you needed to learn at that particular stage. We are connected to these friends and they mysteriously share in our spiritual journey, whether or not they are aware of it.

As women, we are relational creatures. Yet in this hectic, time-pressured age in which we live, we have somehow been robbed of our nourishing relationships with other women. I believe we have an innate drive to reach out to others. I also believe we are in an era of change concerning values and attitudes toward friendships. Women everywhere are longing for the emotional guidance, encouragement, and sheer pleasure found in close relationships.

We seem to know intuitively that we need deeper friendships for our psychological well-being. We desperately yearn for stronger, closer nurturing relationships with friends, mentors, and peers throughout every stage of our lives. With some careful planning, effort, and skill, it will happen. While we cannot choose our families, we can select our close friends. These can become some of the happiest and most fulfilling and rewarding relationships of our lives. And as a result, the other significant relationships in our lives are intensified.

How do we enrich our lives with close friends?

1. We must be able to share our true selves honestly—our values and interests, where we've come from and where we're headed, our strengths and our weaknesses.

2. Wait to share challenges, problem areas, and personal history until a bond and trust in the friendship has begun to blossom.

3. Obviously it's not enough to sit at home waiting for friends to come knocking on our doors. There are many networking organizations, classes, courses, and clubs that bring like-minded people together. We may meet friends through our jobs, a local college, the neighborhood church, or a hobby such as hiking, photography, craft making, or cooking.

4. If you are a professional working woman, you can devote a lunch hour or one evening a week or even a weekend now and again to enriching your friendships. Make a point of scheduling various activities instead of waiting until it just happens.

5. If you are a mom at home, invite other mothers in for lunch or tea on a weekly basis. You may even start a mom's support group of other expressive, astute, and creative like-minded mothers in your area. Meet monthly or biweekly and take turns acting as baby-sitter for the group to cut costs. This is a wonderful time to share ideas and hone communication and listening skills as well as offer encouragement and understanding.

6. Remember that this is a two-way street and be aware of the law of reciprocity. Both give and both take. If one is always the nurturer, she is bound to feel taken advantage of or imposed upon.

Gardening

Gardens are sanctuaries that nourish our souls. They are safe havens where reflection comes easily, retreats where outside cares fade away. Gardening is a bountiful source of rare pleasures. It is comforting and inspiring, relaxing yet refreshing at the same time. All of our senses are nurtured together. The combination of scents, sounds, sights, and textures has the ability to renew us. The sweet smells of moist earth and fragrant rose petals, fresh air and lavender, lilacs and a newly mown lawn, are brought together to soothe us. Even the solitude is something our souls cry out for. Here, where shade and sunlight meet, all our gloomy feelings and tensions are released into the air and float away. When the work is done and we sit for awhile on a bench, watching and listening, we are caught in a kind of reverie. Here we take time for reflection.

Gardening is something nearly all of us, whatever our age or lifestyle, can benefit from. Recently, while on a plane flying to one of my speaking engagements, I sat next to a dear woman who was almost ninety years young. It was obvious that she enjoyed life and it didn't surprise me a bit when I discovered during our conversation that she loves to garden. It was early spring at the time and after visiting with her family for most of the winter, she was going home to tend to her hundreds of rosebushes and the other flowers she loved. She confessed that she'd been thinking about them all winter. She said, "I spend my spare time planning next year's gardens in my mind. I visualize the layout, and imagine the birds singing, the sun shining down on my face, and the scent of the moist earth as I prepare the soil for planting. I always know there's lots to be done and I get so excited about it!"

I'm sure that it was a combination of the joy of anticipation, the outdoor exercise, the fresh air, and being surrounded by sun, soil, and growing things that kept her so youthful and healthy. And to top it all off, she'd won the Annual Garden Award in her neighborhood for the past eight years.

Like so many other avid gardeners, she had discovered that it's almost impossible to fret or feel any tension when you're in your garden. She described hers as a world of its own, with hummingbird feeders, birdbaths, sundials, white picket fences, swinging garden gates, and winding, moss-covered cobblestone pathways. Gardening is a wonderful creative outlet that fulfills a need to be outdoors and involved with nature.

Working in a garden has an added benefit. It provides a natural source of exercise, with all the stretching and bending and deep breathing. I can almost picture her dancing on the lawn, romping through the water sprinkler, and leaping from one flower bed to another! What a great way to stay young and vibrant. What a wonderful haven, safe from the cares of the world.

Many gardeners simply enjoy sharing their works of art with passersby, knowing they're bringing pleasure to the neighborhood. I have a friend in the country who grows herbs because they seem to fit in with the hillsides and natural stone walls on her property. She says that visitors tell her the herbs make them feel comfortable and peaceful.

So many gardeners admit that they can hardly wait to come home at the end of their workday to spend time gardening. Even though it, too, is work, they find it more relaxing than anything else they could be doing with their spare time.

You can spend a fortune on a garden, or you can simply get an old crate and fill it with soil. The plants will grow all the same and you'll still be a gardener. I think we all experience that marvelous fascination when we plant a seed and it actually grows! Gardening gives you a chance to work in partnership with God, cocreating something very real. It also allows you to see a project through from start to finish—one thing very few of us can say about our lives these days. Besides, it's tranquil, gives us hope, and is a reason to look forward to next month . . . next spring . . . next year. "I do not understand how anyone can live without one small place of enchantment to turn to" (Marjorie Kinnan Rawlings).

Vacation Expectations

Everyone needs to get away once in awhile. Anticipation of the adventure aspect of a vacation is as important as the experience itself. Sometimes, simply looking forward to a break in our daily routines, struggles, and challenges is all it takes to enable us to endure and get back on track again. Anticipation plays a major role.

When you think of it, we are often happier planning a vacation and getting ready to go than we are returning. We feel better going out for dinner than when it's over and empty plates are staring back at us. Children are happier filled with expectancy on Christmas Eve than they are the next afternoon, when the excitement of anticipation has passed. A great benefit of your vacation is being so excited that you can hardly wait to see new places. It's the prospect of meeting new people and doing new things.

Many vacations can become year-long projects. When you're preparing for your annual trip, you'll find that time flies, and experiences that might ordinarily get you down don't have the same power over you.

I am one of five sisters and once a year we get away to catch up, have fun, and enjoy the freedom of being able to act silly for a few days! During the year we spend time planning, talking about, and getting excited over our "Annual Sisters Weekend Getaway." Where we go, or even what we do for that matter, is not as important as the fact that we do it, and that we look forward to it all year long. During the vacation, we feel remarkably free, with no restrictions. We've learned how to transcend into a new world in a very short period of time and just "leave it all behind"! Getting lost in the activity of the moment seems to make time stand still. We get a fresh appreciation of each other's special qualities that we may have taken for granted. Even though it's only a short getaway, it can provide the sustenance we need to go back to our individual worlds feeling rested and invigorated with a brand-new perspective on life.

Every vacation can be a wonderful opportunity for assessing life's experiences. When you return home, you'll find that you get even more enjoyment from routine events. You'll also always have the memories. My sisters and I have made it a point to put together a photo album of each of our getaway vacations, from start to finish. The others used to tease me because of my insistence on taking a picture of each event, all along the way, so that we would have a sort of "picture-book" story when it was over. Now, years later, when we can look back on those first few weekends, we're all thankful for something that can make the memories so vivid. And nowadays camcorders give us one more way to relive the feelings. Your life can be enriched in many ways, before, during, and after your vacation.

Become a Master of Play

Women sometimes lose their unabashed love of playfulness when they enter adulthood. Some of us tend to see this behavior as childish when we see it in the men in our lives and so have a difficult time leaving our serious side behind. For others, inhibitions hold us back from doing something outrageous or silly just for the fun of it. Either we fear embarrassment, or we don't give ourselves permission to play because we feel guilty if we are not accomplishing something.

Yet play is essential to achievement. It's also a necessary element in stress reduction, emotional well-being, and total health. The capacity to marvel at the wonders of the world and the ability to play are childlike qualities. There's a big difference between acting *childish* and being *childlike*. As children, we play using the right hemisphere of the brain—the artistic portion. Then later, through our education system, we learn to rely on the left brain, which, as we discussed in the last chapter, is the analytical center. We need to relearn playfulness, to restore and stimulate the right side of our brains. A start is to see the fun side of everyday situations and escape the "dailyness" of routine.

Without play, our lives are dull or full of tension. Sometimes we condition ourselves to absolutely dread what we have to do and actually end up turning our lives into an arduous task. Why make life more toilsome than it already is? What you can do instead is make a decision ahead of time to have fun and enjoy each aspect of your life.

It's possible to deliberately program your moods to look forward

to daily activities, including your work! We're all programming ourselves all the time anyway—either positively or negatively. We tell
ourselves, "A woman's work is never done," "I can't stand my job—
it's the worst thing that has ever happened to me," or "I just wish I
didn't have to go there today." (It is hard to stay motivated when you
have predetermined in your mind to hate something.) We can start
deciding to live for the moment and play along the way.

My hectic speaking schedule can get quite exhausting at times,
especially when I have to conduct several back-to-back workshops
that last all day. At the end of the program, I have a limousine waiting to take me to the airport so I can fly to the next city, spend the
night, and then start all over again the next morning. When this
happens four or five days in a row, over a two- or three-week period,
there's a good chance that I'll become drained and weary and that's
not fun. To stay exhilarated in spite of the challenges, I play at being
a vacationing retiree! I can pretend I'm just traveling around the
country on vacation or enjoying my retirement, and imagine that
what I am really doing is visiting with hundreds of people in each
new city (my audiences!). It takes the pressure off and makes my
work much more pleasant and exciting.

Even when things go wrong, as they have a way of doing, one
thing I have learned is that the *art of playfulness* means not taking
yourself or your circumstances too seriously. In many cases, after an
exasperating event, you know you'll be telling friends and having a
good laugh about it someday, so you may as well start now.
Consciously decide to narrow the gap between the incident and
when you begin to see it as funny. And have a good laugh at yourself, too. If you haven't lately, someone else probably has!

One of my most hilarious predicaments wasn't so funny at the
time. It was one of those speaking tours where everything that could
go wrong did. The tour was a week long, and each day something
devastating happened, from the power being off all day in the
entire city, to 250 workbooks not showing up at my next stop, which
meant having the hotel photocopy enough for every participant.
The fiascoes continued and each day's event seemed to be more
exasperating than the one before. Eventually, on the last day, when
I was to return to Toronto to give the keynote address at a large con-
vention, I thought nothing more could go awry. I was wrong. My
flight was delayed because of engine trouble. By rerouting me, the
airline would be able to get me to my destination that day, but too

late for my engagement. I called my client to explain and asked if someone could keep the audience entertained until I landed and then drove the ninety miles to the venue they had selected. They agreed. Once I arrived at the airport, I had a limousine take me to where my car was parked. As I hurried to get out of the limousine, the handle broke off my briefcase, which then went flying across the parking lot. It opened up and everything fell out, including about twenty red rubber clown noses that I carry with me to hand out in my stress-management seminars. They bounced all over the place. People in the lot kindly grabbed them and brought them back to me. I didn't have time to explain why I had so many of these odd props in my briefcase, so I have no idea what they thought this crazy lady did for a living! Later that afternoon, I decided to capitalize on the situation and told the whole story as part of my presentation, using it to make a point about not taking yourself too seriously. Within minutes, the entire audience was laughing hysterically! When I got off the stage, someone handed me a piece of paper on which was written this phrase: *"Angels fly because they take themselves lightly!"* This made perfect sense to someone who was writing a book about the freedom of having wings. Now, I laugh about almost every predicament and really have learned to lighten up. With a little practice, you can find ways to see the lighter side of life and use humor to brighten the lives of others, too.

Another way to create your own fun with whatever you're doing is to play professional. If you're working in your kitchen, baking or preparing dinner, pretend you're doing a cooking show on TV; household chores could become a commercial for a cleaning product or new appliance; or even shopping for a new computer program could turn you into a market researcher. Tasks will be more enjoyable and you will have a chance to see ordinary, routine activities in a new light.

When I have been on a lengthy speaking tour, I normally come home to dozens of business telephone messages that need to be returned. On top of that, there are a number of personal calls I want to make to family and friends. Since talking on the phone is not my favorite way to spend my time, I used to find myself dreading this aspect of my job and then procrastinating. Now, I have found a way to make the task more pleasant. Once the business calls are completed, I make personal calls from my bathtub! I climb into a warm bubble bath with my cordless phone, a list of numbers, and a cup of tea. This way, I actually look forward to a quiet time of chatting with the special people in my life. (My sister suggests I don't start making business calls from the tub, too, since my voice echoes and she can hear water splashing!)

Play is a great way to change your perspective and bring balance into your life. It is a terrific strategy to take the pressure off. Instead of feeling anxious and in a hurry to get things over with, you'll stay relaxed, free from stress, and enthusiastic about what you have to do. Not only will you feel uplifted and encouraged, but your effectiveness will probably improve along the way, without any extra conscious effort.

Free Time

You need free time in your life and it's up to you to create it. There are times when you must hide out, take a day off from the world, and spend time alone. Unfortunately, in most cases, no one is going to come and offer you the time to do it! Much of what you gain in life is determined by how much you want it. It's the intensity of your desire that will control how much free time you have. If you really want it, you'll get it. You'll find ways to control outside circumstances that influence how you spend your time. What you need are some effective habits and skills to help you recognize and stop the time robbers in your life. Solitude is a rare luxury. Here's what some women told me they do when they are feeling frazzled and need to escape.

- When Evelyn, a franchise owner, has a few minutes to herself, she slips away to her office at home, sets up her oil paints, and *plays.* She finds that even a short time of painting tranquil water scenes and landscapes calms her and helps to get her life back in perspective.

- Frances takes time from her hectic sales career to drive out into the country and go horseback riding. She says it's refreshing and almost like being in another world. No one knows where she is and she purposely doesn't wear her watch or take her pager.

- Ginnie catches up on reading—magazines, journals, books, and newspapers that have piled up over the weeks.

- When Helen is able to get away from her job, she finds that walking is the best way to get a needed break. When the weather cooperates, she walks outdoors, along city streets, enjoying interesting yards and gardens. In poor weather, she walks indoors through the local shopping center or at home on a treadmill.

- Judy says she luxuriates in her hot tub, which is in the solarium. Then, during winter months, she comes in to sit in front of a roaring fire with a freshly brewed cup of flavored coffee and a mystery novel.

These women admit that taking time out is not easy and it does take discipline, but the rewards are so great that it's worth the effort. There was a time when, if I tried to escape from the world for awhile, maybe by hiding out under a big, comfy afghan with a cup of herb tea and a good book, my inner critical voice would taunt me by calling me lazy. I was convinced that while everyone in the whole world was out there making progress in their lives, I was wasting mine hiding under a blanket. Even though I was taking time out, I wasn't able to reap the benefits because of the guilt I was feeling. Now, I quiet that voice by giving myself permission to recuperate.

It does me good to remember how my mom managed to work free time and breathing room into her busy life. We would come home from school on Friday afternoons, which was traditionally cleaning day at our house, and the smell of furniture polish and floor wax would greet us as we walked through the door. But what we would see was Mom sitting alone in the middle of the living-room floor, surrounded by cleaning supplies, dusting rags, and the books she had removed from the bookcase in order to dust the shelves. She'd be munching on an apple and totally engrossed in a mystery, autobiography, or historical novel. A good book was something she just couldn't resist even though there were other things clamoring for her attention. This picture is vividly etched in my mind and reminds me what a great example she was of knowing the value of taking a break and creating one's own free time without guilt.

Silence

Times of quietness and seclusion are not only pleasant, but essential.

They revive our problem-solving capabilities, leaving us relaxed, creative, happy, and renewed. Those priceless times of privacy give us the opportunity to look inward, to not only understand ourselves better but to improve our understanding of others. Silence can speak to us in ways the outside world never can.

In our hectic, fast-paced world, it's not always easy to *do nothing*. Try to take fifteen minutes every day to be still and alone. In fact, right now, close your eyes, quiet your mind, and simply sit in silence for two minutes. You'll experience benefits almost immediately. It does take some effort at first for even that short time, but eventually you'll feel comfortable for longer periods. Try sitting in silence before the fireplace or simply light some candles and shut out all the lights. Listen to the logs crackle. Watch the candlelight flicker.

We get addicted to background noise and often don't even realize it's there. Absolute quiet can be disconcerting at first and you may be tempted to at least have the radio or television turned on. Instead, use these times to meditate, or do some journalizing to record any insights you received after you've had several minutes of tranquillity. When you're driving, turn the radio off now and again. Our cars can be great places for meditation and prayer. Those moments of silence provide opportunities to listen to our inner voice. When you're going for a walk, enjoy the quiet. Tune in to your senses and pay attention to everything you see, hear, smell, and feel.

There's a big difference between being alone and lonely. When we master the art of being alone, we begin to discover who we are, who we want to be, where we want to go, and what gives us pleasure. By caring for yourself in this way, you'll soon get in touch with what you really feel. It's then that you'll be able to care more deeply for yourself, others, life, nature, and everything around you.

Invest in Exercise

Yes, exercise is an investment, and a positive one with many rewards. Women who exercise regularly report results and benefits in many areas such as higher energy levels, the ability to release negative stress, increased self-confidence, and improved memory and ability to concentrate.

When you begin to exercise on a regular basis, doing something you truly enjoy, you will find that you need less sleep yet feel more rested, eat less and crave healthier foods, and enjoy peak levels of alertness more often. You will be able to overcome depression and bounce back after adversity. Most of all, you'll experience a wonderful sense of personal freedom and control! It's the days when I feel I really don't have time to follow through on my exercise program that I have learned I absolutely must do it. When I am experiencing *project overload,* I find that exercise enables me to stay more focused on the project. I get more done in less time, and I'm more effective.

Exercise also promotes an increase in creativity and problem-solving abilities, a fresh excitement in our intimate relationships, and inner peace. Even though exercise is not a total cure for despondency or unhappiness, lack of it can be a great part of the cause. For instance, when you think of it, physical *inactivity* has been used throughout the centuries as a form of punishment!

Any change takes time. Give yourself a chance before expecting to see results. By the way, the good news is that the more out of shape you are, the faster you will notice results!

Try Giving Yourself Away

Acts of kindness enhance your journey, connect you with others, and are a wonderful source of self-nurture. Each time you make an effort to enrich someone's life or further his success, you can't help but nourish your own soul.

Look for ways each day to show someone you care. When you start to develop the habit of giving to others, you will notice countless opportunities appearing in everyday occurrences—someone needs a hand carrying an armload of parcels, a waitress or flight attendant needs a word of encouragement, your child or partner needs a hug, a co-worker needs to be reminded he is doing a great job, or someone with fewer groceries needs to be let in line. You can stop by and talk with someone in the hospital who may not have any visitors or take some baked goods to the neighbor who always seems to be alone. Maybe there's someone special who would appreciate a love note or a single rose on the windshield of his car.

I'll never forget the day I was feeling frustrated with some business challenges I was facing. When I answered a knock at the front door, I was surprised to see the florist delivering a huge, brightly colored arrangement for me. It was sent from a very special friend for no particular reason. This gift couldn't have come at a better time and I will always be grateful for her thoughtfulness.

Acts of kindness have tremendous power. We never know when our action, whether it's a smile, word, or gift, could be just what it takes to offer a person hope. Someone in one of my programs came to me at the end of the day and told me how upset she had been earlier. By the time she arrived, everything had gone wrong, from her son being in a terrible car accident in the middle of the night to not being able to find a parking spot that morning, making it necessary to walk quite a distance in the freezing rain. She said that when I took her hand and shook it, a comforting warmth flooded through her entire being. That handshake calmed her and prepared her to enter fully into the program so she could benefit from the day. Without my even knowing it, one simple action was enough to make the difference!

Giving seems to come naturally to women. For some, charity comes in the form of mentoring, leading, or being role models. You will always reach higher levels if one of your aims is to assist others in fulfilling their ultimate goals and reaching their full potentials. For others, it means giving of their talents, energies, or finances. Some of us have more time than money; others have more money than time. In any case, we all have something to offer. This innate altruistic attitude is an essential element in the process of growing our wings.

Form Support Systems

We need each other. Consider what science has discovered when studying geese as they fly in *V* formation to go south for the winter. As each bird flaps its wings, it creates an uplift for the one following. By flying this way, the entire flock greatly increases its flying scope over what a single bird would cover when flying alone. If a goose happens to fall out of formation, it suddenly feels the pull and resistance of trying to fly by itself. It quickly gets back in line in order to benefit from the lifting power of the others. We, too, can get where we are going more quickly and with less effort if we travel on the thrust of one another. Like geese, we'll always go farther if we choose to fly with those who are headed in the same direction.

When geese honk from behind, it is taken as an encouragement to those in front to keep up their speed. What an important lesson for us! We can choose to spend more time encouraging other women, and less time fault finding, criticizing, or tearing them down.

Whenever the lead goose gets tired, it rotates backward in the formation, allowing another goose to fly ahead and take its place. That way, the weary one can take advantage of the lift from the others, and regain its strength. For women, part of the joy of giving to others is that knowing our load will be lightened by taking turns and sharing responsibilities when it comes to demanding jobs. That way, no one carries the full burden. No one needs to become overtired. It's difficult for anyone to lead *all* the time.

When a goose is sick or injured and falls out of formation, two other geese fall out and follow it down to provide help and protection. They stay with the fallen goose until it is able to fly again and return to the formation. Women with wings stand by each other in the same way.

What meager, barren, and unrewarding lives we will lead if somehow we miss this truth and rely only upon our own strength and abilities in order to fly toward our destinations. If we choose to live in our private worlds, each for her personal gain and convenience, we will fulfill only a portion of our tremendous potential. Once we begin to acknowledge that each person is a unique child of God with much to offer, we can fully appreciate her valuable contributions and accept that we need each other.

PAMPERING PLEASURES

These nurturing rituals are not meant to be complete or absolute answers to breaking through your limiting emotional barriers or to solve all your troubles. They will, however, uplift you and release you from continually coming back to the same problem, headed towards certain destruction. Along with these nurturing habits, here are some easy *pampering pleasures* you can practice daily to keep you flying toward your ultimate desires.

1. *Listen to uplifting, soothing music.* Listening to music evokes a total-body response—inside and out. It can reduce or quicken our heart rates, raise or lower blood pressure, and affect our nervous systems, digestion, and muscle tension. Beyond that, music influences our thoughts, feelings, and moods. Aside from hearing the tune, we experience the vibrations, and that's why music affects the entire body.

Music that relaxes is truly a personal matter. Naturally if your association with a particular piece of music is a positive one, it will most likely be comforting to you. Yet how often do we continue to listen to a certain song that brings back memories of a broken heart or some other sad experience even though we know it's only adding to our suffering? Instead of making the effort to change either the song or our response to it, we persist in torturing ourselves. Although I am not recommending the suppression of negative emotions, music can be the ideal antidote for stress, if we will only select it carefully and allow it to work for us. Music can be therapeutic if we give it permission to touch the very essence of our beings. It stimulates our inner-healing mechanisms, and that's when our harmony and strength are restored.

While some songs are melancholy, we can always choose music that will heal, music that acts as a catharsis, purifying and comforting. The ancient Greeks built their theaters next to places of healing and patients were encouraged to listen to a range of music that would take them through a progression of emotions. A blend of comedy and tragedy aided in their rehabilitation. "Where words fail, music speaks" (Hans Christian Andersen).

Music is like a balm for our spirit. It can invigorate, uplift, and encourage, increasing our determination to make the most of our potential. It can also calm us. Certain instruments, such as the piano, harp, flute, and particular pieces of baroque music, with a rhythm of one beat per second are found to be especially relaxing to most of us. It seems the music that reflects our own heartbeat and breathing tends to be more calming.

There is music for your every mood—to celebrate, unwind, or grieve. As a remedy for stress, it will make you think more clearly, breathe easier, feel more rested, and experience a fresh sense of positive expectancy. Music is very personal. In any case, read your body, notice how you're breathing and feeling, and find the music that will nourish you. Music that's right for you will fill and revive your soul.

2. *Listen to inspiring and motivational messages on audiocassette.* Just a few minutes of a good message on tape can alter our attitude for hours. When I listen to a favorite speaker time and time again, I find that it's almost like having a good friend with me, someone I've gotten to know who is encouraging, supporting, and coaching me.

Choose to listen to your favorite speakers and you'll have friends for life who will be inspirations, sources of strength, and faithful teachers, guiding you in shaping your future. By gaining even one creative idea each time you listen, you can acquire a fresh perspective, and alter your mood for the day. I have listened to some of my tape programs over two hundred times and I am excited to think about how much I still learn each time!

3. *Look at your favorite photos that bring fond memories.* I can't help but smile and feel good all over when I look at pictures of our children and grandchildren. They bring back memories of all the fun times and cute things they've said and done over the months and years. I feel that they are near to me when I study their pictures. Likewise, my photo albums of our "Annual Sisters Getaway" are practically worn out, because I've discovered I can relive those special moments anytime I want. Just looking at them, I laugh until the tears roll down my cheeks! Snapshots of family get-togethers, vacations my husband and I have enjoyed, and even my silly cats are guaranteed to brighten the most dreary moments. Our lives are enriched when we reflect on pleasant memories, and we can do it through photographs, whether it's family times, trips, or people who are special to us.

Marion is a personnel consultant whose after-work hobby is assembling her photo albums. She has a special table set up in a spare room and can go there to work whenever she feels like taking a break. She divides her photos according to themes—an album for summer picnics over the years, another for special occasions and family dinners, one for all the birthdays, and so on. She has fun adding descriptive labels and other decorative touches. These picture storybooks are a joy for not only Marion but for all her family and friends to browse through.

4. *Escape for a few minutes by reading a page or two of a good book.* Books are friends, filling in what might otherwise be lonely moments. They're also like counselors and can be an encouragement, inspiration, and education. My mother often reminded us that as long as you have a good book nearby, you're never alone. When you read, practice *constructive daydreaming.* Form a picture in your mind about the material you are reading. See yourself taking part. Hear what's going on. Feel what's happening. When you involve the right half of the brain, even a few minutes of good reading can alter your state of mind and provide a temporary refuge. "No man can be called friendless when he has God and the companionship of good books" (Elizabeth Barrett Browning).

5. *Reward yourself with a bouquet of fresh flowers.* Jennifer believes in the adage, "Instead of waiting for someone to bring you flowers, plant your own garden," and takes it literally. Not only does she treat herself to a bouquet on the way home from work every now and then, she sometimes calls the florist and has them delivered to work. She greets the delivery person by exclaiming, "Flowers? For me? I must be doing something right!"

6. *Light some candles and enjoy a cup of herb tea.* Helen treats herself by brewing tea in a china pot and serving it in a fancy cup and saucer. Most of us get out the good china and light the candles only for company. You deserve to be treated as well as your guests. A warm cup of herb tea, especially chamomile, can act as nature's sedative. Even the ritual of preparing tea can be soothing. Boiling the water, holding the hot cup in your hands, and basking in the steam that rises up can be immensely calming. Put your feet up, close your eyes, and drift off to your own fantasy land for awhile.

7. *Get outdoors and go for a brisk walk in the nearest park or even in your own yard.* There's something about nature that draws us when the barriers seem insurmountable. It's almost as if there is some unseen force calling us to a secret place where we can gather our thoughts and settle ourselves once again. My husband and I live in the country and we sometimes forget what a beautiful spot we have right here under our noses. Just walking through the woods on our two-acre property every now and then, and even viewing it from different directions for a change, gives us an entirely new perspective on our normally familiar surroundings and current situations.

In fact, anytime we turn our attention to nature and immerse ourselves in the beauty of our environment, it can have a calming influence. Watching the waves on a beach or the clouds rolling by, standing in a sunny meadow, or wandering deep into a forest where leaves rustle in the breeze, we actually begin to tune into and connect with nature. Outdoor sights, sounds, and scents can inspire us and refresh our souls, and in a very special way, we actually share in some of nature's beauty and power.

8. *Learn a joke, practice it and tell at least one person.* Browse through your favorite cartoon or joke book and read humorous literature. The more you expose yourself to these things, the faster you begin to develop your own unique sense of humor. Make a point of learning at least one funny story and tell it to a few people. You'll not only brighten your own day, you'll make a difference in the lives

of others as well. Women who are prone to constant illness and depression are usually those who take life far too seriously. So, find your funny bone, loosen up, and learn how to giggle!

9. *Take time for a massage.* One of the most pleasurable and practical ways of dealing with stress is massage. It's also a wonderful way to reawaken our sense of touch. Of all the senses, touch is the first to develop and the last to abandon us. Touching is a universal language we all use, either consciously or unconsciously. It is the way we express how we feel about ourselves and others and can mean anything from approval to intimacy, understanding, and love. As a child, when you injured yourself and needed to be consoled, you instinctively wanted a hug, more for emotional comfort than anything. Today, when we see someone who is hurt, upset, or crying, our first reaction is to touch. Intuitively we know that touch is healing, stimulating, and comforting.

Physically, our earliest and most instinctive way to lessen pain is to apply pressure. It's also a natural remedy for stress. Massage is one of the oldest and most effective ways of dealing with many types of aches and physical discomfort.

For quite some time, I have had the privilege of treating myself to a weekly massage and the benefits are phenomenal! The smooth working rhythm of a massage helps to relax muscles and release tension, promote circulation, and cleanse the body of toxins. One of my clients commented that, for a woman, the bliss of a good body rub is enhanced simply by knowing that nothing more will be expected of her and she can relax, trusting her body to a trained professional!

A well-performed massage by a registered therapist will have healthful benefits for your whole person—body, mind, and soul. Some professionals combine the treatment with aroma-therapy oils, music, and soft lighting. The whole experience can provide a heavenly oasis in your life, relaxing your mind, invigorating your body, and uplifting your soul. Every woman should have a professional massage at least once a year!

If you want to try massage with your husband, there isn't anything more relaxing than giving your body to his loving hands, receiving freely and with total abandon. Encourage your partner to consider exchanging massages simply for the pleasure of the massage itself and nothing more. The benefits of a good massage may be minimized by a feeling that something else will be expected, even though lovemaking may follow naturally. When it does, it can be an exceptionally beautiful and fulfilling experience. You and your spouse can learn the art of massage together. There are many good instruction books available today, although it isn't that difficult if you want to try it on your own. All you really need is some uninterrupted time; a warm, dimly lit room; some lubricating massage oil scented with rosemary or clove; and a caring touch. Through massage, you'll soon move your relationship into a heightened sphere of intimacy.

10. *Get out a cookbook and try a new recipe.* Sometimes we merely need to get back to simple, basic pleasures, and it seems cooking is a marvelous way to do that. My life feels at peace when there's something cinnamony baking in the oven, or a dinner casserole cooking. Even browsing through cookbooks seems to have a therapeutic effect for me. My sister says that, for her, just being able to start and finish something in one day is refreshing, since completion is such a rare commodity with her frenzied life-style. We all need it in our lives in order to feel fulfilled. What a treat it is to set some freshly baked apple and cinnamon muffins on the counter to cool, then stand back and say, "I did that!"

11. *Pet the dog, talk to the bird, watch the fish, or cuddle the cat.* "Our cat literally saved our lives." This is what Eleanor told me as she shared her story of surviving a devastating personal crisis that included financial challenges and ill health. At times, she and her husband would suffer bouts of loneliness and depression that would literally overwhelm them. Watching their playful kitten and laughing at her many amusing antics lifted their spirits and helped them to stay strong in their struggles. Even the daily act of caring for another living thing protects us from despair. Pets definitely have a positive effect on our emotional as well as physical health. By magnetizing our attention, they provide a break from negative thought patterns that produce stress. They give us a reason to smile! Pets also provide a calming influence and have a stress-reducing effect. Whether your pet has feathers, fins, or feet, it can become a caring, nonjudgmental companion. Pets have a wonderful way of interrupting our cares. They bring us back down to earth and remind us of what it's like to be lighthearted.

Pets that love to be touched and held provide additional advantages. The mere act of petting an animal seems to benefit us as much as our pet. The stroking seems to have a healing effect, as though we were the ones being touched, and can play a major role in satisfying our need for close physical contact.

My friend Diane was thrilled to tell me that the general atmosphere in their household greatly improved when they brought their puppy home. The new family member seemed to open up a new level of intimacy among family members. It's not surprising, since even when we're simply talking to our pets we smile more, we slow down our communication, our voice tone is gentle, and we come across more relaxed.

If you want unconditional love and steadfast companionship, try looking to pets. They don't criticize us or find fault with us. They don't try to change us. They allow us to be ourselves. Our pets are truly agreeable friends, forgiving and loving no matter what. Because they are totally accepting of us, we can let our guards down when they are around. With this simple, relaxed outlet for emotional expression, our worries seem to fade away.

I have fond memories of my dad stooping to pet the family cat while fondly calling her a "time waster." To be sure, she was, but one he knew the value of!

12. *Go to your private "mental vacation spot."* We all have a favorite place that we'd like to go to whenever we're feeling tense or disappointed and just can't face the world. It could be real or imagined. It might be an island in the Caribbean, a cabin up north, or a spot by the river where you can watch the sailboats glide by. What I've discovered is that you *can* go there anytime you want—in your imagination! The amazing thing about the subconscious mind is that it cannot tell the difference between fantasy and reality. When you appeal to all five senses, it becomes a very genuine experience. I like to imagine I am sitting on the front verandah of my aunt and uncle's cottage, where, as a girl, I would visit each summer. In my mind, I can hear the waves of the lake slapping up against the shore and the gentle creaking as I rest in the rhythmic motion of the rocking chair. My mouth puckers when I relive the taste of freshly made lemonade. I can smell the popcorn being made in anticipation of an evening of fun and games. In only a few seconds, it's possible to make a round trip and feel as refreshed as if it had really happened.

13. *Plan a day just for you.* Perhaps you enjoy browsing through bookstores or having a cup of cappuccino in a cafe or visiting art galleries. If you do, find some time—even a few hours every now and again—to do just what you like. It may be going to the library or park to read poetry, doing some "just for fun" shopping, golfing,

or driving through the countryside. Even though we do need others to make our lives whole, before we can become involved in the give and take of any intimate relationship, we need to be happy alone first. My greatest times of solitude are spent reading, writing in a journal, sketching, playing the piano, or simply sipping on a cup of herb tea in the screened porch that overlooks our wooded property.

A young mother once confided to me that she hires a sitter for a few hours every two weeks just so she can go off by herself to read or write or merely think her own thoughts for awhile. You may have thought it would be frivolous to spend your time and money this way, but without those private times of silence, our *unnurtured self* feels stifled and cries out for healing.

Author Anne Morrow Lindbergh summed it up beautifully when she wrote: "I find there is a quality to being alone that is incredibly precious. Life rushes back into the void, richer, more vivid, fuller than before."

14. *Create a place of your own.* I believe that every woman needs her own spot—a secluded refuge, a sacred space to spend time on those special activities that nourish the soul and define the character. Our children have their own rooms to retreat to and our husbands have workshops or garages. But even if we do have a studio, sewing room, or office, it's usually public domain, available to the rest of the family. Find a place that's yours, even if it's a small corner of a room, and let others know that it's off-limits.

Judith is a woman whose marriage was suffering. She felt she needed space to breathe during the turmoil, until the relationship was at least on its way to recovery. She and her family lived in a sprawling farmhouse on several acres of wooded land. Although the home was big enough for a family of six, two dogs, three cats, and a den as well as an office for two home-based businesses, she felt that there wasn't one room she could call her own—a place to go for comfort, a place to escape for even a short while.

One spring, she decided to clean out a small cabin at the back of their property and furnish it with odds and ends she found in corners of the basement or at country flea markets. Here, in this quaint retreat, she could spend the night or just a few hours. Oil lamps flickered warmly in the evenings, and a small camping stove was all she needed to make herself a pot of tea or even a meal. In her secret haven, she could permit herself to cry or laugh without bothering anyone. She could work or daydream, write in her journal, or just sit still, listening to the sounds of nature in the bush. Sometimes she would invite family members or friends. Other times it was enough just to be alone. It was her sanctuary and she had no need to explain anything to anyone. As rough and simple as it was, the quiet woodland hideaway enabled her to see her difficult situation in a new light. Having a place of her own brought healing to her heart and helped salvage her marriage.

15. *Treat yourself with a present.* Make a list of 100 gifts you can give yourself! Being good to yourself doesn't have to be expensive or take a lot of time. Close your eyes, slow your breathing, and reflect on the phrase "innocent pampering pleasures." What do you think of? What can you do for the sheer pleasure of it? What is there that you can become so involved in that causes you to lose all track of time? When is it that the rest of the world goes away and you haven't a care? Think of those times when you're not even aware of the reality around you! When you're ready, open your eyes and write down all the ideas that pop into your mind.

Here are some ideas women have shared with me that might get you going if you're feeling stuck.

Watch the sun set.

Look at old photographs or other memorabilia.

Walk barefoot through your backyard.

Learn a new language.

Lie on the grass or roll down a hill.

Rearrange one room.

Go to the beach and build a sand castle.

Take your umbrella and stroll in the rain.

Jump in rain puddles.

Jump in a pile of autumn leaves.

Light candles at dinnertime.

Make love outdoors under the stars.

Plan a theme party.

Plan to surprise someone.

Write a love note to someone special and put it where he or she will find it.

Eat a popsicle.

Do something that doesn't come easily to you.

Sing, whistle, or hum.

Pack a lunch in a wicker basket and enjoy a picnic alone or with a friend.

Have breakfast outdoors.

Go to a fair.

Ride a roller coaster at an amusement park.

Fly a kite.

Spray paint wicker baskets and fill them with silk flowers.

Take a walk under the stars.

Play hide and seek with a child.

Put on some "big band" music and dance around your living room.

Write a poem, song, or short story.

Take an art course.

Make mud pies in the sandbox.

Buy some clown makeup and paint your face.

As you practice some of these steps, you may discover new ways of escaping for awhile, at least long enough to bring your feelings and reactions under control again. As complex as it can be, your unique feminine emotional intensity can actually help you in growing your wings. Through nurturing yourself and programming pleasure into your life, you can start to appreciate the depth of your inborn sensitivity and use it to benefit yourself and others. Your new wings are unfolding. Now you can begin to dream and plan and set rich, meaningful goals for your flight.

CHAPTER 5

W
I
N
Goals
S

Where there is no vision, the people perish. (Prov. 29:18)

WITH A HEALTHY SENSE of self-worth, an awareness of your insightful abilities, and an abundance of self-nurturing skills, your wings are growing stronger. Now that they're almost fully formed, the next question is, Where are you going?

Can you imagine the tragedy of having beautiful, mighty wings that have the power to take you anywhere you choose, but not having the faintest idea where you'd like to go? So many women do sprout their wings, yet never experience the full benefits of having them because they don't have a vision for their lives. They're not exactly sure what they'd like to see happen. Perhaps they don't know they have a choice. Maybe they are not aware that vision is what makes the difference between *living* and *being alive*.

Many of us spend more time writing to-do lists, watching television, or standing in front of the closet deciding what to wear than we do planning our lives. Other times, we focus on past memories or hopes for a better future, but have no current targets. When this happens, our daily activities turn into a blur of handling problems, coping with crises, and dealing with day-to-day tensions rather than soaring toward our dreams. We say we'd *like* to have a healthier life, more energy, a different job, or better relationships, but our desires at this stage are nothing more than vague wishes. One major element in turning wishes into realities is having a goal. In other words, goals are wishes that have grown wings!

Here are the six most common reasons why goals are not set:

1. *We don't know how.* Goal setting is not generally taught in schools. Unless our parents or a special teacher or group leader introduced us to this concept, chances are, we have never been informed of the process of setting goals.

2. *We don't recognize the value.* The benefits of setting and achieving goals were not emphasized for most of us in our growing-up years. Naturally we *desire* those things that will improve the quality of our lives, but without activating the goal-setting process, we may never obtain them.

3. *We feel that we are too busy.* If we don't know how to set goals or don't appreciate the value of achieving them, we will always fill our days with other seemingly more important activities. Then we begin to believe we simply don't have time to even *plan* our futures let alone work toward certain targets. The truth is we will always find time to accomplish what we perceive to be the most significant items on our agendas.

4. *We are not sure what we want.* It's been said many times, "You'll never hit a target if you don't know it's there." Most of us have not been taught or encouraged to spend time thinking about what we truly desire for our futures. As a result, we neglect to make those few simple decisions with definite specifications that could greatly alter our direction. It's not until we are thoroughly clear about what we want that a goal will become obvious and believable.

5. *We are programmed not to expect too much from life.* That way, we won't be disappointed. Most of us are not in the habit of asking and expecting to receive. It isn't easy to start dreaming big when we've been conditioned to think small. Remember, those who anticipate getting a lot from life usually achieve what they expect.

6. *We remember past negative experiences with other goal-setting attempts.* Perhaps there have been goals that didn't turn out the way we had hoped they would. Now, remembering and contemplating those dreams that were never realized, we are doubtful about setting future goals.

Whatever the reason has been in the past, this is your moment of power. You can begin today to design, direct, and create your future through your goals. Otherwise, daily pressures, other peoples' expectations, and perceived limitations, will always have more control over your life's events than you do, which ultimately leads to disappointments.

"The greatest thing in this world is not so much where we are, but in what direction we are moving" (Oliver Wendell Holmes). Everything you accomplish in life is determined by your goals. Even though there are lots of other factors contributing to the outcomes in your life, taking charge of the direction of your flight is the most crucial. Become someone who knows exactly what she wants in life, confidently selecting end results, without limits or compromise.

A goal is simply a target you aim for, a predetermined destination. There is nothing mystical about goal setting. You've been doing it all your life, whether you realize it or not. Some of your past goals have turned out okay; others have had disastrous results. In order to use your wings effectively, choose to focus on your successes, have some new targets in mind, and know what steps to take to achieve your desired results.

Having goals means you get to decide where you'd like to go in your life's journey. You can determine which new habits you want to develop, which behavioral patterns and attitudes you want to change, which possessions you want to acquire, and which activities you want to integrate into your life-style. You have the opportunity to decide if you'd like to travel the world, own a business, write a book, learn to play a musical instrument, be an encourager of others, get fit, or start a foundation for a worthy cause.

Goals represent what we desire most in life. The only pitfall is that they can become self-defeating if they keep us so focused on where we are headed that we lose sight of the beauty that is unfolding right before our eyes. It's exciting to set, strive toward, and eventually attain a goal. It's equally rewarding to reflect on where we've come from, appreciating the experiences that brought us to where we are now.

Using your wings effectively means knowing when to change direction, release goals that are no longer right, or reach for new targets altogether. It all begins with having a dream, one that is truly yours and not someone else's dream for you. Take time to examine your heart's desires. Find a quiet, relaxing place—a sunny corner by a window, the back porch, a spot by a lake, or even a warm bubble bath—sit still, and consciously slow your mind. Begin asking yourself what you truly want in life. What would you like to accomplish? Which things would you like to change? Think about the strengths you have that would help you in attaining these goals and consider why you desire them.

Listen to your intuition—that small voice within that is not affected by your doubts, insecurities, or other people's opinions. What is it telling you about where you should be headed? Your natural insight will always guide you in a direction that is right for you. The desires revealed to you through intuition will be realistic and reachable, yet will always cause you to stretch and grow. You will soon attempt to accomplish what you never before thought possible! Looking within is one of the best ways to start your goal-setting process. Your insightful nature, your connection to heavenly wisdom, acts as a guiding light, illuminating your path to a better life.

As you go through this process, begin to define your life in terms of your goals. When you do, you will notice an increase in your level of passion, confidence, and motivation.

GO AHEAD AND DREAM!

Keep thou thy dreams—the tissue of all wings
Is woven first of them; from dreams are made
The precious and imperishable things,
Whose loveliness lives on, and does not fade.

Virna Sheard

One of the most intriguing facts I know is that every great creation on the face of this earth started with a dream. Just as an architect has a vision of a future building and a fashion designer has an image of her creation before she even begins, you too must have a dream. To *get* what you want you must *know* what you want. You'll never hit a target if you're not sure what it is.

Dreams make the difference between those who are average and those who are outstanding. For many women, it's a stretch even to dream—about a better life, a happy home, meaningful relationships, financial independence, great health, career success, or personal fulfillment. Yet dreams are free and available to everyone. They are the starting point of all achievement.

The main reason why most women don't use daydreaming to change the direction of their lives is simply that they are not aware it is within their means to do so. Goals begin with knowing what you want, what would have to take place to make it so, and the belief that it's all possible.

Start by letting your imagination run wild. *Forget reality.* Dreams must be free of limitations. Anything you can imagine, backed with deep feelings, has the potential of coming true. Allow yourself to think about a future filled with grand promises. Challenge yourself. Don't hold back simply because you can't imagine *how* it could happen. You don't have to understand how in order to start concentrating on what changes you'd like to see. Focus on the ways it *can* happen, instead of why it cannot. Remember, if it's possible for anyone, why not you?

Someone once asked me two questions that dramatically impacted my life and changed the direction I was headed. They were simply: "If you could do or be anything in this world, and you knew it would be impossible to fail, what great things would you attempt?" and "If you were able to create your *ideal life,* what would you dare to dream?" These were the questions that started me thinking in ways I never had before.

What I discovered was possibly the most exciting concept I'll be sharing with you in this book, and that is that you have been given the potential to plan, organize, and create many more of the events in your life than you might have believed possible. Through your choices, you have a great degree of control over your future. When you provide a target, your mind will automatically move toward it. This may seem like a mystery, but so is your entire being and the tremendous ability God has planted within you. Dreams, desires, and objectives produce a magnetic pull and we attract into our lives what we focus and dwell on.

WHY WE DON'T PERMIT OURSELVES TO DREAM

If you've ever been called a daydreamer, it probably wasn't a compliment! During our growing-up years, at home or in school, dreaming was definitely not promoted. In fact, if you were found daydreaming, chances are, you were corrected and discouraged from the practice. Even today, it's still not something that's encouraged.

Do any of these statements sound familiar? "Get your head out of the clouds!" "Daydreamers don't amount to anything." "Be logical!" "Use your brain."

Is it any wonder that we find it difficult to believe that our dreams play a role in attaining the absolute best for ourselves? We end up trusting only the tried and true, and our dreams fall by the wayside.

SYMPTOMS OF HAVING ABANDONED YOUR DREAMS

Most of the women I speak to are suffering from "daydream malnutrition." They have either forgotten how to dream or simply don't know that it's a fundamental yet powerful way to transform their lives. Here are some signs that suggest you may not be dreaming enough.

Procrastination

When women don't have dreams, they often put off making major decisions or taking any form of action in favor of doing the small or meaningless tasks. They keep *busy* instead of *productive*. It's dreams that provide the sense of mission we need to build momentum. It's dreams that give us the motivation to get up and moving regardless of how we're feeling. Without clear goals, we won't be prepared to take risks or have the ambition to follow through with the necessary steps to succeed.

Depression and a Pessimistic Outlook

Without dreams, many women work themselves to the bone for things they don't even truly want. They reach for the stars and pay the price of success. Part way there, they start asking themselves if this is actually where they want to go. Then, pessimism sets in. Nothing can bring on depression quicker than finally attaining something and discovering that it's not satisfying after all. Dreams can help us to stay on target and remind us to check back on our true values and the reason why we wanted to achieve the goal in the first place.

Sarcasm

Women who use sarcasm are often frustrated dreamers experiencing deep disappointments. Without a dream, life is just one purposeless incident after another. Sarcasm covers up their true

feelings. They are often angry with the world and usually feel bitterness toward life for being the way it is. My heart goes out to these
women with bruised and damaged wings. They need to know that
having a dream can bring the magic back into their lives.

Criticism

Normally, the most critical people are those who are not happy
with the way things are going in their own lives. Being critical and
judgmental can also be a sign of envy of those who *are* living their
dreams. To free our imaginations, we must abandon all temptation
to give in to faultfinding or needless bickering. These negative
habits rob us of our own confidence. They also limit our ability to
connect fully with others or recognize the ways in which they might
be able to contribute to our own dreams for a brighter future.

FORSAKING A DREAM

Even though it's important to keep dreaming, there are times
when you need to forsake a particular dream. It's important to know
when to abandon one in favor of another. Staying adaptable allows
you to make changes when necessary.

How do you know when to let go? Remember that worthwhile
dreams are fulfilling and exciting, and at the same time come with
their own set of problems and challenges. Leave your dreams only
if they have lost their meaning to you. Never change direction simply because you're experiencing trials and turbulence, for even
though the way is rough right now, it doesn't mean you won't eventually reach your destination.

Take a few minutes to consider some of the dreams you may need
to sacrifice. Then, list in your note pad any abandoned dreams you
would like to rekindle.

It's also a good idea to examine closely the barriers to reaching
your goals. Sometimes all it takes to conquer these obstacles is an
awareness of them.

CONQUERING FEAR BARRIERS

Fear is the most powerful negative emotion we can experience
and is our number-one barrier, keeping us from our dreams. Every

time we set a goal and then take action toward achieving it, we are risking and risk can cause fear. While men tend to see taking risks as both dangerous and exhilarating—a hazard as well as an opportunity for possible gain—women tend to consider only the potential loss and think in terms of what it may cost.

Many of us, as girls growing up, learned to be afraid of a number of things. We feared embarrassment or looking foolish. We were afraid of what might happen if we tried something different, or the extra time and energy a new venture may have involved. Now, as adults, we fear more demands on our already-hectic lives. We fear not being able to live up to our own or others' expectations of us. So many needless fears are holding us back from taking flight with a clear target in mind. Most of them can be summed up in these four categories: fear of

F—ailure
E—xpected Pain
A—chievement
R—ejection

Failure

No one wants to fail. We'd like to succeed all of the time. Women need to learn that failure does not mean the end of the world. Men, from the time they are little boys, are conditioned to accept failure as part of learning. They are encouraged to attempt various activities in which they would undoubtedly fail and have to pick themselves up and start over, having gained from the experience. The truth is we can learn more from our failures than we will ever learn from our successes. Since I've discovered that failure is a growth experience, I have decided not to label my setbacks that way. Instead, I choose to say I've learned a lot of ways *not* to do something again!

It's a good idea to keep a "next time" file for important projects and ventures that you know you will be repeating. It might be making a sales call, giving a presentation at your staff meeting, negotiating your fees or salary, coordinating a banquet or conference, or dealing with a difficult person. As soon after your experience as possible, whether the outcome was positive or negative, take some time to evaluate your performance. Note first what you liked and then what you would change.

Critique yourself honestly, and ask others whose opinions you trust for their sincere comments as well. When you are ready to attempt the project again, your "next time" file will act as your "recipe for success." By referring to it and following your own suggestions, you will be able to avoid some of the pitfalls that stymied you in the past. Of course, this time, expect more exciting stumbling blocks because you have new lessons to learn!

You can benefit from every failure, mistake, setback, or embarrassing experience by following these five steps.

1. Ask yourself what was good about your performance.
2. Determine what you learned from the experience.
3. Decide what you will change or do differently the next time you are in a similar situation.
4. Close the door to the past, without regrets.
5. Look forward to your next opportunity to shine now that you know so much more than you did before!

To get up and running once again after a failure or setback, focus on some of the times when you experienced total success—a great day with the family, a good golf game, or the time you won an award of distinction for your work. Write down what it was and the qualities you drew on that enabled you to succeed. Validating your own worth and talents in this way equips you with the stamina to go back and try again.

And remember to evaluate your successful performances as well!

Expected Pain

The fear of *expected pain* is also commonly known as worry. One of the most self-destructive behaviors we can have is worrying about what might happen in the future, which only leads to a sense of frustration and helplessness. We could literally scare ourselves silly contemplating *expected pain!*

Women tend to worry in one of two ways. Either we automatically assume that our efforts won't make a difference anyway and we end up feeling powerless and victimized, or we believe we should be able to control every outcome and take on *all* challenges and problems as our own. Then we become anxious about conditions or issues we might never be able to resolve.

Worry is so destructive because it has a tendency to set off a chain reaction. When that happens, within seconds we are living out the worst possible outcome in our imagination even before we have all the details.

For example, imagine that your supervisor has just called you into her office to do a performance evaluation, and you know that these reviews are not scheduled for another few months. Immediately, you create your own mental movie, beginning with distorted or negative thoughts. You imagine that you must have done something wrong, which you assume will result in your termination, which means you won't be earning any money, so you can't pay the mortgage, in which case you'll probably lose your home, and end up living on the street with everything you own in one huge plastic bag! In only a matter of seconds, you have taken yourself from a pretty good position to utter devastation, even though it is simply in your mind.

Until we have enough information, it's useless to open ourselves up to the harmful effects of worry. There's just as much of a chance that you are going to be commended for the fine work you are doing. But even if the outcome was a negative one, you're better off getting all the facts first and then doing what you can about the situation.

Worry, or the fear of expected pain, can leave us feeling helpless and depressed. Over extended periods of time this can affect not only our mental but also our physical well-being since harbored negative emotions attack the immune system. When we don't act on problems that are within our control or if we continue to focus our attention on events we can't change, we increase our vulnerability to all sorts of diseases ranging from arthritis and allergies to high blood pressure and ulcers.

Worry is the most useless emotion we can have. It's like rocking in a rocking chair—it takes a lot of effort and we don't go anywhere. If we worry about something and it never happens, we've wasted a lot of life energy in the process. If it does happen, we haven't changed a thing by worrying. With wings, we'll choose to act on problems that are within our control and stop wasting time and energy being concerned with those that aren't.

Worry really means we are anticipating negative outcomes. We're afraid of what *might* happen. We look pessimistically into the future and create fatalistic images in our minds. One technique to help move us away from worry is to use our imagination to form positive pictures. Try seeing yourself in the fearful situation and then imagining a satisfactory outcome. For example, if you have a fear of water and you worry about what might happen if you try to swim, picture yourself in a pool filled with warm water. Close your eyes and see yourself floating. In your imagination, relax in the warmth and revel in your weightlessness. Enjoy the sensation of being totally unencumbered. If you worry about your children and what may happen to them when they are out of your sight, picture them safe from harm, protected by an invisible shield and happily returning to you at the end of the day. Do this exercise as often as you can, periodically during the day and again just before falling asleep at night. Handle each worry this way, one at a time, and it won't be long before you'll be able to live *worry free*.

Another technique is to give yourself a reality check. Ask yourself if your worries are justified and supported by facts. If you are troubled about your health, ask yourself if the symptoms you've fretted about in the past have always resulted in disease. Is there any evidence that illness is inevitable? When you are worried about failing to fulfill your obligations at work, ask yourself if you've failed before. If not, you can stop tormenting yourself and set your focus instead on improving your skills. If you have failed, go back to the situation and determine what you can do differently this time.

If you do feel justified in your concerns, you can move on to the technique called the *worst-case scenario*. Instead of just worrying, go ahead and imagine the most terrible possible outcome. When you're anxious about losing your job and becoming destitute, picture just how bad it could be. Consider all your choices in that situation and you may be pleasantly surprised at the options available to you.

Marianne said that, when she was laid off from her position in a hospital laboratory, she was astounded at the opportunities that were presented to her. She wished that she had allowed herself to envision some of the positive choices ahead of time instead of worrying about the possibility of being out of work. There are so many alternatives that can open up to us if we trust our potential and focus our attention beyond the fear.

You can get your situation back in perspective by asking yourself these three questions:

1. What is the worst thing that could happen if my concerns were to be realized?
2. What will this mean to me ten years, five years, one year, or even a week from now?
3. What are my choices if it does happen?

In other words, if the worst really occurred, would it be all that bad, could I cope with the outcome, how long would it affect me, and what can I do to move forward?

Then there's the *procrastination method*. Noreen has developed the habit of putting off worrying and scheduling time for it in her date book on some other day. For example, she promises herself that since she doesn't have time to be troubled right now, she'll get to it on Thursday evening, from 7:30 until 8:00, and she actually makes an entry in the appropriate spot. Then, she starts her "worry list," and whenever anything else comes up that she might be tempted to fret about, she adds that to the list and saves it for Thursday. What usually happens is that she simply is not in the mood to worry at the scheduled time, or something else has come up in the meantime, so she has to put it off and reschedule her worrying! This is one time when it's actually a good idea to procrastinate!

Another benefit to scheduling time to worry is that, often, problems have a way of working themselves out before you get to them. Alternatively, you may just want to sit down and have a good old time of fretting. After about thirty minutes of it, even *you* are going to be tired of hearing about all those worries! Imagine how you'd feel if a friend called you and asked you to listen to a solid half-hour of her cares. It would become a little tedious after awhile, especially if there was no attempt to make changes.

Whenever the fear of *expected pain* begins to burden you, try to work some area of familiarity or certainty into your life. Pockets of emotional safety here and there seem to provide a temporary escape and shelter you from the harmful effects of worry. Whether it's doing some form of exercise, curling up in front of the fire to watch a good movie, working on a favorite hobby, getting lost in a good book, or talking things over with an understanding friend, simply adding some measure of reliable comfort to your life can be a source of encouragement and contentment.

Finally, there is such a thing as *constructive* worry. The discomfort it causes spurs us into action and provokes us to do some serious brainstorming and problem solving. When we embrace worry and make it work for us, it can be an effective and valuable tool in creating new opportunities. Turn anxiety into a positive force by controlling it before it controls you.

Achievement

We can get so accustomed to not succeeding that accomplishment is as unfamiliar as failure is comfortable. We know that success usually comes with a price tag, whether it's less energy because of increased demands, or less time to do some of the things we truly enjoy. It may be that now we will be expected to continue moving beyond our comfort zones, accepting more responsibility and taking bigger risks.

Even when we have been blessed with achievement and affluence, we often have a difficult time allowing ourselves to accept it all. We either acknowledge it apologetically or denounce certain aspects of our success by pointing out our flaws and imperfections.

Sometimes we sense that professional relationships will suffer when we leave the status quo behind to step out from the crowd. By assuming any type of leadership position, we automatically set ourselves up as targets for criticism or rejection. As long as we stay in line, blending our ideas and opinions with those of others, we are not threats. By achieving success, we are making a statement and others may not be supportive. The cost of accomplishment may be temporary loneliness, until we make new associations with those who are also achieving success. "Birds of a feather . . . " still holds true, but the flock we get together with is a choice we must make.

Friendships can also be part of the cost of achievement. Many women build a circle of friends who reinforce each other's complacency, keeping anyone from making changes. Some associations are built on similar or shared problems, and when one tries to break out of the rut, there is the threat that this common thread will be broken. Within groups, it's almost as though there's some hidden oath or unspoken agreement that no one should get ahead because it means leaving others behind. Without realizing it, they feel threatened if one moves forward and subconsciously the aim is to keep anyone from growing.

We then feel we must somehow get everyone else's support before we choose success. Our belief is that if we are too happy or accomplished, we won't be accepted. What we don't recognize is that through our efforts to move forward, whether we're successful or not, we can encourage others and spur them on to pursuing their own new challenges and risks. *Rather than seeing achievement as a*

barrier between you and your friends, see it as a valuable opportunity to clear
the path for others and to act as a positive role model.

Even within our families, there may be a general feeling of disapproval for *forgetting our place.* We might hear statements such as
"You won't last long; in our family, we've never been welcomed into
those circles" or "You might think you've arrived, but you're only
fooling yourself."

Madelyn, the general manager of a restaurant franchise, shared
her story with me. She confided that once she had made it to the
top and achieved her goal within the hospitality industry, she was
shocked to discover that her family began rejecting her. None of
her relatives had ever attained such a level of success in the business
world and they were obviously feeling threatened. Because of their
own insecurity, they had chosen to shut Madelyn completely out of
their lives. She admitted that although she was never tempted to
leave her newfound success simply to appease her family, one of the
most devastating experiences of her life was receiving rejection
instead of praise. However, now with her wings, she is able to give
herself the approval she needs and depends less and less on the
recognition of others.

Since success comes with a price tag, you may be tempted to hold
yourself back. What you can do instead is focus your attention on the
long-term gains as well as the purpose you are fulfilling by succeeding, rather than dwelling on the cost of achievement. As much as I
love what I do as an international speaker and author, my career has
involved its share of sacrifices. There have been canceled weekend
engagements, the occasional missed family event, many twelve-hour
days spent at the computer, and times when I worked around the
clock to meet a client's deadline. But the rewards are worth it. I feel
fortunate to have the support of many people who care about me—
a husband who encourages me, supportive children, an understanding family, and patient friends who believe in the work I do. It wasn't
always that way. I too have paid the price of achievement. Because
success may cost us in our personal lives, we must be totally focused,
committed, and sure of what we want before we go after it.

Fear of accomplishment for women can also be closely connected to the fear of self-reliance. When we begin to succeed and reach
higher levels of achievement, there's no reason to blame anymore.
We're no longer victims of circumstance. Success means taking
responsibility for our outcomes, both the good and the bad. Even

though we know that it doesn't help to blame, sometimes it's easier to play the role of the victim than to move ahead and create our own circumstances—challenges and all. When you think of it, there really is no glass ceiling these days when every woman has the choice to start her own company of which she can be president!

Achieving excellence is a continual process of changing and evolving. Any transformation is uncomfortable for a time, even if it's a positive one. For instance, the success of starting a new job, being promoted, beginning a new relationship, or getting married all bring unfamiliar pressures and to be dealt with. Yet to stop growing is to stop living. Success begins with a willingness to pay the price. You can find strength by seeking spiritual guidance along the way. Know that it is always God's will that we propser in all good things and that we become all we were created to be.

Rejection

Many of us have a hard time dealing with any form of disapproval. Why is it that we seem to have this innate need to be pleasing to everyone all the time? What can we do about it? Let me share with you how I had to learn to handle rejection in my speaking career.

At the end of some of the corporate workshops I conduct, participants complete evaluation forms on which they are asked to rate not only the program content, but also the speaker, on everything from professional appearance to the use of humor and the ability to hold the group's attention. Although negative comments are the exception rather than the rule, simply because of the law of averages we know that not every comment will be positive. Yet those are the ones that stand out from the rest. Many of my friends have confessed to me that they don't think they could handle even that amount of criticism or "rejection" on a regular basis. There was a time when I didn't think I could either.

What I had to do was decide early on in my career as a professional speaker that I would learn from every evaluation, and seek out ways to use this input to develop and alter my programs. Rather than seeing the comments as *personal* criticism or rejection, I now use the ideas to add or eliminate material and change my delivery style in order to improve my presentations.

By looking at it in this way, I am able to offer more to my listeners the next time I present the same course. I can discover how better to meet the needs of the audience when I pay attention to the comments. It's not an easy thing to do, because negative remarks still sting, but the results are worth the effort.

Fear of rejection, according to many therapists, is one reason why some women sabotage their love relationships. Apparently, inherent fears of being rejected prompt a woman to do one of two things. She will either stay in a relationship that is not right for her rather than face being alone, because she feels it's the lesser of two evils, or she'll unconsciously turn a good situation into a bad one through her behaviors. In spite of the fact that things may be going well, because of her own feelings of inadequacy she doubts whether she deserves a pleasant, untroubled relationship or that it could last for her. Without realizing it, she produces emergency situations that will eventually tear the relationship apart and by doing this, she creates a self-fulfilling prophecy. Then she may say something like, "See, I told you relationships never work out for me!" But at least she has, in a sense, controlled the rejection.

Women also fear being rejected for "rocking the boat." So, they choose to keep any new ideas to themselves. If they want to break away from traditionally acceptable roles, they wonder if they will still be liked and affirmed.

The fear of rejection locks us into a "sacrificial" mode of thought, in which case we run ourselves ragged with *busyness*. We agree to take on multiple roles, perhaps being a wife, raising a family, running a household, and managing a career, while also doing charity work, submitting articles for the company newsletter, becoming a committee chairperson for the local business group, comforting friends in need, and volunteering to host the family reunion in our home each year—all at the expense of our own well-being. Rather than risk being rejected for saying no once in awhile, we continue taking on new duties. At the very least, we could delegate tasks or even leave some things undone.

UNCERTAINTY

Most of our fears can be summed up in one word—*uncertainty.* Generally, women fear the unknown and, as a result, hang on to every measure of security and order in their lives. *Since we hold tight to anything we perceive to be solid or genuine, we won't let go of an idea whose time is passed.* Some of us stay in dead-end jobs and tolerate destructive or even dangerous relationships, and all because we worry about entering unfamiliar territory.

Whenever fear of change takes over your emotional state or your choices by paralyzing you, try fantasizing in reverse. Imagine yourself in your existing situation a number of years from now if you continue the way you are. If your emotions are ruling you today, how much more serious will it be later if you don't make some positive changes? If you find your job unrewarding now, how will it be then? If current relationships are devastating you, consider how much more detrimental they will be in the future if you don't confront and clear up harmful issues. Ask yourself what will happen in your life if you don't take action. Determine which of the above fears is causing you to hesitate and establish why you are holding yourself back.

Identifying your concerns and attaching labels to them is the first step in conquering them. The next step is to take action and just do it. Every change marks the end of a stage in your transformation. Yet every end signifies a fresh beginning—one that has the potential to be richer, because you have gained from your past experiences. "Do the thing you fear the most and the death of fear is certain" (Ralph Waldo Emerson).

TURNING DREAMS INTO GOALS:
AN EIGHT-STEP PROCESS

Here is an exercise you can do almost anywhere and anytime that is convenient to you. Find a comfortable spot, get a pencil and pad of paper, and settle in for an hour or so. Use this time to search deep within yourself and contemplate your heart's desires. Throughout the process, remember to dream, and dream big. Stretch your imagination to the limit! The purpose of these steps is to ensure not only that you express your needs and desires, but that your dreams are focused and firmly established. You may think that because you have your goals in your head it's not necessary to write them down. Yet it has been my experience that lofty wishes, floating around in our minds, rarely materialize.

1. *Create your wish list.* To do this, begin with a dream about your ideal life and then think about what would have to change or take place in order for you actually to experience it. Where would you

live? What would you do to earn your living and what would your work environment look like? Which people would share your life with you? Knowing where you're headed is the first step in getting there. I find that it helps to imagine I am at the end of my life and someone is interviewing me in order to write my biography. You can do this, too, by asking yourself what you would like to be able to say you had accomplished or experienced in your lifetime. Plan now to be an interesting senior with lots of exciting stories to tell!

Don't concern yourself at this point with your financial status, current living and working conditions, or others' expectations of you. You can consider these elements later in the process.

For dreams to fly and work their magic, they should begin with action verbs. For example, would you

- start your own business?
- turn your hobby into your profession?
- change careers?
- learn to play the saxophone or the drums?
- play in a philharmonic orchestra or a band?
- sing in a choir?
- go back to school?
- get your degree?
- enroll in a photography course?
- renovate your home?
- buy a house? Buy a boat? Buy a houseboat?
- buy property in the country?
- climb a mountain?
- build a cabin, a playhouse for the kids, a tool shed in the backyard?
- own a horse?
- learn how to oil paint?
- join a gym and get fit?
- learn to scuba dive and explore the mysteries of the sea?
- play golf, tennis, or volleyball in a tournament?
- take gourmet cooking lessons?
- fly an airplane?
- drive a race car?
- invest in a new car?
- get to know a famous person?
- go on an island vacation or a cruise?
- meet and marry the person of your dreams?

- start a family?
- give large sums of money to your favorite charity?
- write a book, poem, or song?
- grow a vegetable garden?
- conquer your fear of heights, water, elevators, or public speaking?
- collect antiques?
- start a foundation for a worthy cause?
- invite your friends to an elegant dinner party?

Remember, at this stage, there are no limits. We'll be analyzing the list later in the process to determine which goals are feasible and which are not. For the time being, nothing is impossible in your dreams! Take a few minutes now and make your own list. Start with a blank piece of paper and continue writing as long as the ideas are flowing.

You will stop the stream if you allow yourself to focus on boundaries, such as limited time, money, knowledge, talent, opportunity, confidence, experience, or support from those you would like to be able to count on. Naturally there will always be confines in real-life experiences. The truth is that most of these can be overcome. However, you don't have to conquer them before you begin dreaming. It doesn't cost you anything at this point, beyond a little time and effort. Besides, giving yourself permission to dream is the best way to spot opportunities you may have otherwise missed.

When creating your list, consider every aspect of your life and your various roles—at home and at work. Include intangible as well as tangible items. Contemplate your personal life—mentally, physically, spiritually, and emotionally. Think about your needs.

One of the items on my dream list a number of years ago was to have a large country kitchen. I imagined this may be possible by taking down the wall between the existing kitchen and the dining room. Both rooms were quite small, yet combined they would create a good-sized kitchen, and I really didn't mind the idea of forfeiting a formal dining room. Another dream was to become an international motivational speaker and author, traveling around the world, inspiring others to make the dramatic changes that would improve their lives.

At this "dreaming" stage, I wasn't quite sure if either dream was feasible because of a number of issues. For my country kitchen, I didn't know if the wall between the two rooms was a supporting wall, which would mean it couldn't be removed. Could I come up with the finances to cover such an undertaking? Was I sure we would want to stay in this house long enough to make such a major renovation worthwhile? In my dream to be a speaker, I wondered if I had enough experience to start and operate this type of business. Would people pay to hear me talk? Who would hire me? How would I survive financially while I was building the business? But the rule for successful dreaming is "no limits," so I canceled all of those thoughts from my mind for the time being and continued to imagine, asking myself, "What if?"

2. *Determine your purpose.* Something almost miraculous begins to happen when you have a definite motive for pursuing your goal. There's power in having a specific and steadfast incentive. Even the most routine tasks can take on new meaning when you have a purpose. Being seriously committed makes the difference between a wish and a goal. Resolution results from understanding the significance of reaching that objective. It is purpose that motivates us to do whatever it takes, for as long as it takes.

There were several reasons for my kitchen dream. Our family enjoys getting together for special occasions and I look forward to every opportunity to entertain them in our home. When we are all together, it is quite a large group and growing all the time. Everyone always wants to congregate in the kitchen so, in the past, I often found myself attempting to prepare a meal with over twenty people squeezed into this small space. I didn't want them to leave, but always felt we would be more comfortable in a larger room. Aside from that, cooking for me is a hobby—very relaxing and a form of self-nurture. I delight in experimenting with new recipes and menus and knew that it would be even more enjoyable with the convenience of well-designed work areas as well as more space to get and stay organized. Another reason involved lighting. The windows in the original kitchen were small and didn't allow in much light. In addition to well-planned, improved artificial lighting, larger windows would be desirable to open up the room so we could enjoy the view of our wooded property. I imagined being able to enjoy our meals while observing the beauty of the four seasons, the magnificent old trees on our land, and the many varieties of birds attracted to our feeders.

As a speaker and writer, I hoped to encourage men, women, and young people, giving them the techniques and strategies they need in order to experience satisfaction and peace of mind in their personal and professional lives. Another part of my purpose was to help companies grow and prosper by giving employees the tools they need to achieve excellence in all they do.

When you know why it's important to accomplish your goal, you will always find a way. With enough reasons, you can achieve almost anything.

3. *State each goal in the form of an affirmation.* The left side of the brain takes its instructions in the form of words. Affirmations are simple one-sentence statements worded in the positive and the present tense. For example, the affirmations I created for my dreams went like this:

"I appreciate entertaining family and friends, cooking gourmet recipes, and eating meals in front of the large windows enjoying the view from a bright, new country kitchen, by Christmas 1994."

"I enjoy my exciting, prosperous career traveling around the world and meeting wonderful people as an international motivational speaker, by January 1990."

Other affirmations might be "I enjoy my two-week vacation, basking in the sunshine on the beach in Montego Bay, this coming winter" or "I operate my own successful business and make a great living as a graphic artist, by this time next year." Phrase it as though it is currently happening, rather than "I wish to" or "hope to" achieve something. Also, state what you *do* want rather than what you *don't* want. The brain won't respond as easily or quickly to the reverse of an idea. In other words, instead of saying, "I no longer smoke," declare, "I am now smoke free." Rather than "I am not claustrophobic," pronounce, "I am comfortable in close quarters." Another technique is to write yourself a letter dated one year from today and say something similar to, "This has been a terrific year! I have achieved _____." Fill in the blank with a description of your *ideal* year. Did you make some new friends, lead a youth group, change jobs, buy a new home, or go on a dream vacation? Did you attain your ideal weight, sing in a choir, learn to play a musical instrument, or publish a book of poetry? Use your imagination and forget limitations. The only boundaries are the ones you impose.

4. *Envision your success.* Purposeful visual imaging is a powerful tool to support your affirmations. Your words are the seeds you plant, but you also want to have a conception of the harvest you are expecting. Just as the left side of the brain operates through words, the right side takes its instruction in the form of pictures. Seeing

yourself achieving your goals in mental representations provides balance and now, along with your verbal statements, you will be utilizing both hemispheres of the brain. In other words, you will achieve what is commonly known as whole-brain thinking.

Imaging is one of the most dynamic techniques you can use to clarify your desired outcome. Norman Vincent Peale, in his book *Positive Imaging,* suggests that envisioning success consists of vividly picturing in your conscious mind a desired objective, and holding that representation until it sinks into your subconscious mind, where it releases great untapped energies.

Experts tell us we cannot only star in our own life's movie, we can write, direct, and produce much of it! Goal setting with mental images is one way to play center stage in our own life drama. Instead of reading your horoscope or seeking the advice of a fortuneteller, why not create for yourself some clear representations of the changes you'd like to see taking place?

These pictures become instructions to the brain. Because the subconscious mind doesn't differentiate between what is imagined and what is real (that is the job of the conscious mind), it accepts what you tell it and sets out to produce your desired results. Due to of the universal law of attraction, you are like a magnet, continually attracting the very people and situations into your life that enable you to fulfill that image.

We all think in pictures. If you're not sure you do, ask yourself if you have ever worried, relived an embarrassing moment, or had a sexual fantasy! *In fact,* it would be difficult even to think without using some form of mental imaging. Those representations have power, whether they are positive or negative, right or wrong. Always concentrate on what you want rather than what you don't want. Think of prosperity, not poverty; health, not illness. Be sure what you are imaging supports and enhances your personal belief systems and core values, and will not hurt anyone in the process. Otherwise, you may attract into your life something that will never satisfy or could even be harmful. An old adage puts it best: "Be careful what you wish for—you just may get it!"

Olympic teams and athletes are trained to improve their skills through visualizing positive results. Golfers often report increased success when visualization is used. Imaging is not new. It has been researched in the health and medical fields and has been practiced by peak achievers for centuries. Carrying a strong mental picture of yourself as a fit and energetic person can protect you from illness. You can use positive imaging to overcome fears, refine skills, increase your confidence, or turn your goals into realities.

Here's how it works. You can actually create an internal picture of yourself in the future and mentally rehearse upcoming events—whether it's dealing with a difficult person, making a presentation at a staff meeting, closing a sale, or attaining your best weight. Envision your ideal life, meaningful relationships, your dream home, your next vacation, or your new car. Whatever it is that you would like to see happen in your life, start with a mental image. Then, continue to focus on this image while believing that the outcome is really possible. Every time you envision your goal, you increase your confidence that your dream can come true. Eventually, you will achieve just what you have been picturing.

In the Scriptures, Christ taught us to "pray, believing." Remember when you were a child and played "make-believe"? You actually lived out the fantasy in your mind and believed that it was real. You didn't hope it might be genuine. You simply knew it was! Well, today you can use this same technique. Begin by seeing yourself in your mind's eye, in your current situation, and then move into your desired state. When you visualize, fill in as much detail as possible. See your new image in living color. Appeal to your emotions and all five senses.

I began to do this for my kitchen. In my mind, I imagined walking through it exactly the way I wanted it set up. I saw myself using my appliances, sitting at the table set with coordinating linens and china, loading the dishwasher, and cooking—anything I expected to do there. I saw the brilliant colors of the tiles that I envisioned behind the stove, the navy-blue walls, the antique white woodwork and English country-style cabinets, the dark oak floor, and the paisley wallpaper border. I felt the warmth of the sunshine coming through the windows and smelled exotic stir-fries on the stove or cinnamon muffins in the oven. I heard the laughter and lively conversation of my guests and saw them relaxing with me at the dinner table.

In my career dream, I saw myself wearing a red business suit, carrying a leather briefcase, and getting on an airplane. Since I had never even owned a briefcase, I went to the leather store and held one. I wanted to add to my image the feel and smell of leather. I visited dress shops and tried on red suits. I envisioned myself on a stage, at the podium, calm and in control, and saw huge audiences receiving what I had to say, and becoming inspired by my messages.

I created these images as often as I could during each day. Every detail was visualized, over and over again, until I was actually living the dream. Then it was only in my mind. Today it's a reality!

Imaging is a simple and fun way of getting started on your goal-setting journey, but it will do more for your success than nearly anything else you can do. Lack of action is one of our main barriers and envisioning ourselves successfully living out our dreams will transform us from just dreaming to doing.

5. *Set time frames.* Break goals down into monthly and weekly action steps that can be measured. You will want to have a start date and a target date for each phase. Also, break long-range goals into bite-size intervals, so that by completing individual segments, you get the positive reinforcement you need to stay motivated and on track.

A method that has always worked for me is to begin with the end in mind. In other words, once I know my desired outcome, I start with the target date and work backward until there is something I can do today and every day until the goal is completed. Let's say you want to submit an article to the company newsletter and it is due in three months, on March 30. You might decide that by the end of February, you should have the rough draft written and ready for final editing. In that case, by the end of January, you should have collected your data and compiled all needed pieces of information in a file in order to begin outlining the article. Now you know that within those first three or four weeks, your job is to seek out statistics, books, and reference manuals that will provide you with the tools you need to research your topic. You can begin today by calling the library and starting a file to save all the material you'll be gathering. By placing time frames on the various stages, you'll have checkpoints or guideposts to let you know if you are still on target.

Even though my kitchen goal had a target date of December 1994, I had to determine short-range and intermediate goals within the framework of the larger one. By listing all of the action steps necessary to complete the project, from calling contractors and getting quotes to researching appliances, choosing colors, and selecting light fixtures, I was able to prioritize them and assign a time span to each one.

Target dates for my career goals went something like this: to be a motivational speaker with my own business by 1985, to be speaking nationally by 1988 and internationally by 1990, and to be a published author by 1997.

It seems to be human nature that we are more effective, work more efficiently, and get more done when our deadlines are approaching. If we were given one year to complete a project, chances are, we wouldn't begin until the eleventh month! So, break large goals into smaller ones and determine lots of intermediate plans and targets for each bite-size piece.

6. *Commit your objectives to paper.* While wishes are merely random thoughts, writing them down makes them concrete and gives them validity. Amazing things happen when we get our goals in writing. Once they are on paper, they crystallize and become real. Not only do written goals promote commitment on our part, but they seem to activate the universal law of attraction. We automatically begin to magnetize into our lives the necessary conditions to fulfill our desires.

A close friend told me recently that one of her written goals was to try one new recipe each week. Almost magically, recipes began appearing in her life. Whether they came from friends and associates or through magazine articles, she was delighted to find that she was guaranteed to have yet another new recipe to try every single week! Outcomes may seem to be coincidences. In fact, a written goal is similar to a seed planted. You will always reap what you sow.

The act of writing something down helps to clarify the thought because it requires us to use the logical left hemisphere of the brain. Some of the most successful women I know tap into this source of precision by writing their goals over and over again on a regular basis, sometimes daily, feeling free to revise them if and when necessary.

Once you have them in writing, put your most prominent current objectives on cue cards. Post them where you can see them or carry them with you in your handbag or briefcase. Choose the goals with the highest priority from your dream list and those that have passed a reality check. These are the things that excite you the most and would bring you the most satisfaction and pleasure. They are also attainable, yet cause you to grow at the same time.

Remember to be specific when writing your goals. It is crucial to create clear and accurate descriptions of what you want. Definite plans produce definite results. Fill in all the details. Most of us have obscure goals. For instance, we say we'd like *more time, improved health, more money, a better job, a vacation, or a new car.* But our minds don't respond to these "fuzzy" images. They need something more definite.

How explicitly you state what it is you want will determine whether you get it. "To achieve my ideal weight" is not as effective a statement as "my goal is to weigh 130 pounds by June 30." A goal to "exercise more" is not as powerful as "to walk for thirty minutes a day, four days a week." Imagine what would happen if you asked your husband to take your clothes to the cleaners and left it at that. You wouldn't consider asking a moving company simply to deliver your furniture to your new home. We know they need more instructions. Directions to yourself have to be clear and precise as well.

7. *Assemble a project workbook.* For my kitchen goal, it was a tremendous help to have what I call my integrated planning workbook. I actually began assembling it twelve years before the project even got started. Then, it was simply a "dream book" that enabled me to believe that someday this room in my imagination could truly materialize! In my workbook, I collected everything from my own rough outlines and other ideas to the conceptions I discovered in books and magazines. Eventually, actual computer renditions were included, which were done by our cabinetmakers and taken from my original sketches. As well, I cut and pasted pictures from decorator magazines and saved various brochures for appliances, cabinets, countertops, window treatments, lighting fixtures, and floors. These provided many innovative solutions and concepts I may not have thought of otherwise. On each picture, I would circle or note in some way what it was that specifically interested me. I also collected paint, wallpaper, and fabric samples and saved numerous articles on topics such as choosing the most appropriate appliances, which questions to ask when interviewing a contractor, ways to survive the renovation, and how to budget the entire project.

This started out as merely a fun way to outline the project but became an extremely beneficial tool when I explained to tradespeople or a salesperson exactly what I was attempting to achieve. It was simply a matter of showing them in the workbook. What a pleasant surprise it was when several of those individuals expressed gratitude for having their jobs made easier this way. Another added benefit was that I was able to achieve a truly customized kitchen.

Another section of the planning book was for telephone and fax numbers of all those who were involved in the project, from the plumber and bricklayer to the plasterer and painter as well as any retail outlets we dealt with. A separate compartment held receipts for purchases that had been made and all warranties and instruction manuals. One of the most exciting and rewarding parts of all was inserting the *before, during, and after* photographs. Seeing what was accomplished made the long hours, the financial investment, and all the inconvenience worthwhile.

My career project workbook contained any articles I came across that pertained to the topics I wanted to specialize in along with a list of books I could read to increase my understanding. I collected brochures that had been used to promote other programs and speakers, and compiled an index of leads and potential clients, including contact names, addresses, and phone numbers. There was a special section for marketing ideas, including my personal sketches of possible logos along with samples of different types of stationery. I researched current "hot topics" and saved this information in another segment. In the back of the workbook, I added pictures that represented every aspect of this career, including other speakers on the platform, airports, airplanes and hotels, exciting destinations, business apparel, meeting rooms, and book covers of some of the most popular motivational books.

I admit I have always been a "project" person. Yet aside from being a fun way to see the goals become realities, the workbooks definitely made it easier to stay focused, remain on track, and continue to visualize the desired results. My objectives became specific and measurable, and the workbooks, while acting as overall blueprints, also served as permanent records of the progress.

8. *Be prepared to persevere.* Seeing your goals become realities will not normally happen in an instant or be a spontaneous experience. Yet, in today's "microwave world," we tend to look for the fast and easy way. Most of us wish for a quick fix to make our lives better, whether it involves breaking a bad habit, getting in shape, improving our finances, or healing a relationship. But in truth, there are no quick fixes, at least none that provide lasting results.

Women in generations before us knew that good things took time—bread needed to rise, a stew needed to simmer, gardening and sewing quilts demanded patience, friendships required long-term commitment. Quality was more important than getting something done as quickly and easily as possible. It's not so much that the "good ol' days" were better, but perhaps we have lost some of the values that enriched the lives of women before us, such as patience and perseverance.

Today, if there's an easy way—a program or a pill—we'll take that route. We say:

> "It takes too long to save money. I'll just get another charge card."
> "Why wait until we're married when we can make love now?"
> "Working out our differences is hard work. Let's get divorced."
> "I'm not ready for the responsibility of a child, so I'll choose to have an abortion."
> "Working for a living takes too much effort. I'll buy lottery tickets, or hope to be the guest on a game show instead."

When I first began dreaming about renovating those two rooms and starting my own company, I had no idea how long it would take to see things materialize. They were merely fantasies for a number of years before they became specific, written goals with target dates assigned to them. Throughout the entire procedure, I had to persist with my plans and stay hopeful when things were not going as smoothly as anticipated. Many times I found myself wondering if they really were going to happen. I can tell you today that the years of dreaming and patient scheduling are now providing rewards far beyond what I could have imagined or hoped for! I know today it was worth the wait.

In this age of fast foods, fast credit, easy divorces, and rapid financial profits, any advancement we might experience is often short-lived. With our diminished self-control, we are left with failed marriages, debts we can never hope to repay, sexually transmitted diseases, and a world filled with pain, poverty, and despair.

Transformation, reworking your life and all your goals, will happen gradually and with patience. After all, caterpillars don't become beautiful butterflies in a day. *When you begin to practice self-denial or delayed gratification in order to have the things you truly want, that's when you'll catch the current that will get you airborne and then sustain you, even during times of turbulence.*

It's been discovered that those who are truly devoted to their dreams, and who act with dedication and determination, are more likely to develop a hardiness that protects them in tough periods and gives them the stamina to fly above the storms.

Sometimes we look at others' successes and see only the final results. What we don't observe are the long hours, persistence, conviction, struggles, sacrifices, and setbacks involved in getting there. When you choose to persevere, you will not only be more successful in attaining your goals, but you will notice an increase in your levels of endurance and tenacity when you deal with future challenges.

KEY ELEMENTS OF GOAL ACHIEVEMENT

Starting metamorphosis to recreate your life doesn't always require drastic measures. It doesn't mean you must change your name, dye your hair, and move to another country. It doesn't necessarily mean leaving a relationship, quitting your job, or parting with *anything*. It may simply mean doing some of the same things in different ways. And your goals today may be different a year or even a month from now. New opportunities will come to you. Fresh choices will have to be made. Give yourself permission to pay attention to that voice inside you. Stay connected to your inner spirit, the source of godly wisdom, and listen to the guidance you are being given.

> All great achievement begins with "I desire," moves on to "I believe," and is completed with "I can." To continue on the path of success, follow through with "I knew I could" and "I'm thankful for it all!" Then ask, "How will I improve next time?"

Once you have decided specifically what it is you want to achieve, have it in writing and have assigned a target date, your brain will respond to the *intensity* of your feelings. Women are good at fierce feelings! It's our nature to fully experience emotions that are deep, potent, and filled with zeal. What we must do is carefully direct those feelings with insight.

Here are six keys to ignite your passion, keep it burning, and thoughtfully guide it, so the results you produce are positive and profitable:

Key 1. Really want it.
Key 2. Really believe it.
Key 3. Repeat it to yourself.
Key 4. Reward yourself.
Key 5. Reflect on it.
Key 6. Revise it if necessary.

Let's take a closer look at each key.

Really Want It

Strong emotional drive sets your goal in motion. Desire will get you places. Dreaming without feeling will not. With the necessary level of emotion, you can focus your thinking abilities to get the greatest effect. Start with a creative concept and fuel it with deep desire. It's when a dream becomes all consuming, and develops into a magnificent obsession, an overpowering passion, that things will begin to happen. Desire is our primary motivating force.

For years, I had wanted to learn to paint with watercolors. I studied other artists' work, got books from the library on the subject, and even purchased some of the necessary supplies. I remember saying, "I want to do this so much that I feel as if there's a painting inside me trying to get out!" My desire was at times overpowering and relentless until eventually, I did have the wonderful opportunity of seeing my dream come true. My longing was not to develop a new career or to earn a living with my artistic work, but simply to paint for my own enjoyment. Now, I find that it's a wonderful way to escape from the world for awhile. And it all began with a clear goal backed by fervent desire.

However, I must admit I have also said that I would like to learn to play the harp—one of my favorite musical instruments. And woodworking is something else I'd like to try my hand at someday. I've been talking about both of these for a long time now, yet have accomplished neither one. I'd prefer to tell you that the reason is I don't have time or I can't afford to invest in the necessary equipment or materials. It would be much simpler to lay the blame there. The truth is I know deep down inside that the only thing holding me back is my lack of desire. In other words, how much do I truly want what I say I want?

It's always easier to come up with excuses, but I know that when I really *desire* to play the harp or work with wood as much as I wanted to learn to paint, I'll do it! Somehow I'll find the time and the money. The simple truth is that my desire hasn't reached that level yet.

Ask yourself if you long for your dream with your whole being. Only a heart that is sold out completely will be willing to do whatever it takes to implement the necessary steps. Dreams are not usually brought to fruition when a heart is divided or indecisive.

Also, if our goals do not line up with or support our highest values or if they conflict with our personal integrity, chances are, we won't be able to muster that kind of desire either. Eventually, we may even sabotage our own success. Even if we should somehow attain our goal, chances are great that it will never bring the satisfaction we hoped for.

There are very few people with great desires. Wishful thinking is more common, but it is without effect because the element of fervor is missing. The amazing thing is that when we truly want something, when we want it as much as we want air to breathe, when we yearn for it as we might crave our favorite food after a long fast, we'll somehow find a way to make our dreams come true.

Really Believe It

Once you are compelled by desire to go after your dreams, it's the power of believing that sets your potential in motion. Unless you are in a frame of mind where you are convinced you're going to succeed, it's probably best not even to attempt a new venture. Thoughts of doubt or fear are just as powerful in attracting trouble and failure as positive thoughts are in attracting achievement. Lack of belief that you really can attain a goal is your only true limitation at this stage.

You might think that certain events have to take place before you can even begin to believe in your objective. Instead, the opposite is true. You must first believe it and achieve success in your mind. You must *be* that person, living out your dream in full color even though it's merely in your imagination. When you can envision the fulfillment of whatever you desire, just as though you already possess it, your belief sets creative forces in motion. I call this the "habit of confident expectation."

For example, if you're going for an interview, first go through every stage in your mind and see yourself performing at your very best. Visualize the other person responding to you in a positive way. If you work in sales of any sort and are about to go on a sales call, close your eyes and see yourself perfectly relaxed and in control. See your future customer responding positively toward you and then signing on the dotted line.

Maybe you want to wear great clothes. Activate your belief system by purchasing fashion magazines and visiting clothing stores that sell garments of the best quality. Actually try on those you want to own and get a clear image fixed in your mind of what you look like and how they feel.

Perhaps you want to own a better home. Go to open houses in the neighborhood where you'd like to live. Walk through them and imagine living there. If you'd like to remodel your existing home, visit the furniture stores and browse through decorator magazines. All this will build your belief until you feel inside that you can really attain your highest aspirations.

Flood your mind with pictures and sensations of the realities you want to experience. Don't worry for now whether or not it's possible or if you can afford it. Just concentrate and allow your mind to dwell on what it is you want. Get the picture. Get the "feeling." Appeal to all five senses. What would this look, smell, taste, and sound like? Imagine how you will feel when you have achieved your goal. Will you be experiencing pride, joy, contentment, excitement, or self-confidence, for instance? The emotional intensity of your belief is the key that unlocks the technique of goal setting and gets things working more quickly.

In your mind, live out the "end of the story." Imagine a positive, happy result, just as though you had read the end of the book first. Now you can relax, knowing how it all comes out in the end. There's no need to worry. When things appear to be going wrong, you already know how it turns out and that everything will resolve itself for the good of everyone involved because you've chosen to picture it that way. This is what faith is all about. It's almost an *irrational confidence*. It may seem preposterous, but if you believe that it can happen or if you believe that it cannot, you're right in both cases. To a great degree, it's your conviction that makes it so.

Repeat It to Yourself

Our brains respond to repetition. Mind experts tell us we need to hear any new concept seven to twenty-one times before we begin to internalize it and truly believe in it. By repeating your goals to yourself and affirming that they are possible, you transform your beliefs into deep convictions. You will become absolutely convinced that you can attain whatever it is you are believing and desiring.

One effective way to do this is to provide constant reminders to yourself. Post your written goals along with inspiring slogans and

simple phrases on cue cards where you can spot them at a glance—
your date book, bulletin board, walls, and briefcase. Imagine how
empowered you will feel to persevere with your goals when there is
an uplifting motto that meets your gaze every time you look around
the room.

A number of years ago, I started the habit of displaying success
books in every room of the house for this very reason. As I go from
room to room, I see titles that remind me of *winning,* our *unlimited
potential, optimum health,* and the *power of our imagination.* They ignite
my creativity and inspire me to continue with my goals. Today, there
is a huge range available of miniature books that are easy to carry
with you and filled with positive affirmations and quotes. They're
ideal for those times when you're away from home and need a quick
reminder.

Every night just before falling asleep and again in the morning
upon awakening, concentrate on your primary goals and repeat
them silently to yourself several times. By doing this, you'll strength-
en your belief and build your desire. The more urgent your hunger,
and the stronger your conviction, the quicker you'll experience
results.

Reward Yourself

Do something nice for yourself. Give yourself some recognition
and a pat on the back for your goals as you accomplish each step.
Too often, we jump from one objective to the next without basking
in the sunshine or enjoying the fruits of our labor. Depending on
the goal, treat yourself with some special awards. For some achievements, it might simply be time off, away from daily routines.
Consider a miniature vacation, a picnic just for you, a day in bed
reading, or going to a restaurant for your favorite meal. Try leaving
your watch at home and having a day with no schedules. When I've
completed a major goal, I like to take one full day to do just what I
want—either visit or call a special friend, browse in a bookstore,
enjoy a cappuccino in a cafe, or visit a tourist town with antique
shops and art galleries. Rewards can include anything that makes
you happy, whether it's a day at a spa, eating chocolate brownies, or
watching a funny movie!

When our first grandchild, Kurtis, was born, my daughter and
her husband lived in another city about an hour's drive away. I

would treat myself every now and then by going to visit the new baby right in the middle of my workday. If I could meet my goal of accomplishing at least one major task in my office, for instance getting my bookkeeping up to date, or completing four hours of writing, or prospecting for ten potential new clients, then I would reward myself.

When we honor ourselves this way, it gives us the motivation and stamina we need not only to enjoy what we have but to go on to other dreams.

Reflect on It

Another way to celebrate your success is with gratitude. Devote some time to pondering and meditating on your accomplishments as well as all that you've been able to overcome to get where you are today.

The problem with continuously striving toward bigger and better goals is that it's possible to get so caught up in where we'd like to be next that we forget to reflect on what we've already achieved. Thinking about the strides we've made and where we've come from helps us to be more appreciative of our present circumstances. By taking time to recognize how different our life is now, we can awaken new levels of inner peace.

The other day, I was leaving my country home just as the housekeeper arrived. I got in my new car, drove to have my weekly massage, and then met some friends for a quiet luncheon. The next day, I was to fly to the west coast to do a series of speaking engagements. As I was driving along, I began thinking about my life as it is now and how it has changed so drastically in a relatively short period of time. I reflected that it wasn't very long ago I was cashing in soda bottles to buy stamps so I could mail in my phone bill. It seems that only yesterday I owned an old rattletrap of a car in which the rearview mirror kept falling off and had to be manually held in place while I was driving. Occasionally, the door would fly open as I rounded a corner, and my seat-back would fall down every now and then without warning! As well, at that time I was just starting out in business, and no one else knew this but I had only one business suit to my name. I wore it everywhere, simply added different blouses or accessories, and had it dry-cleaned often. A complete and stylish wardrobe was merely a dream that seemed far, far away.

What a difference—then and now. In those days, loneliness and an empty longing were feelings I'd grown used to. Today, with my wings, I enjoy a satisfying life, rich with family ties and close friendships, one filled with blessings and opportunities. There are always new barriers to be conquered, but I now have the strength and insight. I need to overcome them. (And, by the way, today I also have a couple of business suits in my closet!) That day, I needed to be reminded of how far I had come. I was prompted to quiet the urge to focus solely on what I wanted to achieve next and say a prayer of thanksgiving for my many blessings.

Sometimes we get so caught up in where we're going and what else we want to do or have that we forget to look back to where we started. Once we begin to apply the principles of successful flying, our dreams come true so quickly that it's easy to forget what it took to get there. Reflect for a few moments on how far you've come and the barriers you've conquered. Perhaps you have special memories, a photo or some other keepsake, you can refer to that will start you pondering the steps of your personal journey. Some of my favorites are the rocking chair where I nursed my babies, the cozy afghan my grandmother crocheted, cards from my husband on special occasions, and loving notes from my children, parents, or other family members over the years. You may want to take time for a solitary walk on the beach or sit under a tree in a quiet park with your journal. Think back to a time in your life when you wondered how you would ever break through and compare it to some of the pleasures you are able to delight in today. I'm sure you'll find, as I did, that many of your present joys come to you in direct proportion to your past sorrows. As gigantic as your trials were then, so tremendous are your blessings today. If it happens that you are still in the midst of your troubles, take comfort in the hope of these truths. They are powerful and will work for you, too.

Revise It

There may be times when it's necessary to update a goal. If you are wondering why you wanted a certain objective in the first place, or if your external circumstances have been drastically altered, it might be time to modify your dream or shift direction.

Because of the old stereotypical image of women "always changing their minds," or old childhood programs that you "always start projects and never finish them," you may be hesitant about revising your plans. However, your goals are not written in stone. Change can be good. Check in with yourself once in awhile during the process of striving toward your dream. If the direction you're headed still feels good, keep pursuing it. If not, perhaps it's time to revise it.

The purpose of goal setting, aside from reaching your target, is to experience personal growth along the way. As you create a new vision for your life, your understanding will reveal to you the need for balance in that development. Your goals will be multifaceted and include all dimensions of your life. You need to first see the big picture. You'll want to lay out everything you have dared to dream for yourself in some orderly fashion. Start by analyzing where you are now to determine where you are headed. A specially designed and fully integrated planning system will set your goals in motion. Then to keep you on target, you need a strategic action plan.

CHAPTER 6

W
I
N
G
Strategies

> Ideals are like stars; you will not succeed in reaching them with
> your hands, but like the seafaring man on the desert of waters,
> you choose them as your guides, and, following them, you
> reach your destiny. (Carl Schurz)

HAVING A VISION is a wonderful way to set your personal metamorphosis in motion. It is not only admirable but essential to have mighty aspirations and grand ideals. Yet goal setting is the easy part. All these noble plans, splendid ideals, and powerful secrets to success will result in very little of value without action. They won't make a bit of difference if you continue to live as you always have.

Remember what Henry David Thoreau said about building castles in the air. He encouraged us by saying that is where they should be and our work need not be lost if we will now put foundations under them. In order to build your castles and their foundations, and to experience the results you're after, you can restructure your life with a step-by-step plan. An effective, productive life doesn't merely happen. Now that you have transformed your ideals into specific goals, design a flight path for each one. Definite plans produce definite results. It's time to leave your cocoon.

Having dreams without a clear plan would produce about the same results as flying with one wing. You would keep going in circles. No matter how fast you flew, you'd have no chance of getting where you want to go. The first four ingredients—recognizing your worth, listening to your insight, understanding why and how to nurture yourself, and having clear goals—certainly provide you with an abundance of power and motion. But without specific, well-defined plans, you will have no control over your direction.

An effective strategic plan shows you where you are now and where you want to go from here. It outlines existing atmospheric conditions and indicates to you what the territory looks like along the way. It allows you to take charge of your future. Your strategy becomes a series of incremental steps you take along the way that will contribute to the fruition of the dreams you hold in your heart. *How* you use your capabilities and your life energy determines the consequences you'll experience. Women who consistently produce extraordinary results have a specific set of action plans. They have a *system* for success—not one that forces them to toil, fight, and agonize day and night, incessantly striving to reach the next plateau, but rather one that provides the means for them to slow down and delight in the journey, with time for themselves and those they love.

Over and over again I hear from women that one of the most difficult aspects of flying above life's barriers is staying on course. Even if we know exactly *what* needs to be done, doing it faithfully and regularly is the challenge. We all experience times when we fall back into self-limiting patterns and behaviors. Whether the cause is internal strife or external pressures, we never fully escape the obstacles that cause us to veer off target occasionally. There will be days when we lag behind and feel disappointed in ourselves. Other days it seems we are run ragged and totally out of control. Those times when we feel harried, frazzled, or out of balance may often seem to outnumber those when we feel on target. That's when we find ourselves wondering if we'll ever get back on course again.

One thing we can be sure of is that setbacks will continue—wings or not. Even airline pilots tell us that when they're flying a plane, it's off course much of the time. This is a normal occurrence and happens partially because of shifts in the wind. Eventually, though, it does get back in line and successfully reaches its destination.

When you're flying off course, don't waste your energy feeling weak. Instead, acknowledge what it was that caused you to drift and gather all your resources to get back on target. Having a strategy will empower you to evaluate the obstacles that pulled you from your mark in the first place and to create new patterns to keep you from falling into the same trap so you can continue moving in the right direction.

CREATING YOUR OWN FLIGHT PATH

Life will pass you by unless you stop to do some serious reflecting and take back control. Start by giving yourself permission to imagine what it would be like if you could soar above this chaotic, frantic pace and enjoy what you work so hard to attain. Don't settle for an average existence, merely *coping* or *getting by*. With wings your life can be exceptionally rich and full.

Bird migration is a wonderful example of flying according to a specific pattern. Billions of birds each winter stretch their wings and soar over thousands of miles to destinations that have been predetermined. Come spring, with their migratory instincts, they retrace their flight and return at the appointed time. We have only a few of the instincts of nature that birds have; however, we do have the power to choose our own flight path. If you're striving for a healthy, balanced, and prosperous life, set your internal compass in that direction and then embark on the flight that will lead you there. Since you and I have limited time and energy, a strategy will assist us in organizing our efforts in such a way as to give us maximum rewards for our investment. *You have been given everything you need to soar to new heights. It's the* direction *of your flight that is your responsibility!*

We all have our own internal and external strategies. Most of us are using them at a subconscious level, often unaware of the choices we have available to us. If we ever attempted to accomplish all the things we are literally capable of, we would probably astonish ourselves. We usually get lulled into doing what we've always done, following the crowd or allowing others to determine what is right for us.

Developing a strategy really means taking charge of the choices we make with the resources we have available to us—whether it's our innate abilities, time, physical energy, or finances and material possessions. It means being leaders instead of followers by focusing on our hearts' desires, and not what others would want for us. Decide what would fulfill you. Then take action, do your best, and relax, contented with what you have accomplished.

REDEFINING SUCCESS

"It is not enough to reach for the brass ring. You must also enjoy the merry-go-round" (Julie Andrews). Women today are longing for full, rich, and rewarding lives. They're asking themselves what is true success, what does it mean to prosper, and what is really important after all? Some ask, "Am I defeating my own purpose with this stress-filled life-style I've created? Is the life I'm now living really worth the anxiety I'm experiencing?"

Everyone wants to be more successful. As humans, we have a natural desire to do, be, and contribute more. Success means different things to different people. We need to devote time to determining our own definition of prosperity and what it means to us to achieve "the good life."

Society has sent the message that there's happiness to be found in financial wealth and material objects. If we are not careful, we can easily be swept along by the belief that we must keep doing, getting, and accumulating. The goal of advertising is to get us to shop, shop, shop. Treat yourself. You deserve it! After all, you only live once. We become convinced that true joy is just around the bend; that contentment is to be found in the next purchase or accomplishment.

It is easy to become trapped into defining achievement according to advertised images. We have been bombarded with *the illusion of success.* Everywhere we look—on television, in magazines, in the movies—there are images of women who are supposedly enjoying life. They are executives or presidents of large corporations, wearing the latest fashions, driving luxurious cars, and living in expensive homes filled with lavish furnishings. Even when we are able to obtain all this, we sometimes find that the greatest pleasure came from the planning, the anticipation, and the challenge of achievement. As soon as we get what we were chasing, we realize that it doesn't really change anything except our bank account.

When your primary focus in life is to get and do more, there's a price to pay. Women today are weary of constantly struggling to earn higher positions and more money at the cost of having less time and energy to enjoy the benefits those things can provide.

What seems to be happening now is a revival of values and a desire for the simple pleasures in life. In the midst of fast-track living and global uncertainty, women are seeking quiet times, alone or with loved ones. Even in the art world, we are seeing a resurgence of poetry as well as Renaissance-style paintings depicting a slower pace—afternoon tea on the verandah, evening strolls through the park, family picnics along the riverbank, or leisurely conversations with friends at a cafe. We are yearning for weekend pleasures like hobbies, crafts, gardening, afternoon theater, or a walk in the woods. We miss getting together with friends over quiet, relaxing dinners, or being able to sit by a still lake to watch the sun set. We are longing to enjoy the fruits of our labors.

There is a peace so many of us are yearning to find in our lives today. Many women who are incredibly wealthy and successful by society's standards are leading lonely, sad, and miserable lives. In reality, to be wealthy is to be free of stress, worry, and doubt; to be at peace with yourself and your life; to feel fulfilled in whatever you are doing; and to have no need to strive continuously for a more lavish life-style. *We cannot separate success from serenity. They go together.*

One strategy for dealing with our fast-paced, changing world is to know, with certainty, exactly what a prosperous, abundant life means to *you.* You need to feel in control, and then proceed with boldness to attain that life. Society, family, and friends do not know better than you do what you need to do with your life. Only you will know what is truly right for you. When you do, transformation takes place and true freedom is born.

Choose to leave the status quo behind and free yourself from stereotypical assumptions of what is a "normal" or "acceptable" life-style. Begin right now. You will need to work hard to overcome the barriers; to take a stand against the better judgment of others; to bypass what society would have you believe. Define success in your own terms. Is it the big dream home, luxury car, boat, membership at the country club, or wearing the latest fashions? Do you believe that you will be happy if you have a more attractive or caring partner? More exciting vacations? One more toy? Does success come from the prestige and power of certain career titles or positions?

Sometimes when we do manage to get the right job, and all the material possessions associated with wealth and prosperity, we're disappointed because we find out that no matter how much we get, it's never enough. If you've just moved into a new home, there's always a bigger and better one somewhere else. If you're driving your new car, there's always next year's model that you're looking forward to. When you return from your dream vacation, you're longing to start planning your next one. Success in your job usually opens up another level to strive toward. If you're not in charge of your choices, before you know it you're locked into a lifelong battle for the wealth, fame, and influence that will supposedly provide freedom, but is really a trap. You end up living in the fantasy world of "I'll be happy when . . . ," believing that real success is in the next project, the next purchase, the next venture. Look over this list and see if any of it sounds familiar.

"I'll feel happy when . . . "

- I have more time
- I get more money
- I win the lottery
- the mortgage is paid
- I'm out of debt
- I get one more credit card
- I retire
- my boss changes
- my spouse changes
- I get married/divorced
- I have children
- the children are potty trained/grow up/go to school/graduate/leave home
- I get a dog/cat/bird
- you apologize
- you start treating me with the respect I deserve
- I get a better job/raise/promotion
- times improve
- my ship comes in
- winter is over/summer is over/the weather improves
- tomorrow comes
- I turn sixteen/twenty-one/sixty-five with senior's benefits
- my horoscope improves
- my talents are recognized
- I get discovered
- I win at tennis/golf/racing/chess
- I get my new wardrobe/dining-room suite/car/diamond ring
- there's an end to wars, cruelty, crime, and all injustice
- everything in my life falls into balance, my life is perfect, and I can finally start living!

Have you been putting happiness on hold? One of the greatest tragedies on earth is when people believe they will someday "arrive" at success. Instead, there are opportunities every day to enjoy little accomplishments and to discover ways to be truly happy. Success doesn't happen in the absence of challenges and problems. It often comes out of adversity. If we wait for perfect conditions, we may be waiting forever to get the most from life. Imagine what would happen if we waited until we were sure of weather conditions before planting our gardens. There's never a guarantee that we will be free of storms, high winds, droughts, or floods. There is no ideal time. I encourage you to quit stalling. Abandon all your excuses, and enjoy your life wherever you are now.

Help Yourself to Happiness

Everybody, everywhere seeks happiness, it's true,
But finding it and keeping it seems difficult to do.
Difficult because we think that happiness is found
Only in places where wealth and fame abound.
And so we go on searching in "palaces of pleasure"
Seeking recognition and monetary treasure,
Unaware that happiness is just a "state of mind"
Within the reach of everyone who takes the time to be kind
For in making others happy we will be happy, too,
For the happiness you give away returns to shine on you.

Anonymous

DESIGNING YOUR LIFE PLANNING SYSTEM (LPS)

"I long to accomplish a great and noble task, but it is my chief duty to accomplish small tasks as if they were great and noble" (Helen Keller). A number of years ago, I began using a personal planning book that enabled me to focus on the small tasks that I discovered would eventually lead to the fulfillment of the great and noble ones. This planner altered my life in a way no other concept ever has. I named it my *Life Planning System*. In this section, I want to share with you not only how to assemble your own system, but also the exciting ways in which you are going to benefit from putting all the pieces of your life puzzle together in one place.

When you consider your hectic schedule and add to that your new dreams and plans, you may be wondering how you can tackle one more activity like a Life Planning System. I'm sure there are days when you feel as though you are *literally* flying. You may be darting from task to task, switching responsibilities in midstream, flitting from one crisis to another, or always changing priorities. Perhaps you can hardly catch your breath before it's time to move on in a new direction. When the end of the day comes, you are much too exhausted to enjoy it. And now you'll have one more item on your list. However, think of this as a life-altering activity, not just one more thing to do. Having a comprehensive strategy is a powerful way to ensure that you *don't* overwhelm yourself by trying to take on too much. It will protect you from trying to make huge changes in every area of your life all at once. "It's not so much how busy you are, but why you are busy. The bee is praised; the mosquito is swatted" (Marie O'Connor).

So many of us believe that time is our enemy. We say things like, "There aren't enough hours in the day," or "I don't even have a few moments to think, let alone sit down and devise a strategy for my life." This is when a vicious cycle takes place. We are too busy to plan our lives, but without a blueprint, our life threatens to become a continuous blur of one stressful event after another. We find ourselves remarking, "Here it is the end of the day [or week . . . month . . . year] and I haven't even begun what I had hoped to accomplish." When that happens, our enthusiasm disappears. We drag ourselves out of bed each morning, despising the things that were once satisfying and lacking the energy or motivation to change any of it.

When you say, "There is never enough time," you imply that outer circumstances have more control over your life than you do. The truth is that you have the option of allowing them to be in power. It's always a choice.

There's one way to be sure you will take full control of your life. That is to be clear about the future you want to create for yourself and then to devise a plan to make it happen. This is what your Life Planning System—LPS—is all about. Attaining what you desire in life as well as the ability to enjoy your achievements is determined by how well you've designed your plan. If you haven't achieved your hopes, it's probably not that you lack competence. Rather, you lack a strategy. Without a definite system for accomplishment, you set yourself up for disappointment.

You'll know that you are ready to invest the time and effort involved in preparing your own system if you are dissatisfied in any way with what's happening right now. Perhaps you feel that you're standing on the threshold of a new plateau in your life. You may be filled with anticipation and have great aspirations for success. On the other hand, you might be experiencing varying degrees of anger that have left you feeling inadequate or insecure. If you can't remember the last time you had a good laugh, if you're missing a sense of fulfillment, purpose, or joy; if your life isn't fun anymore; or if you are feeling anxious just reading this book wondering how you're going to be able to apply all these new principles, then you are ready to begin assembling your LPS.

It's important that you have an integrated system, in which all aspects of your life's plans are organized together. I have found that the easiest, least expensive way to do this is to purchase a three-ring binder (some styles zip up) and fill it with blank paper along with a set of dividers. On the inside cover, label it your *Life Planning System* for the current year. It's also a good idea to include your name, address, and phone number in case you misplace your system. With your entire life's plans inside, you want to be able to recover it if it is lost. So let's begin!

By working with your system, you will be able to distinguish four main aspects of your life journey.

1. Where you are now
2. Where you want to go
3. How you will get there
4. How long it should take

This is also your goal-setting workbook and it's a good idea to get into the habit of referring to it every day. I can guarantee that you are going to have so much fun assembling it, updating it, and observing the fast and fabulous results you'll achieve that you won't have a problem coming back to it regularly.

To get started, find a secret place to hide for an hour or so, someplace where you won't be interrupted. Take along your new planner, as well as some pens, pencils, and colored markers. If possible, get outdoors into nature or sit in a sunny corner of your favorite room. Allowing yourself to retreat provides you with the critical time and inspiration you need to reflect on your life and begin creating your *new and improved* version.

Start by labeling your individual planner sections. Your LPS is a complete system for planning the major areas of your life and staying on top of events as they develop. It is designed to incorporate your beliefs and ideals into every single area of your life. You'll want to identify ten sections right away and label them with these tabs.

Section 1—Core Values
Section 2—Purpose and Mission Statement
Section 3—Current Circumstances
Section 4—Dream List
Section 5—Goals
Section 6—Visual Images
Section 7—Action Plans
Section 8—Daily Activities
Section 9—Record of Accomplishments
Section 10—Rewards

Now go back to the first section and begin making entries in your LPS.

Section 1—Core Values

Happiness is usually the end result of a goal and not necessarily the goal itself. A good starting place for determining what would bring you contentment and prosperity is to clarify your set of values—what is genuine and honest, what has worth, and what will have lasting meaning for you.

When you emphasize the wrong things in life, it's nearly impossible to succeed. It's true that you may be able to achieve and even enjoy success for a time, but it won't be lasting or fulfilling. There is no way around the reality of values.

Unfortunately, many women today have heard the message that we cannot get ahead without sacrificing values. There's an underlying implication that attaining true success in highly visible corporate positions means forfeiting time for ourselves, our family, our friends, or the many other things that are important to us. If you have bought into this idea, you may have to overcome some questions and uncertainties when you are ready to make changes in your life-style. As well, be prepared for a degree of cultural and societal resistance. You may find it difficult to slow down and work toward a better balance in your life since one of the barriers for women who put concern for their children and family responsibility at the top of their priority list is that they are sometimes judged as being uninterested in their career development. Fortunately, on the other hand, through the efforts of many concerned men and women, we are seeing some positive changes and progress in work arrangements in many organizations for women who do value family involvement, such as flextime, working from home offices, and job sharing.

However, there is still an enormous gap between the standards we are presented with—the way we're expected to lead our lives—and our own dreams and values. From the beginning of recorded time, women have wrestled with these tough choices. They have lived their lives attempting to balance their own true values against the demands others placed upon them. Some have rebelled; others have bowed to the forces that ruled them. In any case, if we do not have a crystal-clear understanding of our personal values, we will eventually lose the very freedom we were seeking in the first place. While it's true that without the right priorities, it may appear as though we have to give up some important things to enjoy prosperity, it's also true that we can have rich and fulfilling lives if we are willing to do some rearranging of the things that really matter to us. Clear values help us in wise decision making.

Often the goals that dominate our lives do not come close to lining up with or supporting our highest values. For instance, if you want to be remembered as an encouraging and dependable spouse, parent, or friend, then goals of material wealth or rising to the top of the corporate ladder would not be the main forces in your life. In our culture today, we are sometimes made to feel that, as women, we are not quite good enough if we're not aggressive, achievement oriented, or totally self-sufficient. What women are discovering when they buy into that philosophy is that there is a high price to pay. We sacrifice not only our families and home lives, but our health, friends, and, most of all, peace of mind. These are the times when adverse situations and forces beyond our control can serve a wonderful purpose. Trials and problems have a way of leading us to reflect on what is truly important in our lives. So many times, the barriers cause us to discover our wings! For instance, illness makes us still so we can listen to the voice within. When we're going through a stressful situation, one with extremely significant consequences, we become amazingly clear in our values and priorities. This new pressure tends to eliminate any meaningless chatter going on inside our heads. Our choices are narrowed down and life takes on a simplicity that it may have lacked prior to the upsetting event.

It becomes much easier to see clearly what matters to us and what doesn't.

Having a strategy, however, allows us to do some planning ahead of time in order to prevent crises. If we don't devote time to health, the result is disease. When we neglect to nurture our relationships, we lose those people in our lives who mean the most. Without long-range financial planning, we are in danger of potential loss and hardship.

It's easy to fall into the trap of constantly reacting to things that are urgent rather than spending time planning in those areas that are important. When you manage your life by crisis, you're always putting out fires, which is a major cause of unnecessary stress and burnout. Effective personal management involves keeping your life in balance, developing perspective, and having a vision of what you want your life to be like. It means being disciplined enough to deal with areas of value, such as family times, personal relationships, health, and money matters, before they turn into emergencies. In other words, we rarely get around to some areas simply because they don't appear urgent, but we can develop the habit of investing in preventative maintenance and long-range planning in those areas.

A great way to begin uncovering your true values is to ask yourself how you want to be remembered when you leave this earth. Sometimes, I like to imagine that I am nearing the end of my life, and someone is interviewing me to write my biography. What exciting things would I like to be able to say I've accomplished and to share with others?

Your values might include some of the following:
- inner peace
- vibrant health and vitality
- a meaningful relationship with God
- true friendships
- an intimate relationship with your husband
- family relationships
- close relationships with your children
- church involvement
- career satisfaction
- charity, including contributing to a worthy cause
- financial freedom and security
- travel to interesting places
- recreation

- sports and hobbies
- social events and culture—music, theater, art
- continued education
- personal development
- honesty
- trust and loyalty
- happiness
- confidence
- fame or status
- recognition
- material possessions
- meeting famous people
- owning your own business
- life-style and environment
- creative expression
- sense of accomplishment
- privacy
- self-care
- respect
- love
- physical appearance
- passion and adventure
- independence

Examine your priorities carefully, add your own, and check off those items that matter most to you. In other words, in which areas are you willing to spend your time and energy in order to improve and get more enjoyment?

Your values are not your goals. A goal is something you intend to accomplish or change. Values are those things that you believe in and that matter most to you. However, values and goals must be in harmony and work together in perfect alignment. When we achieve goals that don't match our values, we end up asking, "Is this all there is?" Not only do those goals drain us of our mental and emotional energy, but we soon realize they are a waste of precious time. When your actions and choices line up with your highest values, you will experience pleasure and satisfaction when you do reach your goals.

What has the highest meaning to you? If you don't consider and evaluate what it is, you could end up chasing dreams that don't fulfill. The farther your actions and choices are from your core values, the more inner turmoil you will experience and the more difficult it will be for you to function with contentment. It will be hard to stay in flight. Sooner or later, your system will break down—physically, mentally, emotionally, or spiritually.

Give yourself a values-integrity check from time to time. When you notice a conflict or incongruity, ask yourself these two significant questions.

1. Is this value truly important to me?
2. Am I willing to make the choices or changes in my life necessary to uphold this value?

Perhaps you need to speak up when you hear a rumor about someone you care for, change the channel if there's something on the television that bothers you, or throw away the box of cookies you just bought because you previously decided they are unhealthy for you. It's amazing how many times during a day we betray ourselves. We choose or agree to do something that violates our beliefs, act in ways that are acceptable to others rather than be ourselves, hold back when we would rather reach out, or smile even though we're hurting.

Review your personal list of values and either let go of the ones that no longer make sense to you or recommit to supporting those that do.

Section 2—Purpose and Mission Statement

One way to assure you are living in alignment with your values is to determine how you view your life purpose. Then, write out a personal mission statement. Most successful companies have defined and written out their corporate statement. They display it for all to see so employees will understand the true meaning of company goals and be able to fully commit themselves to them. Yours will serve the same purpose.

A personal mission statement will address the major key elements of your life—physical well-being, psychological growth, emotional balance, and spiritual harmony—and will achieve the following three things:

1. It allows you to see the "big picture" of your life.
2. It connects you to others and the world around you.
3 It keeps you moving toward only those goals you feel are worthy and most important to you—those that will be the most satisfying.

Knowing why you want to achieve your highest aspirations enables you to direct your energy effectively and productively. When your greater purpose is to contribute to the world, to serve others, or to make a difference, you'll have a more balanced perspective, which will carry you through the tough times. With a sense of mission, you are in tune with your true self and can stay focused on your desires. A well-defined life purpose creates the energy that will propel you toward your dreams.

Just coasting through life without a clear mission leaves us feeling empty, disconcerted, and dissatisfied. Our thoughts are scattered and we will continually shift our attention. The result is confusion and hopelessness. Activities and accomplishments are meaningless. It's the spark and energy created by a strong purpose that can propel us through uncharted territory, and keep us stable during times of turbulence.

Here are some key questions to ask yourself that will help you to discover your purpose.

- What important things do you want to accomplish before (or after) retiring?
- Will your dreams fulfill your inherent talents, temperament, and emotional needs?
- What dream do you have that would contribute to the world, making it a better place?
- If you suddenly became a millionaire, would you choose the same life-style tomorrow? If not, how would you spend your time?
- If you were given one year to live, what would you want to achieve?
- If you could save only three favorite things from your burning home, what would they be?
- How frequently do you do something special for someone you care about without expecting something in return?
- Are you the kind of friend (or mate) you would want by your side in a difficult situation?

The answers to these questions will help you in your study to know yourself. Then you can more easily define your purpose and write your mission statement. As an example, I would like to share my mission statement with you: "My purpose in life is to leave the world a better place for having lived here; to make use of my God-given gifts and serve God according to His Word; to be an encouragement to my husband and my daughters, their partners, and their children; to enjoy my family relationships and build meaningful friendships; to inspire my readers, audiences, and anyone who comes to me for guidance to see themselves as the miracles they are, to believe in themselves, and to become all they were created to be; to lighten up, have more fun, and travel the world; and to live one day at a time, ever mindful of how short a time we have here on earth."

As I reread this, I am reminded that a written mission statement is not a guarantee we will always live in such a way as to fulfill every aspect all the time! I wish I could say I consistently live up to each factor. Instead, I have discovered that this statement serves as a guiding light, providing checkpoints where I can measure my progress, thereby gently bringing me back on target so I can continue moving toward my ultimate purpose.

Section 3—Current Circumstances

You've probably seen the maps at shopping centers and amusement parks that have arrows with the words *You Are Here.* We need those because we can't go anywhere else until we know where we are now. To begin planning your future, you have to have a clear picture of where you are. In other words, what does your life look like today? One simple and concise way to get a comprehensive image of your overall life pattern is to list the various aspects of your present life-style on one page in this section of your LPS.

Consider all your roles, activities, involvements, and relationships. For starters, divide this segment into four categories: work, home, personal, and community/church involvement. Write down your roles in those areas as you think of them. Your desired outcome is to have your life as it is today outlined on one piece of paper. One woman's initial "picture" might look something like this.

1. *Work:* Business owner, insurance agent, office administrator, sales manager

2. *Home:* Wife, mother, daughter, sister, aunt, mommy to the dog, homemaker, chef, hostess, shopper, decorator, organizer

3. *Personal:* Friend, artist, musician, runner, student of health, nature lover, reader

4. *Community:* Church choir member, Big Sister, board member for a local girls' home, Cancer Society chairperson

As each new role surfaces, jot it down quickly. Include whatever is important to you. If you get stuck, just think about a typical week in your life and the many hats you wear, activities you are involved in, and relationships you have with other people and the outside world. The next step is to take one item at a time within each of the four categories and expand on it by identifying the various activities and people connected with it. This will provide you with a full description of how you currently see yourself. To get you started on your own list, here is my example of the first segment.

Work

- Keynote Speaker—Speak at conferences and dinner meetings; conduct in-house seminars, public events, and workshops; produce audio- and videocassettes; build relationships with speakers' bureaus; research and develop new material; maintain contact with existing clients; follow up on leads and referrals; prospect for new clients
- Writer—Books based on seminar material, corporate needs analysis, and audience surveys; columns for business magazines; articles for company newsletters; market research; collect statistics
- Public Relations—Contact media; arrange press releases; do TV and radio interviews; write newspaper articles; join networking organizations
- Office Manager—Hire, train, and meet regularly with office staff; work closely with accountant and lawyer; supervise activities

Complete your own and continue on with each category. This is basically an outline and a modified version of what is known as "mind mapping" or "patterning," a technique that has been used by life-management experts for years. It's a wonderful way to see your life at a glance and gain a clear understanding of what you have been accomplishing until now. It's important to view all aspects of your life before making future plans or prioritizing activities.

This type of outline is great for analyzing what has already taken place in your life. There is a more traditional method of mind mapping that not only makes it fun and easy to instantly scan your life, but helps in generating new ideas as well.

To begin your mind map, print your name in the middle of a blank piece of paper and draw a circle around it. Now add spokes radiating from the circle and label them with the main aspects of your life, for instance personal, home, community, and work. Next,

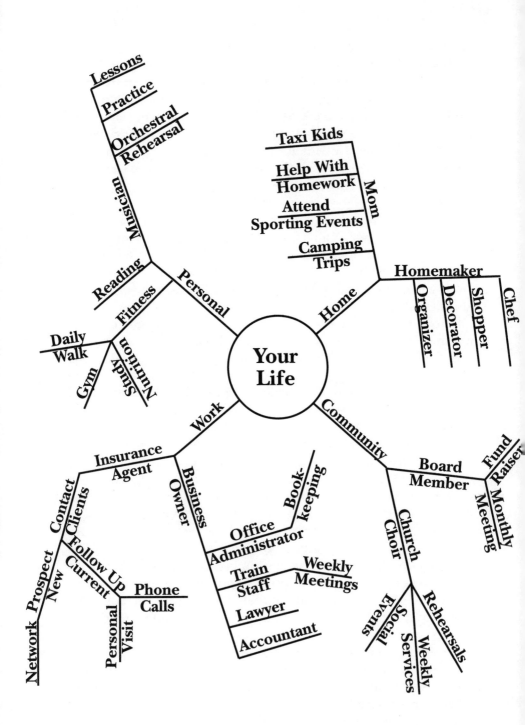

branch out from each of those spokes and name the various roles involved in those areas of your life. Continue branching away from the center by adding activities, people, and objects connected to the roles. When you think of more roles and activities, add more branches. As you work on this and begin to concentrate, ideas will come to you so quickly it will be challenging to write them down fast enough. To get them all down, avoid too much detail. The trick is to generate and capture ideas without analyzing them. That can come later. What you are aiming for at this point is a broad and global overall pattern.

This is a simple technique for collecting, externalizing, and organizing your thoughts. There is nothing complex or mystical about mind mapping. It seems this is the way our minds work naturally, and it is helpful to get those concepts on paper so you can have a concrete visual image. As you study your map, you will see patterns emerging. It will soon become apparent to you what is missing from your life, what you want to do and haven't, and what you have started but never finished. These will become your dreams and eventually your goals. Here's a sample of what a mind map might look like.

Section 4—Dream List

I always think of wishes as being the objects or activities in our lives that we merely hope to achieve or regret having left unfinished or even unstarted. We believe if we could do or have them, our lives would be enriched, but somehow we never get around to them. Wishes are generally random thoughts that nag at us and possess little or no power. They can leave us feeling frustrated, angry, depressed, or bored.

Writing down your dreams, on the other hand, is a powerful way of crystallizing your wishes. Dreams become concrete when you get them down on paper. Mere wishes are whimsical and dissipate into thin air. Dreams materialize and have the ability to become goals, generating personal satisfaction and the positive emotions of enthusiasm, motivation, and self-confidence. Dreams empower us to hold up through the storms and turbulence along the way. Aside from providing the assurance you need to get you over the barriers, outlining your dreams can help you detect opportunities you may have otherwise overlooked.

At the top of a page, write the date and the title *Dreams*. Then, keeping in mind your present life situation in each of the four major areas, consider what would have to change or take place in order to improve your future. Answering these questions will get you started:

- What would you like to do or have?
- Who would you like to become?
- Where would you like to travel?
- What would you like to offer the world?
- Whom would you like to enjoy your journey with you?

Let your creativity soar. Nothing is too absurd or far-fetched at this stage. Don't evaluate how your dreams could come about or even the probability of achieving them based on your existing situation. Don't think too hard and, for now, imagine there are no limits—not time or money; not knowledge or talent; not confidence, support, or opportunity. List everything that comes to mind no matter how outrageous. Refer back to chapter 5 for more ideas to get you started. There are dreams that have been hovering in the back of your mind until now. Get them all down and keep writing until you have exhausted your imagination. Dreams that are wrong for you will surface later when we measure them against your core values.

Section 5—Goals

Take your dreams to the next level. The difference between dreams and goals is that dreams are created in a spirit of playfulness while goals must carry enough weight to make them of true value to you. Your dreams included anything that could be imagined whereas goals will focus primarily on practicalities. A dream is the big picture and is often realized after a series of related goals are accomplished, much like pieces of a puzzle fitting together. You may have many lofty dreams without seriously evaluating them, while your goals will require commitment and will cover definite areas of your life. You will want to have goals for

- stimulating your creativity
- building financial freedom
- maintaining vibrant health and vitality
- creating fulfilling, rewarding relationships
- feeling loved and contented
- moving ahead in your career

- getting organized
- having more time
- tapping your internal resources
- traveling to your favorite spot
- developing your spiritual nature
- continuing your education
- leisure time
- home improvements
- material possessions (car, furniture, art, jewelry)
- pampering yourself
- updating your appearance and wardrobe

For goals to work their magic, they must line up with, support, and enhance your personal values. This strategy involves aligning your goals with your values and ensures you will not be chasing dreams that will not satisfy. Begin goal setting by comparing where you are currently to where you want to be in each of the particular areas of your life that you want to change or improve. Then, select those goals with the highest priority, the ones at the top of list. Now, go back to the values list to be sure each goal is supported by your greatest values. Let me share with you how I put this effective values-alignment step into practice using the goals I shared with you in the previous chapter.

Dream #1—*To have a large, bright country kitchen with a view*
Goal Statement: Remodel the existing kitchen and dining room by turning the two smaller rooms into a single one and adding several large windows
Values: Family times
Get-togethers with friends
Convenience
Creative expression
Viewing nature

In this case, achieving the goal would result in a spacious kitchen, which in turn would mean guests would be more comfortable and entertaining would be easier for me and my husband. In a well-designed work area, gourmet cooking as a hobby would be a fun and pleasant creative experience. As well, larger windows would provide better lighting and also the opportunity to enjoy the natural beauty of our property. This goal and my values were definitely in alignment.

Dream #2—*To have a career as an international motivational speaker*
Goal Statement: To travel around the world, presenting keynote addresses at conventions as well as providing in-house, corporate training workshops that focus on professional and personal development, goal achievement, and self-motivation
Values: Career freedom
Creative expression
Inspiring others
Traveling to interesting places

Many aspects of operating a business and being my own boss could provide the independence I value. Developing new programs and materials would allow me to tap my creativity. By designing and presenting innovative success strategies and techniques, I could motivate others. Also, being an international speaker would provide many opportunities to travel and meet new people. Again, these goals were supported by some of my highest values.

By turning dreams into specific goals and then comparing them to your values, you can be certain that each one will be a worthy investment of your time, energy, creativity, and finances. As a result, you will experience true pleasure and satisfaction as you enjoy the rewards of your accomplishments.

When our values and goals conflict, it is difficult to stay focused. Achievement and advancement will always be a struggle. Either we sabotage our own success or we attain our goals and then find they aren't fulfilling.

We all have limited resources at our disposal, whether they be time, energy, talent, or finances. We can waste our resources by trying to attain goals that will not give real meaning to our lives. Remember, as you grow, your values may change, and when they do, it's important that your goals change along with them.

Section 6—Visual Images

Crystallize your thoughts by backing up each goal with a corresponding picture to represent what it is you want to achieve. Aside from the mental images we talked about in the last chapter that will help you to envision your success, you can use this section of your LPS for collecting actual, physical pictures of your desired outcomes. Solidifying your goals with pictures is an extremely powerful strategy, one that will bring quick results without requiring a lot of conscious thought or effort. Besides, it's a fun way to organize your goals and watch your dreams materialize.

I was first introduced to the idea of a what is sometimes called a "dream board" or "treasure map" by a speaker at a conference I attended in Dallas a number of years ago. I was so excited about this new strategy that the first thing I did when I arrived home was to assemble my own. At that time, I didn't have an LPS, so I pasted a few pictures on one of those small cards that comes inside a new pair of stockings. (Obviously, I wasn't thinking very big in those days!) On mine, I glued a picture of a watch, set of luggage, coffee table, and dishwasher. I posted it where I could see it daily.

At the time, I was a sales trainer so I took my "dream board" with me to show my sales team at our next meeting, encouraging them to get started on one of their own. Within the next year, everything on my card had become a reality! Others on the team were experiencing incredible results, too! Needless to say, my next dream board was much larger. I have been thinking big and creating a new one every year since then. Now, I use this section of my LPS to design a dream collage. I mount the pictures representing my current goals and view them on a regular basis.

The images you choose may represent both tangible and intangible items. In any case, you should see yourself in the picture, in your ideal circumstances with your goal appearing in its completed form. For instance, Grace, the woman at the conference who introduced this concept to me, said one of her goals was to increase her level of confidence. So the picture she chose was of a woman who appeared to be exuding assurance and self-esteem. She knew the value of putting herself in the picture, so she glued a photograph of her head to the body. Another goal was to have a loving, harmonious family, so she included an image of a cheerful family enjoying an evening of fun gathered around a board game. Other pictures represented a home in the country, an island vacation, and a new car.

You can make your dream board by creating a collage of photographs or of pictures you have collected from travel and new-car brochures, fashion catalogues, decorator magazines, books, or cards. You can also draw or paint your own images, including color swatches and paint chips, and anything else that will help you get a solid visual image of your goal. Use personal photographs to put yourself in the picture, showing yourself achieving your desired results—singing in a group, playing a musical instrument, vacationing on a beach, traveling to different parts of the world, getting on an airplane, downhill skiing, white-water rafting, or riding a horse. I designed a potential cover for the book you are now reading, complete with my photograph and the words *National Best Seller,* long before it had been wholly written or accepted by a publisher.

Show each goal in its finished form so that it is believable to you. Make it as bright and dynamic as possible. The mind reacts to intense color. This promotes an emotional response and helps you to accept that the goal is possible. Adding affirmations to your images adds power, too. Say something like, "I now enjoy my vacation on the beach," or "Here I am operating my own company and earning plenty of money." Also, remember to give thanks and acknowledge that every good thing comes from our Creator.

Fashioning visual images this way is a powerful technique for realizing your goals. Reflecting on your pictures every once in awhile is all that's necessary to keep the dream activated. You will find that, whether you post yours on the fridge or your bulletin board or put them away in your binder, much of what you visualize will eventually come into being just as you imagined!

Section 7—Action Plans

Once you've turned dreams into goals, aligned those goals with your values, and created a visual image of what you want to happen, it's essential to devise a set of action plans. Your goal is the target you are striving toward, but along the way many essential steps are involved in reaching it. An action plan is simply a list of all the necessary steps and successive actions involved in achieving your goal, allowing you to pursue each step as a separate project. In this section of your LPS, with all the strategies required for completion recorded in one place, you can regulate the procedure and track your progress quickly and effectively.

Start by devoting one page to each of your major current goals, those that have top priority. In a one-sentence description, clearly state your goal and note whether this is a personal or professional goal. To achieve balance, you may want to start by choosing one career, one family, and one personal goal. Note the date you are beginning as well as the expected completion date. Always give yourself a deadline. It seems we work best within a fixed time frame.

Next, sit quietly, relax, and take time do some personal brainstorming. Make a list of all the action steps that come to mind, as you think of them. The order is not important just now, only that you write down everything that will be required in order to accomplish this goal.

Let's see how this works. Perhaps one of your dreams was to turn your hobby—floral arranging—into a career that would net you $30,000 per year, enough to allow you to leave your present job. This would lead to a goal that could be written as: "To establish a successful business, owning and operating a florist shop." Write this at the top of your Action List page, noting that it is a professional goal. Add today's date and also assign a target date. Now go ahead and list all the action steps you must take. Many times, some form of research will be the first step, which would involve gathering additional knowledge. All steps, like goals, will begin with action verbs such as *investigate, establish, conduct, apply, find out,* or *decide. For example:*

- find out which licenses you need for the floral business
- determine the capital requirement—expenses that must be met to form the business
- establish what equipment you will need and obtain costs from retailers and manufacturers
- investigate financing sources and options, including government support and funding
- make a list of potential investors, if necessary
- determine fixed expenses required (rent, utilities, etc.)
- conduct your own market research to ascertain who is going to buy your service, what it is they want, where they will go to get it, how much they will pay, who else sells it, and how much profit you want to make
- determine a suitable location, considering zoning laws and whether you will lease or purchase
- examine the advantages and disadvantages of buying an existing business or operating a franchise versus starting from scratch
- establish a relationship with banks, suppliers, an accountant, and a lawyer
- decide how much merchandise will be part of your inventory
- write a detailed business plan and a budget including expected monthly operating costs and income
- decide how and where will you advertise your service
- determine your business image and design a promotional package
- apply for appropriate tax numbers—retail, corporation, sales

- attend seminars and study literature on starting a new business and being your own boss
- join associations and networking groups in your community and within the floral industry

Another example, a personal one, would be organizing and coordinating your family's annual reunion and picnic. Your action steps, in any order, would be

- set a date
- determine your budget, consider all costs, and decide who will pay for what
- develop your guest list
- select a location for the picnic as well as hotel accommodations, if necessary
- determine "rainy day" alternatives
- delegate tasks to other family members
- design a written invitation for out-of-town relatives
- coordinate guest arrival times
- compile a name and address list for mailing invitations
- plan a menu
- decide on a theme and colors for decorations
- prepare a shopping list
- plan the agenda
- decide on games for children and adults, and select prizes

Each question that needs answering becomes another step. Every supply you must gather is another action item. Once you get going, you will find that your mind is continually coming up with new activities to add to your list. I'm sure that as you read these you can come up with your own ideas to add to these lists!

For now, the activities are listed in random order. Once you have completed your list, reorganize items according to priority. Simply go down the list and note beside each one which must be accomplished first, second, and so on. Depending on the particular goal, I sometimes find it helpful to work backwards from the final step. Some steps will obviously precede others. When one task is dependent upon another being completed, you'll assign a higher priority and do it first. Some tasks will be parallel, meaning they can be worked on at the same time. You can group those items together, giving them the same priority.

On this list, you'll also make a note of the date you plan to begin each action as well as your proposed completion date. It's all right to use a pencil for this part because you may have to change the steps along the way. Remind yourself that this plan is not written in stone. Make changes as necessary throughout the project. As you work through your project, additional action steps and tasks or subtasks will become apparent. You can insert them into the overall plan as you go by assigning the appropriate priority.

Many steps in your plan will have subtasks and you can list these various related activities in a separate miniplan. For instance, for your new floral business, the step of creating marketing and promotional material will include such subtasks as hiring a graphic artist, designing a logo, writing a brochure, choosing a printer, and having letterhead, stationery, and business cards printed. Likewise, in the personal goal of organizing a family reunion, the step of selecting a picnic location might involve the subtasks of making telephone calls to all possible sites, listing the pros and cons of each, and checking all available dates as well as requirements to hold the date. As you list each subtask, you are creating a step-by-step pathway toward the achievement of your goal.

An additional project-management technique I discovered that works well for prioritizing these subtasks is to record each item on a yellow sticky note, the type we use to leave messages on. Then you'll be able to group tasks in clusters that have the same rank or other common factors. These handy notes also makes it easy to regroup anytime you need to.

As you complete an activity, simply remove the sticky note, or cross it off the list if you are using the traditional method. This clarifies your direction and is also gratifying.

One of the greatest secrets of women with wings is they break goals down into manageable written action steps. This makes goals specific, measurable, and achievable. All of our goals can be accomplished this way, yet the toughest part for most of us is conquering inertia and simply getting started. A clear description and understanding of those first few steps will provide the momentum and direction we need to continue. The true difference between women who achieve average results and those who reach outstanding levels of fulfillment is the motivation to take that first step.

Section 8—Daily Activities

All goals can be accomplished by breaking them down into bite-size, manageable action items and then taking steps daily. Yet, unless the steps are connected to our daily agendas, we may never get around to working seriously toward them. We can get so caught up in the day-to-day busyness of life that we'll find ourselves saying, "Here it is the end of the day and I still haven't managed to accomplish anything towards achieving my ultimate goals." The answer is to regularly transfer top-priority items from your Action List to a daily activity planner. Otherwise, these tasks are easy to postpone because everything else has a way of appearing to be more urgent. By including your top goal activities on your daily to-do list, you are more likely to take them seriously and eventually achieve them.

This section of your LPS is the place to record and prioritize your daily activities, including those from your goal list. Rather than writing to-do lists on random pieces of paper where they can easily get lost or jotting those items on a weekly or monthly calendar, keep them in this portion of your system and refer to them each day.

Compiling a daily activity plan involves two steps. The first is to make lists of all the activities you plan to accomplish in the near future, business as well as personal. This includes every activity from writing a letter or making a phone call to a trip to the shoe repair or post office. I actually divide these lists into three categories labeled *Inside Activities, Outside Activities,* and *Phone Calls.* As new items, tasks, or phone messages come in, they can be added to the bottom of the list. The second step is to look the list over and prioritize only those activities you plan to work on the next day. A time-management habit I practiced for years was to take those top-priority items from that list and transfer them to a separate daily activity sheet. An alternate method is to mark them with a highlighting pen and label them *1, 2, 3, 4,* etc. in the order you intend to accomplish them. When each one is completed, cross it off and move on to the next priority. The next day, continue with the same procedure. Another system I have used in a similar way is to create a basic to-do list in a computer file and simply delete each item as it is completed. Use whichever system works best for you. The most important factor here is that each day your action plan includes at least one step that reflects a major current goal.

Your dreams, goals, and action plans are what get you off the ground but it is your daily activities that keep you flying and produce a sense of direction and accomplishment.

Section 9—Record of Accomplishments

Once a year, take a page in this section and label it *Goal Achievement* for the current year. Go back over your goals, plans, and activities, and assess your progress. Note your accomplishments in each area and take the time to enjoy the great feeling that goes along with achievement. Goal setting is as much about who you have become and feeling good about yourself in the process as it is getting what you want from life.

This is also an excellent time to review your dreams and values and reread your life purpose and mission statement. Revise them if necessary. Use this time to take inventory of your knowledge, skills, characteristics, and wishes. By retreating and regrouping, you can chart your future direction, gain a fresh focus, and add any new dreams.

Ask yourself some important questions about where you want to go next and what you would like to change about your life. Take stock of your strengths as well as your weak-link areas. Ask, "Is my life in balance mentally, physically, emotionally, and spiritually? Is it in balance personally and professionally? Am I satisfied with my relationships at home? On the job? Is my financial situation healthy? Am I physically fit? Am I continually growing in knowledge and awareness? Am I spending my time wisely and effectively? Do I enjoy the time I spend with those I love and care about? Do I spend enough time with them? Are my 'I love yous' up to date?" There is tremendous impact in asking yourself the right questions.

By now, through recording your accomplishments and analyzing the results, you will have what you need to place a new *I Am Here* arrow along your road to reaching your life's dreams. You will be able to see clearly how much you have progressed and accomplished throughout the year. This step will give you the strength you need to continue planning your future. You will know without a doubt that you can overcome whatever barriers may lie ahead.

Section 10—Rewards

It's time to celebrate and enjoy your success! You have worked hard and earned the joy that comes with achievement. Too often, when we complete one goal, we throw ourselves immediately into the next, without pausing to reap the rewards. Unless you take time to enjoy your accomplishments, you will become stressed and overwhelmed at the thought of continuing. Don't forget to nurture yourself in this way. It is encouraging and refreshing. You need to give yourself a big hug and offer a prayer of thanksgiving for what is good about your life.

A major drawback to setting goals is that they keep us waiting in the balance for future successes. Goals, if we allow them, can rob us of the joy and celebration of what we have already accomplished. If we get caught in the trap of continually preparing for "future triumphs," our happiness always eludes us because it lies down the road somewhere. We won't ever fully enjoy what we have in the present. Even though we'll always want to strive to improve and to achieve excellence, we must also take the time to appreciate what we have right here and now.

One way to remain eternally grateful for what you have is to remember where you've come from. While it's useful to have money and all the things it can buy, it's also good to make sure you haven't lost sight of what it cannot buy. Set aside a portion of each day to count your blessings. Give something back by reaching out to others. Consider those who are less fortunate, and pledge to make a contribution, even in some small way. Contemplating these things first thing each morning is an inspiring way to start your day. Something I've learned to do when I go for my morning walk is to spend the entire hour naming those things I am grateful for. When this practice was first suggested to me, I wondered if I would be able to fill the hour. What I found instead was that I could easily continue being thankful well beyond that hour! You will find too that, once you get started, there's no end to the blessings that will come to your mind.

While designing your strategic plan toward the new and improved version of your life, you will be increasingly aware that you control your life's outcomes. You won't waste any more time searching for joy and peace in outside sources. When you discover that the answers lie within, you will be ready to spread your wings and begin your flight.

CHAPTER 7

The Beginning

> Don't be afraid your life will end; rather, be afraid that it will never begin.

"THE BEGINNING" IS AN UNUSUAL WAY to end a book. Yet, now that you have experienced metamorphosis, with your wings complete and strong, you are poised and prepared to take flight and rise to new heights. In the same way that "commencement" at school means "the beginning," yet comes at the end of a long, intense period of learning and growth, so is this your opportunity to begin. This is your commencement.

LET YOURSELF GO!

The way to truly *begin* flying is to let yourself fall. There's no need to struggle anymore, no need for worry. Think of the baby eagle, whose parents push it from the nest. At first, it flutters with apprehension, wondering what will come next. Then, with amazement, it discovers that it is falling into an invisible sea of support that is capable of holding it up. Now, as it relaxes and catches the current, flying happens with ease and confidence. This same support is waiting to sustain you when you are ready to surrender.

Letting go is not an easy thing to do. For you, it may mean releasing old habits or comfortable attitudes—ways of seeing and doing things that aren't working for you but are still a major part of your life. It may be a matter of giving up the belief that you have to do it all, or that you have to do it by yourself. Letting go could mean you've lost a loved one to disease or death, or a relationship that still has meaning for you but not for the other person. Maybe letting go represents holding back while a wayward child discovers her own wings. Perhaps it means watching your teenage son make some of the same mistakes you made, or seeing an elderly parent going through the natural changes of aging and feeling helpless to stop the process. Letting go may mean forgiving someone who has wronged you even though you feel that person doesn't deserve to be forgiven. It may mean letting go of blaming "busywork" or poor health as an excuse for not moving forward with your dreams.

In any case, letting go is a process that begins with awareness. It may take time. It definitely takes faith. And it requires the understanding that in letting go you are not admitting defeat. Nor does it mean you are condoning inappropriate behavior. Instead, it acknowledges that you are ready to move forward, free from worry, doubt, or bitterness, knowing that you have done all you can. It doesn't require that you stop caring about others. It does mean you will allow those you love the most to go ahead and make their own choices. It means recognizing that you can't change others, empower them or do it for them. Rather than sheltering them, you can allow them to face their own challenges, accept responsibility, and learn from their experiences.

Letting go is not to blame or feel powerless, but to change all that is within your control and accept that which is not. Letting go doesn't mean you will have a clear understanding about every problem. Rather, it's the realization that you don't have to have an answer for everything. In some situations, understanding will elude you. As much as you feel the need to "know why" you didn't get the job, your husband left you for someone else, you've been rejected by a friend, someone started a rumor about you, or you weren't invited to the neighborhood party, you may never know. There are some things you simply won't be able to comprehend. They will remain a "mystery." Rather than trying to resolve them, choose to believe that when things don't seem to go your way, it is because there is a better plan for your life than even you could have designed!

LEARNING TO APPLY LIFE PRINCIPLES

Part of letting go involves tapping the powerful laws of our universe. These principles are constantly in operation—whether we recognize them or not. For instance, you will always reap what you sow. As in the ebb and flow of the tide, what goes out must come back. You will attract into your life what you focus on and expect according to your deepest intentions and desires. Other people normally will rise to your expectations. You have the privilege of teaching people how to treat you by the messages you send out to them. These are all universal principles. *In order for our dreams to happen, we must acknowledge that these laws are in effect, recognize that they are operating for our good, and cooperate with them, not defy them.*

Whatever "the beginning" represents in your life, one principle is that this invisible sea of support is waiting to catch you when you let go and relinquish your control. It's when you stop striving and start relaxing that you can open yourself to what God has planned for your life. Then you will be set free, totally free, to enjoy the journey.

Perhaps you are not yet sure that you are able to let go. Use your journal to guide and encourage you in your surrendering. As your thoughts come, know that you are connected to a powerful source of truth and wisdom. Ask for direction and expect to receive it.

Letting go results in freedom. Start by making a list of those areas where you want to experience liberation. Write whatever pops into your mind, without analyzing or attempting to understand those thoughts. Don't concern yourself with details at this point. You may be amazed at what's within you that you had not been aware of until now.

After this creative, intuitive exercise, move into the next stage—logical life planning. Letting go is a rational decision to relinquish the need to know the outcome of every situation or be in full control of everything and everybody. Letting go frees your mind from the emotions and frustrations that constrict your thinking. You will clear the way so that answers can come, not only *from* you but *to* you. Instead of dwelling on the confusion of a situation or your compulsion to have all the "right" answers, turn your attention to generating new solutions. Here are some intriguing questions to ask yourself, covering twelve major areas of your life, that will help you align yourself with your true potential.

1. Personal Growth

What choices can you make to be free and totally responsible for your success and happiness?

How can you achieve a state of mind that allows you to release the unlimited potential you have within you?

What must you do to take charge of your character or alter your temperament?

In which areas do you exhibit attitudes and behaviors that represent those of your family members, which may be limiting you from being genuinely your own person?

How can you lighten up, take yourself less seriously, and improve your sense of humor?

What steps can you take to tap into your creative self?

Who would you like as your mentor?

Which three people can provide valuable feedback to assist you in reaching your objectives and fulfilling your purpose?

How do you describe your main purpose or mission in life?

Envision yourself with a positive self-image, with qualities such as wisdom, serenity, and creativity. Begin to feel good about your life, job, and relationships. See yourself as you want to be—pleasant, relaxed, resilient, warm, positive, optimistic, or funny. You become what you think about.

2. Physical Condition and Appearance

What nurturing habits can you create to live as richly as possible each day?

What can you do to get more fun and enjoyment from your life?

Which type of exercise do you like and how can you arrange your schedule so it allows you to do it regularly?

What nutritional program can you plan for yourself that will improve your eating habits?

What do you notice is taking place in your life when you find yourself eating unhealthy foods?

Are your perceptions of your life's events helping you to handle negative stress and gain endurance?

What steps can you take to improve and update your looks and alter your wardrobe?

See yourself participating in whatever activities you would choose that would require you to be in excellent physical condition. Envision yourself as a healthy, beautiful woman, radiating vitality, walking and moving with grace and poise.

3. Intimate Relationships

How do you plan to spend more time with the people you care about?

What can you do to improve your communication with others?

How have fears, doubts, and insecurities affected your relationship with your spouse and children?

How can you be an encouragement and a positive role model to the people who mean the most to you?

Do you strive to care more about others' feelings than being right?

How can you plan to listen more openly and actively, without judging?

How will you express your admiration for your spouse as a person?

What can you do that will demonstrate your affection in many ways each day, including physical intimacy that isn't necessarily sexual? (It could just be holding hands, hugging, or touching.)

What can you do to treat your partner as the most important person on earth?

Are you fun to be around?

Do your mate and children look forward to spending time with you?

"If you would learn the secret of right relations, look only for the divine in people and things, and leave the rest to God" (J. Allen Boone). Women are ingenious at seeing the potential in everything and everyone. We are always expecting miracles and have a habit of anticipating the best in situations and in others. We can transform ordinary conversation into an event where sparks fly. With a little imagination, some paint and wallpaper, and an interesting color scheme, we transform a house into a home. Dinner is transformed into a special occasion with some candles, music, fresh flowers, and pretty china. A picnic lunch in the park is turned into an adventure and a drive in the car is transformed into a song fest or a guessing game.

Equipped with your new wings, you can begin to apply this incredible ability to transform in healing and nourishing your marriage, family, and home. With wings, you will understand that the barriers you encounter in your relationship with your spouse are there to enlighten both of you and reveal to you the lessons you need most to grow together. You'll be able to fly higher and travel farther together. The challenges and obstacles you encounter won't frighten or consume you because, with wings, you'll know that there are supernatural arms of love stretched out beneath you. You'll be more open to moments of intimacy, both physical and emotional, because of your acceptance of your true self—with weaknesses, limitations, and all. When you have nourished your own spirit, you will be ready to nourish your mate's, too. Your flight into a long-lasting, committed relationship can be one of the most liberating paths you will ever have the opportunity to follow.

With wings, you will make your home a warm, comfortable place for your family to retreat to because you will take responsibility for your own happiness and not expect others to provide for all your needs. You will love yourself, for it is in loving yourself that you are able to give love to your family. You will always love them for who they are and never expect them to be who they are not. You'll let them know you appreciate them by saying "thank you" often, and verbalizing what you are grateful for. Most of all, you won't wait until they express love to you in the same way before you give love to them.

4. Family and Friends

What specific things can you do right now to create better family relationships?

Who can be part of your support system and how can you build that relationship?

Which unproductive people do you need to spend less time with?

Which three special friends do you want to commit to in building long-term relationships?

How can you demonstrate your happiness for others' prosperity?

What steps can you take to overcome trying to be all things to all people?

How can you rid yourself of the false belief that other people's approval is necessary for your well-being and self-respect?

Who in your life is fun to be with and uplifts you when you are down?

Although we can't do the changing for others, we can create an atmosphere conducive to change. As someone once noted, "There are only two lasting bequests we can give our children—one is roots; the other is wings." Instead of limiting others by labeling them or putting them in boxes, we can create an environment in which they have the desire to become loving and strong within their own sense of self-worth. It's then that others can come into their own by being with you! Everyone has the same opportunity and equal potential for radical change and you could see a drastic turnaround. The other people in your life are also searching for a life of magnificent possibilities, and you may play a key role in the direction of their flight.

Choose and build your friendships with care. Birds of a feather really do flock together. The most fulfilled people are magnetized to other fulfilled people. With our own sense of worthiness, we attract others who are also aware of their worthiness; with our confidence and inner peace, we attract the same; when we criticize ourselves, or complain about the things that are happening to us, we attract those who are also dissatisfied with life. The first step in creating positive, rewarding relationships is to look *within* in order to change what we are bringing into our life *without*.

If you're wishing that the people already in your life could be sources of strength and encouragement to you, the truth is that they can be. There is always hope. People do change. No one has to remain the same, if he chooses not to. And that is the secret. Try not to confine the potential of others by your expectations of them.

5. Career Development

What needs to happen in your life before you will consider yourself successful?

What do you want to accomplish in the next three to five years?

How could you create a career from something you have a passion for?

Which major work experiences do you need in order to reach your goals?

When you reach your goals, what will it take to stay at your new level?

What can you do to have a more positive attitude toward the job or position you currently have?

What exceptional performance or service do your customers/clients/supervisors expect from you?

What systems can you implement in order to obtain helpful feed-back from customers, employees, and suppliers?

How can you improve communication with others to better understand them and inspire loyalty?

What part-time, job-sharing, or home-office opportunities are available to you?

What are you doing on a regular basis that will get you where you want to go?

How can you take more initiative and become more self-reliant?

Envision yourself doing something you really want, not what others want for you. See yourself involved in what you believe is a worthy investment of your life energy. With wings, you can look forward to going to your chosen work each morning. A lot of physical and mental energy will be generated and you will find that you are renewed daily.

6. Spirituality

Where do you think you came from and where do you think you're going?

What blessings do you have in your life that you can be grateful for?

What are your God-given talents and how are you using them?

How can you substitute the "doom and gloom" you hear daily with positive, inspiring information in order to transform your state of mind?

What can provide absolute security in your life?

What life principles can you rely on to achieve inner peace and remain free from anger, guilt, and worry?

Who in life, including yourself, do you need to forgive?

What would it take for you to forgive unconditionally?

Are you happy with the choices you make in situations when no one else will ever know?

How can you develop the skill of listening to your voice within?

How would you like to be remembered when you pass on from this life?

"People see God every day. They just don't recognize him" (Pearl Bailey). You and I are spiritual beings, and during our time on this earth we live in human bodies. Therefore, it is impossible to separate our spiritual selves from everyday living. When we attempt to disconnect in that way, we limit our opportunities and it's not possible to fulfill our potential. We miss small miracles and wonders.

You can enhance your spiritual journey by developing the habit of taking some time each day to sit quietly and meditate. Relax. Be as silent as possible. Acknowledge the spiritual side of your nature and contemplate your link with God, the source of all wisdom. Take along a prayer journal and your Bible or some other inspirational material. Spend time reading. In your journal, write the answers and possibilities that occur to you in your silence. Create your personal list of ethics and develop a code of behavior that complements them. Envision yourself living out in detail the internal values that mean the most to you right now.

7. Finances

What can you do today to create value for yourself and others?

What services could you offer to barter if necessary?

Could you use your talents for sewing, photography, caring for pets, baking, electronics, or woodworking to earn money?

What are ten ways you could earn extra money if you were willing to invest the time and effort?

What financial investments can you put toward your future security?

What steps can you take to ensure financial freedom?

How can you protect your economic interests?

Are you aware of how much your partner earns and the condition of your joint savings?

Could you survive without your partner if it became necessary?

What books can you read or courses can you take regarding financial planning?

Envision yourself earning more than enough money for your personal use. Open your eyes to the abundance all around you. Sometimes we limit ourselves by believing the falsehood that money is the root of all evil. The truth is it's the *love* of money that destroys. Some believe that it is morally wrong to experience financial freedom, yet the more you prosper, the more you have to share with others. Begin to see that the universe offers abundance and there is plenty to go around!

8. Education

What type of information, which is supportive of your highest aspirations, do you expose yourself to on a regular basis?

What three things could you learn that you didn't know before that would contribute to your overall achievement?

Which strategies can you use to improve the caliber of information you program into your mind?

How can you continue to be a student of new skills and knowledge?

Which resources can you invest in that could help your progress?

How can you benefit the most from your local library?

What books can you read, tapes can you listen to, classes can you attend, and courses can you take that will bring you closer to achieving your personal and career goals?

What organizational skills could you learn and start using?

Attending regular classes, enrolling in seminars, and making use of your personal success library or your company's resource center are powerful ways to transform your life. You can create what you want for yourself and reach your goals if you practice self-development on a regular basis. There are so many opportunities out there waiting to be discovered. Women with wings believe in continuous lifelong learning.

9. Travel and Leisure

What cultural events can you attend that you have not experienced in the past?

Which gallery exhibits, local theater productions, lunchtime concerts, or lecture series are available in your area that are either free or inexpensive and easily accessible?

How can you plan relaxation and quiet time in your life on a daily basis?

Which places would you like to travel to?

How much do you need to save monthly to pay for your next vacation?

What sports or hobbies can you become involved in?

Which activities can you become so absorbed in that you lose all track of time?

Envision yourself wherever you would like to be. See you and your partner, family, or friends in a leisure spot of your choice. You need travel and leisure time not only for the obvious physical benefits, but also to stimulate your problem-solving capabilities in order to generate innovative solutions to the obstacles you face.

10. Material Possessions

Which external assets and belongings do you believe can cause you to feel fulfilled?

How can you go about attaining the material possessions you truly want to be part of your existence?

What can you do to surround yourself with the things that make you feel comfortable, inspired, and at peace?

What must you let go of *internally* to be free of the need for "more stuff"?

Which life-style patterns bring you the most fun and peace of mind?

We spend so much of our time in our homes, offices, and vehicles. All day we are at work. Then we spend our evenings in the living room and all night in the bedroom. In between, we are in our cars. These places should be as pleasing, comforting, and nurturing as possible. Quite often, this is not so. Either we are surrounded by clutter and all the paraphernalia we have collected over the years, or we haven't yet managed to decorate our lives with some of the unique things that would bring pleasure to our routine activities.

You don't have to spend a fortune to enjoy where you spend most of your time. Start by getting organized. Decide which possessions you can do without and strive only to acquire those that mean the most to you. Give away everything you no longer need to a local charity. What you are doing is making space for your creative spirit. Then you can add a touch of warmth and originality to the places where you spend most of your time. Photos, postcards, and your favorite quotes posted here and there or tucked under a piece of glass on your desktop can provide instant comfort during the day. Painted wicker baskets in all sizes can hold those items that never have a place. A small antique lamp, a bouquet of flowers, a fresh coat of paint, a new scatter rug, or some unusual picture frames can brighten any room or office. Focusing more on displaying your favorite things rather than buying just for the sake of "having more" is one of the secrets to peaceful living.

11. Contribution and Charity

What possessions that you are not using can you give to someone else to enrich his life?

In which organization can you volunteer your services?

How can you offer your time, energy, or finances to make a difference in your community?

To whom could you become a mentor and role model?

How can you donate regularly to a good cause?

A great universal secret of prosperity is giving to others. What you give away will always return to you—multiplied. You can never give too much away. When you cease holding on tight, and release yourself as well as your finances and possessions into the universe, you will start to receive bountifully. Once we begin to understand that the nature of life is similar to the ebb and flow of the tide, we are able to go with the flow, knowing we will never lose by releasing. Rather we will always gain. As we give out of abundant hearts, we make room for goodness to flow into us. Tithing is the practice of giving back a percentage of all you earn to God, in acknowledgment that every good thing comes from Him. When you tithe regularly, you will have a continuous outpouring of prosperity. God is the unfailing, unlimited source of all your supply.

12. Risk and Change

What are your comfortable habits that keep you from altering your life patterns?

Are you afraid of the unknown, of failing, or of trying something new, and if so, why?

What changes or uncertain circumstances are currently weighing on your mind?

How can you become an "agent of change," spot trends, and see the big picture?

What challenge do you currently face that, if you changed your perspective, would change your future?

Which risks are you willing to take because you refuse to be limited by your fears or others' negative opinions?

What new habits and strategies will you begin to use to create a better future for yourself?

It takes courage to overcome comfortable but deadening

patterns, experience life to the fullest, and live in the best possible way. It takes bravery to accept that you have fears and to take action in spite of them. A great way to stay motivated is to begin moving forward in the face of fear, confusion, or doubt. Become a positive risk taker rather than merely enduring change.

JOURNEYING ON

Your wings are now strong enough to carry you for the rest of your journey. There are no barriers you cannot overcome. Expand on each of these areas, considering your strengths and experiences. Take some time to savor all you've discovered. List some possible strategies and plans to make these resources work in your favor. Use this time to decide exactly what it is you value most in your life. The more precise you are, the more effective will be your results!

It's imperative to take charge of the choices you make with the resources you have available to you—your time, finances, and energy. Having a clear set of values and priorities—knowing what matters most to you—allows you to make the right choices. You may like your life the way it is, most of the time. Perhaps you have a global feeling of contentment about your work, family, and personal situations. To get the full impact of this book, however, you must know specifically those areas that could stand to be improved. None of us has reached divine perfection. We are all aware that we have weak links. For you it might be one of many things—your marriage or career, relationships with your children or other family members, sagging self-esteem, physical well-being, or the ability to achieve inner peace. In creating a prosperous future for yourself, you must be willing to admit that your previous flight path is not taking you where you want to go. Then, move forward to design some plans and make the decisions that will set you in the direction of your choice.

Learn to master your thoughts and belief systems to consistently produce the attitudes and actions that will give you the outcomes you desire. When you become self-directed and success conscious, you will be able to see your goal clearly ahead of you. Then, you will work rapidly and effectively to find ways to make your aspirations become realities. "If one advances confidently in the direction of his dreams and endeavors to live the life which he has imagined, he will meet with success unexpected in uncommon hours" (Henry David Thoreau).

Everything we've talked about in this book will empower you to make the choices that will dramatically alter your life. However, there is one power that will enable you to fly up and over the barriers more than all others. That one motivator is something everyone is searching for—unconditional love.

TRUE LOVE: OUR GREATEST POWER

"We never live so intensely as when we love strongly. We never realize ourselves so vividly as when we are in the full glow of love" (Walter Rauschenbusch). So many women continue their quest for the "full glow of love" in all the wrong places, including our men, careers, family or friendships, material possessions, hobbies, or money. While all of these certainly contribute to our happiness, none will provide sure, lasting love and fulfillment. Rather than continuing to rely on these sources and setting ourselves up for perpetual disillusionment, we can experience true, satisfying love in three ways.

1. *Accept yourself unconditionally.* While you are learning and growing, don't be afraid to admit, to yourself or anyone else, that you are less than perfect. Just as it takes rain to make rainbows, it takes difficulties and struggles to make strong wings. Besides, being imperfect is one of the fragile threads that binds us to one another. If you were perfect, you wouldn't have much in common with anyone else!

Accepting yourself means searching deeply to capture the essence of who you really are. Endeavor to reveal your hidden inner feelings to yourself and then trust them, because you have the intrinsic ability to become all you expect of yourself.

2. *Give unconditional love to others.* We know we can't change others nor can we force them to love us the way we need to be loved. We can only change ourselves, then nurture others and encourage them through being positive role models.

True love means dedicating ourselves to the growth, happiness, and fulfillment of one another. It takes time and depends on giving and receiving. It flourishes during intimate moments of laughing and crying. It never promises instant gratification but it does assure ultimate satisfaction. Love says no with empathy. It is the first to encourage, the last to condemn. It has the wonderful ability to be firm yet tender at the same time.

Don't take for granted those who are closest to your heart. Cling to them as you would life itself. Don't let them slip through your fingers while you explore other possible sources of pleasure. Real love accepts that there will be disagreements and disrupting emotions and circumstances, yet is willing to make a commitment to endure all things. And in that commitment, a love beyond your wildest expectations can flourish.

The best way to keep love is to give it wings. Don't hold on to it tightly. Release your grip and let it fly freely, on its own. As the old adage reminds us, if it is true love it will fly back to you. If it doesn't, was it really yours to begin with? This is the genuine test. Even God Almighty merely gives us His love and does not force us to return it. That is always our choice.

"Smile at each other, smile at your wife, smile at your husband, smile at your children—it doesn't matter who it is—and that will help you grow in greater love for each other" (Mother Teresa).

3. *Accept the unconditional love of your Creator.* Even though we believe in ourselves, have a sense of our personal worth, and treasure our unique insightful abilities, there are times in each of our lives when we simply cannot devise our own solutions. With all our learned strategies, principles, and concepts, it is still possible to lose our confidence. We can go through the cloud banks feeling lost, bewildered, and alone. It's possible to feel disappointed and distressed regardless of how far we have come on this journey of self-discovery.

When I have experienced these times in the past, I knew I had to search for a better way to find contentment. I am now convinced there is a truer pathway than mere self-discovery to a rich, free life. I have learned that all my tools and techniques are only as powerful as my trust in God. There is a direct correlation between my ability to use my innate gifts and my faith.

Whether you are dealing with guilt, self-pity, despair, or worry, or you are feeling helpless and hopeless, or you simply want to increase your ability to use your natural talents, let God embrace you. Let Him carry you on wings of love so you can rest awhile. When you give yourself up to Him, He will take you to wonderful places. He will show you the majesty of the morning wind, the stillness of a peaceful shore, the energy of a glorious daybreak. Let Him, through His love, reveal to you the miracle of your own complex nature and you will be amazed with the realization that life can be everything you truly want it to be.

YOUR SPIRITUAL FLIGHT

You have come full circle in your metamorphosis. You have experienced the joys, the sorrows, the triumphs, and the tragedies of growing your wings. You have discovered powerful techniques that, when practiced regularly, will transform your life. However, as necessary as it is in all areas of achievement, turning over a new leaf, or developing better habits, or making New Year's resolutions is not everything. Here we are at "The Beginning," ready for full flight. Yet we have found that, even with wings, there are limits. It is not possible to enjoy the "ideal life" totally through our own efforts. Even when we do realize our dreams, success on its own can leave us with an emptiness and an unexplained yearning to be fulfilled.

My true *beginning* was the day I chose to end my old life and become a new creation. Wounded by the arrows of heartbreak, embarrassment, divorce, defeat, and feelings of inferiority, I'd had enough of flying alone. I was becoming more and more disappointed in myself and the choices I was starting to make. Disillusioned with what was happening in my life, I began to search wholeheartedly for the answer and, in my seeking, I learned what it meant to trust Almighty God as my support. Just as something unseen could carry the baby eagle, so is God able to provide more security for us than any visible means. I believe that our most promising hope might be found in the truth that the entire universe is operating within a system of natural laws, and that God is the source. Your wings will work for you to the degree that you are in alignment with these laws. Your full potential can only be realized and true satisfaction experienced when you connect with *your source, your origin, your beginning.* This is when life takes on new meaning and your own potential begins to merge with that of the universe. This is how you become empowered to let go, take flight, and enjoy the ride.

"O God, Thou hast created us for Thyself, and we are not satisfied until our souls rest in Thee" (St. Augustine). I encourage you to search for God with all your heart. In your sincerity, He will answer you and reveal Himself and His truths to you, as He has to me and anyone who turns to Him. Whether your faith is great or small, you may be surprised to find out how close help is if you'll just ask for it. The secret, of course, is that it's up to you. It's always your choice.

"Ask, and it shall be given you; seek, and you shall find; knock, and it shall be opened unto you. For every one that asketh, receiveth; and he that seeketh, findeth; and to him that knocketh it shall be opened" (Matt. 7:7-8). I will never forget the day, a number of years ago, that I began to ask, seek, and knock. I was desperate for an answer. Alone in my sickbed, believing I was going to die as the result of a rare blood disease, I called out for an answer. Deep in my spirit, I was prompted to read the Bible. I didn't have one handy, but remembered a small, white, zippered one from my childhood. I began rummaging through some boxes in the basement until I found it. Back in bed, I said a prayer, asking for guidance and understanding since the verses it contained had never made much sense to me. As if divinely directed, I discovered some of the most powerful, liberating, and uplifting truths I have ever read or heard. There were answers to so many of my life's questions. What I discovered were concepts that gave new direction and meaning to everyday life here on earth, as well as all the success principles needed to achieve excellence and inner peace. That day I committed myself to being a follower of Christ. My faith was soaring and I asked for and accepted a miraculous physical healing. I decided then that I would look to Him forever as Master, Savior, and Friend. This is a marvelous and mysterious gift, yet one that is available to everyone.

There are still going to be times when you will feel as though you are falling into an invisible sea, but there is an unseen force that can be your support, if you'll merely let yourself go. How often do you and I search for a visible means of security only to find that we are disappointed in its ability to free us from the anxieties of life—to get us up and over the barriers—and that it's not our answer after all? Instead, begin to trust yourself. More than that, begin to trust God. He has created you for Himself and has a plan and a purpose for your life.

"They that wait upon the Lord shall renew their strength. They shall mount up with wings as eagles; they shall run and not be weary; they shall walk and not faint" (Isa. 40:31).

You are not alone.

You can fly when you choose to.

With wings, there are no barriers!

A Personal Word

CONGRATULATIONS—YOU HAVE DISCOVERED YOUR WINGS. You are to be commended because, by completing this book, you have committed to doing something positive for yourself. By now, you've given yourself permission to feel good about being a woman, to feel good about the choices you will make in your life, and to feel good about living each day with passion.

Thank you for giving me the opportunity to share with you the beliefs that have made such a tremendous impact on my life. Although I continue to struggle with so much of what I have presented here, the effort is worthwhile. Over and over again, I have experienced the reward of picking myself up and trying once more. Now that you know my story, from trials to triumphs, you may be saying, "If Sue can turn her life around with the obstacles she had to overcome, then so can I." I sincerely pray that you will be inspired to transcend the barriers of this world into a life of extraordinary personal freedom, fulfillment, and prosperity—life of magnificent possibilities.

My final thought for you is this. It's time for change. It's time for action. It's time for you to use your mental, physical, and spiritual energy to create the life you truly want. Determine in your heart to use your *wings* to find your special purpose on this earth, because I believe that the greatest joy in life is knowing that you are in the right place at the right time, doing exactly what you were created to do.

May you be blessed with all that your heart desires.
Happy flying! God bless you.